THE BALANCE

THE BALANCE

MY YEARS COACHING SIMONE BILES

AIMEE BOORMAN

WITH STEVE COOPER

ABRAMS PRESS, NEW YORK

Library of Congress Control Number: 2024943657

ISBN: 978-1-4197-7977-0
eISBN: 979-8-88707-564-8

Printed and bound in the United States
10 9 8 7 6 5 4 3 2 1

Abrams books are available at special discounts when purchased
in quantity for premiums and promotions as well as fundraising or
educational use. Special editions can also be created to specification.
For details, contact specialsales@abramsbooks.com or the address below.

Abrams Press® is a registered trademark of Harry N. Abrams, Inc.

ABRAMS The Art of Books
195 Broadway, New York, NY 10007
abramsbooks.com

To my mom, for always making life easier in Our House,
even when it meant it was harder for you.

Contents

Foreword

BY SIMONE BILES

I had just finished competing in the 2015 City of Jesolo Trophy in Italy and our connecting flight through Amsterdam back to the United States had been delayed a couple of hours because of severe wind. The gusts were so bad that Schiphol Airport in Amsterdam had closed all but one runway. Once our flight was finally ready to land, the wind quickly grabbed our plane and started tossing it around. Soon the luggage in the overhead bins started rattling and then the plane dropped before quickly recovering. Then the whole plane shook again and then dropped like a roller coaster before stabilizing. I'm shocked the oxygen masks didn't fall out of the ceiling. With each violent shudder of the plane, you could hear gasps echo throughout the cabin. All of my teammates were tense, and a few rows up my coach, Aimee Boorman, was white knuckling her armrest.

Me? I was cracking up! I don't know why I thought it was so funny; I was only sixteen years old, so that may have been part of it. Looking back, it was traumatizing. With each drop I couldn't help but start giggling, which then turned into loud cackling. I should have been more panic-stricken, but at the time I thought it was kind of exhilarating. It was a roller coaster ride, not a potentially life-and-death situation. After I was jerked into laughter a couple of times, I started to hear Coach Aimee begin to chuckle a few rows in front of me. I would laugh, then she would laugh—and before you knew it, the storm had passed, and we were safely on the ground. We had survived, but because our plane had been delayed, we needed to sprint across the airport to make our connecting flight back to America. There were thirty-five in our delegation running through the airport, including the team coordinator, Martha Karolyi, who had been training for this moment her whole life with her daily power walks. Coach Aimee, on the other hand, wasn't as prepared and had to take off her slides (thank God!) and run barefoot to keep up. We made our flight.

That experience feels like a perfect encapsulation of our time together: a wild and exciting adventure full of quirks and a disdain for sprinting. It was one of many occasions the results of our partnership would take our breath away. We complimented each other and embraced what we both offered. Coach Aimee didn't turn around and scold me on the airplane for being loud and instead let me be myself, and in that freedom she let go of her own stress.

I first noticed that the relationship I had with my coach was different when I was thirteen years old and I started going to Women's National Team development camps. That's when I realized Coach Aimee was special. Not just because she has one blue eye and one brown eye (fun fact!) but for the way that she treated me as a person and how she coached me. When I began to learn all the rules we were supposed to follow at camp, I knew the way I had been coached was different. I would look around the gym and notice how most of my teammates weren't as comfortable or close with their coaches. It makes me a little melancholy knowing that not all of my friends had as enjoyable of an experience as I did getting to that point.

Coach Aimee and I have a special bond. In and out of the gym, we understood each other, but that also happened because she had trained me since I was seven years old. She was my gym mom. I know I wasn't the only person who felt this way and I wasn't the only gymnast she coached this way either. She always did what was best for her athletes personally, even if someone told her it might not work. When I began going to the national team camps, I remember having conversations with Coach Aimee about doing things our way and ignoring what some other people wanted. Almost as soon as I started attending, Coach Aimee and I declined an invitation because she wanted to protect me from the criticism I was receiving that she didn't think was necessary or warranted. On more than one occasion she would pull me from an event final because she thought it was best for my physical or mental health. Coach Aimee went with her heart and stayed true to herself during the process.

Some of this might sound obvious, but if you've paid attention to the world of gymnastics, or even youth sports, you'd know it's not. Coach Aimee understands that every athlete works, processes instruction, and learns differently, and she caters to that. She'll do what works best for *you*.

This system served us well. We were able to travel around the world together and share our accomplishments with each other. It was so rewarding and it's something I'll cherish forever. Of course, this all peaked in 2016 at the Rio Olympics. I think we did pretty well.

I'm not saying there weren't hard times getting there. Some days I didn't want to condition: *Who does?* On other days I would even shed a few tears. Coach Aimee understood how hard the process was, and more than anything she just wants her athletes to be happy and to succeed even if everyone's goals are slightly different. She made it okay for each of us to have our own ambitions and our own peaks. Coach Aimee just wanted all of us to do our best and to be happy and satisfied when we walk away from the sport.

In order for me to satisfy my ambitions, Coach Aimee pushed me to strive for perfection. This was a real struggle because our sport is very repetitive, but it's also hit-or-miss. You either hit your split, or you don't. You wobble or you don't. You stick your landing or you don't. I know perfection is an aspirational goal, but the effort to get there is within the power of each of us, and Coach Aimee expected us to put in that effort. That's something I still try to do in everyday life. I'm not gonna lie: it's not always easy to give 100 percent effort; sometimes it's important to fake it till you make it. Many times that's all you can do. The important thing is to keep reaching for your goals, even on your bad days. Who knows: you might find yourself standing on top of the podium someday.

Most importantly, Coach Aimee treated me like I was my own person. She allowed me to grow and speak up. I was given the space to be empowered. Coach Aimee wanted me to be the best I could be and to be my whole self, and she never let gymnastics become too serious. That's what you'll get in this book from Coach Aimee: her authentic self. She stays true to what she believes even if not everyone agrees with her. That realness is what makes her special.

Coach Aimee has an incredible spirit, and I think anyone who learns from her will feel free to push themselves without feeling put down or judged. When we were starting out, I fell short of my goals a lot, but I always knew she would be there for me—and now I'm excited that you will get to experience that and see what she was thinking at the time.

I'm obviously grateful things worked out in Rio, and I know I would have been disappointed had I not done as well as I did. I also know Coach Aimee would have been there for me regardless of the outcome. Having someone in your corner like that is very liberating. It allows you to really go for it and to put your whole self into your dreams. This book will take you from the beginning of Coach Aimee's life all the way through Rio and beyond. You'll realize it took a lifetime of experiences to become the coach she became. And when you see the totality of a lifetime of work, the weight of the medals becomes lighter. As Coach Aimee would tell me all the time, "It's just gymnastics."

A single competition doesn't define your entire life; it's just part of your life. When you realize that, you're truly set free. This is what a whole journey looks like: the good, the bad, and the gold medals.

The process of writing this book made one thing clear: if I want to be honest with my story, I will need to acknowledge the colleagues, parents, and coaches I've come in contact with throughout my thirty-plus-year journey. And if you've read the headlines lately, you'd be right to assume that not all the characters in this book turn out to be healthy role models.

I'm going to talk about some people who have been accused of both emotional and physical abuse and others who have been convicted for their actions. Also, some of these people have done very kind things for me, which helped my coaching and leadership journey. An honest recount of my history must include our interactions, but I am not talking about them to promote or defend them.

It has been an emotionally tough process trying to figure out how to accurately tell my story while also being sensitive to those who are still in pain. My experiences are not meant to overshadow the accounts of others in the gymnastics community. It's my hope their inclusion will contribute to a better understanding of what being a good, non-abusive coach means.

One of the things I learned writing a book about my life is that, well . . . I have learned a lot and I feel now is the right time to share what

I've learned. In the 1980s and 1990s, I didn't realize what I witnessed was abuse. To be clear, I never witnessed anyone getting hit or touched inappropriately. I witnessed gymnasts being demeaned and put down, which I didn't agree with, but I didn't realize at the time the lasting damage this was causing. This sounds naive, but it's true. Some behaviors in the world of gymnastics in that era would make modern coaches cringe. Many times I knew I didn't feel good about what I was seeing—a coach turning their back on an athlete when they were upset with their performance, or telling them they were worthless because they may have not scored well at a competition—and I vowed I wouldn't coach that way, but at the time I didn't recognize the coaching I witnessed as abuse that needed to be reported.

What's ironic is that while I rejected these adverse coaching processes, I was told repeatedly that I wasn't going to be successful because I was *too nice*. Even after Simone started succeeding, I would receive comments about how I was too easy on her.

At the elite level of gymnastics during the early 2000s, there is not a coach in the United States who can say they have no association with a colleague who has been accused of, is under investigation for, has been suspended for, or has been arrested for and/or convicted of abuse.

I hope by not ignoring the complexities of my relationships in this book it will help future generations.

I acknowledge and recognize that I didn't see the physical abuses that have since been reported, but, to be self-reflective and fair, some information about the abusive and unhealthy environment of our sport was trickling through. *Little Girls in Pretty Boxes* by Joan Ryan, which explores abuse in elite figure skating and gymnastics, was originally published in 1995. Elite gymnast Jennifer Sey wrote about her journey and abuse in her memoir *Chalked Up* in 2009, and Olympic champion Dominique Moceanu shared her story in *Off Balance* in 2012.

In the past, when I heard a story of abuse—such as when Moceanu wrote about being forced to train while injured and told she was "fat" when she weighed just seventy pounds as a fourteen-year-old—I (wrongly) assumed the story was an exception and not common practice.

Today—and particularly at the elite level of our sport—as more brave girls have grown to become strong, powerful women, we have learned that the abusive environment wasn't an exception. In just the case of convicted rapist Larry Nassar, more than five hundred women have now come forward to expose their trauma.

In this book, I will talk about my experiences with a variety of good and bad gymnastics personnel as I interacted with them, but the stories of abuse others have suffered, along with the allegations of harm that are still coming out, are not my stories to tell. What I have done and will continue to do is advocate for the survivors in this sport and *start by believing* when confided in. I was honored when I was asked to appear in the Emmy-nominated documentary *At the Heart of Gold: Inside the USA Gymnastics Scandal.* I was the only elite coach featured and it's my hope that in the future others will follow suit when presented with a similar opportunity. I will also continue to learn and be an example for others as a leader in gymnastics. Sharing my knowledge along with my story is the main driving force of these pages.

The sport of gymnastics is in the process of healing and rebuilding—better and stronger than ever. Coaches from all sports are going through the enlightenment of what works and what is unnecessary. Moreover, parents are also having a reckoning with healthy expectations and boundaries for their kids and the organizations with whom they have entrusted their care. It's time we had an honest conversation.

PROLOGUE

Did I Do It?

Something was off. We were less than six months from the Olympic Games and Simone couldn't twist—on basically anything! I had been coaching Simone for a decade and I could see the doubt suppressing the shine on her always-assured face. This wasn't good! While training, Simone would physically stop herself from twisting during her routines because she was afraid of getting lost in the air. Simone would never crash; she would just stop herself before ever attempting a twist. We didn't have a lot of time. The Rio Olympic Games were quickly approaching, and Simone had the "twisties."

Some people say the twisties are like getting the "yips," which is when a baseball player can't toss a ball to first base or a golfer attempts to swing their club and experiences involuntary wrist spasms, causing the ball to take an unplanned trajectory. This is embarrassing and confusing for a professional athlete, but ultimately pretty harmless. However, when this happens to a gymnast who is flipping ten-plus feet in the air and they lose body awareness in space and time—not knowing if they're going to land on their feet, back, or head—it's much more dangerous.

Simone described it herself years later on the podcast *Call Her Daddy*, saying, "Every day you drive a car, if one day you woke up and you had no idea how to drive a car, your legs are going crazy, you had no control over your body . . . you've been doing something for so long and you now no longer have control." She also took to social media, saying, "Literally can not tell up from down. It's the craziest feeling ever. Not having an inch of control over your body. What's even scarier is since I have no idea where I am in the air I also have NO idea how I'm going to land or what I'm going to land on. Head/hands/feet/back . . ." Having this disconnect between mind and body can be deadly.

On television, gymnasts make it look easy. You see the sparkles, the smiles, and the athleticism. What you don't see is that gymnastics can be life altering or catastrophic if an error occurs in training.

Yep, before Simone introduced the world to the twisties in 2021 at the Tokyo Olympics, she had experienced this proprioception phenomenon in January 2016. You might be asking, "How did she get rid of it?" I wish I had a silver bullet, but I didn't. However, here are a few things I believe helped. First, we identified what was happening to her quickly, which allowed me to make a conscious effort to remove what pressure I could. I tried to make it a nonissue. "Oh, you don't want to twist? We won't twist," I would tell her, and left it at that.

The biggest thing we had on our side was time. I knew the twisties weren't something we could just ignore in hopes she'd be ready to compete. She could need days or weeks in the gym before the twisties passed . . . and in fact it took *weeks*.

I know a lot of coaches who would have pushed their athletes to do their desired skills. I didn't see the benefit. I knew trying to strong-arm Simone was only going to create an opportunity for harm because her skills are so crazy difficult. At the time, Simone was already the back-to-back-to-back world champion. Simone knew how to twist. As her coach, I understood that my role needed to shift. I needed to protect her with the timing and pace of reintroducing skills, all while keeping her confidence up.

The twisties also required a mental health professional to explore the issue, and this is where having a team of professionals is deeply beneficial. Simone was already seeing a sports performance therapist, Robert Andrews, and when she began to struggle in the gym with her twisting, the team assembled. Robert and I went over to the house of Simone's parents, Ron and Nellie Biles, to have a conversation about what was happening. During that productive meeting, we discovered that Simone was nervous and stressed, but the problem wasn't fixed during that session.

I want to be clear that Simone can handle pressure. She is the most decorated gymnast of all time because she repeatedly—unprecedentedly—rose to the impossible expectations and rewrote the record books. But here's the thing: none of it was inevitable. I first began to notice the pressure Simone was feeling a few months earlier, in October 2015.

Simone was competing in her third world championship. She finished her last routine, came over to me, and asked, "Did I do it?"

She then wrapped her arms around me and buried her head in my shoulder as tears began forming in our eyes.

The press started crowding around us and we couldn't immediately see the score flash across the board. Then I got a glimpse. As the crowd erupted at the SSE Hydro arena in Glasgow, and our nervous embrace relaxed, I remember thinking, *This is our moment.* Simone had just three-peated as the all-around world champion at the 2015 Artistic Gymnastics World Championships in Scotland. That made her the only woman ever to have won three world championship titles in a row. And as we have all grown accustomed, Simone dominated the competition by more than a point—a blowout for those not familiar with gymnastics scoring, where medals are typically decided by mere tenths of a point or less.

Her victory was so assured, it seems surprising that she would even ask that question, but there was great relief in Simone's victory. It was less than one year before the Rio Olympics, and—coming into the competition as a back-to-back world champion—the superlatives were piling up fast. Simone was about to become a household name.

Yes, her talent was obvious, but Simone still had to do the work. Simone also had to stay healthy. She had to stay motivated. She had to want to be great. She had to meet the gigantic expectations. Of course, Simone didn't *have* to do any of those things, and that's partly why it all worked. Ask any of the gymnasts I've coached over the years, and they've heard me say, "We're not curing cancer; it's just gymnastics." When I noticed an athlete was stressed, I would ask, "Are we curing cancer here?" And they would respond, "No, it's just gymnastics." Inevitably it seemed to settle them down. I value this saying because it immediately puts things in perspective and allows the athlete to understand that I'm able to see a larger world beyond the sport.

When Simone and I hugged in Scotland, a photographer captured the moment, and the photo was later published in *Inside Gymnastics* magazine. What I love about the picture is that there's a beautiful story there, but you only get the opening line. You can't see my face and you only get a peek of Simone's. It's one of those rare instances where a picture isn't worth a thousand words because you can't see all of the emotions we were both feeling. Through the photo, you can't hear the words uttered by Simone, which I believe say so much. To really grasp that moment, you'd have to have been there. I was, and that's why I want to share my story.

It's hard to remember now, but, outside of dedicated gymnastics fans, most Americans—let alone the rest of the world—had never heard the name Simone Biles before the Rio Olympics.

So how does a legendary athlete come about? What were our days like in the gym? What had I done in my life that qualified me to be the head Olympic coach of the United States women's gymnastics team? What did my family think of all this?

These are some of the things I'm excited to share with you—from the time I swiped a personal photograph from world-famous photographer Annie Leibovitz to dealing with irrational gym parents. I want to show how growing up in the city of Chicago helped shape me and what it was like at the now infamous Karolyi Ranch.

It took over a decade of ups and downs before Simone and I arrived in Brazil prepared to put all of our training on the competition floor. This book will take you on my journey from gymnast to coach to wife and mom. You will have a front-row seat to Simone's rise from when my mom originally spotted her in a field trip to her first elite competition—all the way through her multiple world championships and Olympic experience.

Then there is life after the Olympics. Life after coaching Simone. My move to a new gym. Working under the flag of a different nation. My conversations with parents who think their child might be the next legend.

Many people believe Simone and I just popped up on the international stage one day. In truth, we had a long journey—and I had a full life of coaching before we ever met. It was those experiences that gave me the ability to buck some of the worst trends that have plagued our sport. It was my early experiences and some of the coaching I had, good and bad, that helped craft my views on expectations and navigating the system.

My hope is that my story will strip away some of the veneer of the magazine covers and expose the process that helped cultivate greatness and find balance. I want to share the sacrifices of coaches that often go unmentioned and inspire others to find their own path along the way. A lot of stories have been written and a lot of photographs have been taken. What now seems inevitable wasn't.

My road to the top of the sport had a few bumps and it's my desire this book will fill those potholes so future generations will have a smoother ride. Not every narrative will be tidy, because, as we know, the world isn't that straightforward. What we do understand is that America is great at building champions, but medals don't sparkle quite as bright if we don't let the athletes shine from the inside out. I think about this when I consider how much pressure Simone was under during the Tokyo games. She was *the* global superstar of those Olympics. There was no Michael Phelps or Usain Bolt to dilute the attention. Not to mention the isolation from all the COVID-19 protocols was crippling. I know because I was there coaching the Dutch women's team. (More on that later.) Looking back at our brush with the twisties in 2016, I'm grateful that I stood up for Simone and didn't apply more pressure to the situation. And in 2021, I was filled with pride when Simone was able to stand up for herself. She had grown into a woman who was strong enough to courageously advocate for her own mental health and safety, which I believe will outshine all the gold medals she had previously piled up.

Still, my greatest pride is that, while Simone's tumbling has riveted the world, most recently in Paris, it's the beautiful smile that remained on her face and has become indelible. The secret to our success? Being authentic to ourselves as we Balanced Greatness.

PART ONE
Aimee

Me dancing as part of the Hawaiian Club, Lane Tech High School.
Courtesy of the author.

CHAPTER 1

Growing Up

Gymnastics was introduced into my life out of necessity and convenience. My mom, Veronica (who goes by Ronnie), enrolled me into my first gymnastics class when I was six years old, like Simone, because she needed to keep me occupied while she went to her marketing research job in downtown Chicago. This is not a huge revelation for the millions of parents who drop their kids off at sports practice in the afternoon each and every day on their way to earn a paycheck, but that's how extraordinary things happen: one unassuming step at a time.

I entered this world when my mom was twenty-two and my dad, Dennis (Denny), was twenty-five. I was born in Chicago and then soon we were living in a hippie commune in New Mexico. As an infant, I slept in a teepee surrounded by easygoing, inclusive social attitudes that have stayed within my household ever since. I even attended my first gay pride parade when I was six months old. It wasn't all kumbaya, though. My parents divorced when I was just five months old, and when I was two years old the FBI raided the commune we were living in, although my mother and I don't know why.

By the age of five, I was living in Vermont with my brother, Michael, who's three and a half years older than me, along with my dad and my stepmom, Trudy. While living with my dad, I took ballet classes, which included my first taste of gymnastics. In the summer of that year, while visiting my mom, she mentioned that my brother and I weren't returning to Vermont to live with my dad. So, after all the moving and turbulence, I was finally settled in a city I grew up loving: Chicago.

Three years later my brother left and went back to live with my dad and stepmom, and before long my half sister, Katie, was born to my dad and Trudy. I didn't have a lot of contact with my older brother or my younger sister except at Christmas and when I visited during my summer vacations; I kind of felt like an only child with siblings. Being a pseudo only child of a single parent, I had a lot of independence at a very young age. I was a "latchkey kid," meaning I had my own key to let myself into our apartment when my mom was at work.

My mother made sure she did everything she could for me, and I never felt neglected. It was me, her, and the city of Chicago. I grew up in Rogers Park, a neighborhood on the Far North Side of Chicago, bordering Evanston. The area is a mixture of apartment buildings, single-family homes, shops, and some city parks where fireflies would light up the night sky in the summer. My mom and I lived in a fairly large, U-shaped three-story apartment building in a modest two-bedroom, one-bath apartment with the Metra train tracks across the street. The sound of the train became such a constant in my life that when I would visit my dad in Vermont, the still, quiet country air would frighten me.

Down the street was one of Chicago Park District's six hundred–plus city parks: Pottawattomie Park. At the facility was a standard basketball gym that was turned into a small, makeshift gymnastics center for the local kids in the afternoon. It had a few fold-out mats, a wooden balance beam, and . . . that's about it. This is where my lifelong relationship with gymnastics truly began.

My mom didn't want me to spend much time alone after school, so I would walk with Mike (before he moved) to the park a few times per week and practice some basic skills. I loved it! I especially loved flipping on the floor exercise. (Not to brag, but I was able to do ten back handsprings in a row when I was seven—kind of a huge deal in 1980.) Training on the balance beam, on the other hand, hurt. I suffered a lot of bruises and fell a lot. There was no padding and no leather cover: it was a primitive, lacquered, hardwood beam, and my shins were not happy. Yet I loved gymnastics! If I wasn't in a handstand against a wall or doing cartwheels down the sidewalk, I was sleeping in the splits. I was born to be a gymnast.

Even though my gym had limited equipment—no vault or bars—I was still on a team and occasionally got to compete; when we did, we would just skip the apparatus we couldn't train on. After my first inter-park district meet (where I took first place on the floor exercise *brushes shoulders*) my mom realized I needed more than what the park could offer, so she set out to find me a more robust gymnastics program.

I attended Pottawattomie Park for three years while my mom kept an eye out for a practice facility that was better equipped. My mom was working full-time and we were living on a very tight budget—although I didn't know that at the time. As we entered the early '80s, there still wasn't much available in the way of gymnastics programs in Chicago. Finally, my mom found the Lakeshore Academy of Artistic Gymnastics. The club worked out a deal where my mom would earn credit toward my tuition in return for her working in the office on the nights I trained.

The next hurdle was figuring out how I was going to get from the Far North Side deeper into the city. My mom was rightfully concerned about having her nine-year-old girl get on a public bus by herself, travel thirty minutes, and then walk three blocks to the gym. Seeing how much I loved gymnastics—and seeing that I exhibited a tiny bit of potential—she relented. Before my first day at Lakeshore, we did a dry run. My mom took me on the public bus, showing me where I would sit (either right behind the bus driver or in the very first seat by the door), and then we walked the three blocks with a whistle in hand. This is the moment I knew that if I wanted to follow my passion, I would have to tackle the journey with a sense of independence.

Lakeshore was definitely a step up, and over the next five years it would bring me lots of joy and eventually profound rejection. When I first entered the facility, I was in love, even if it wasn't the type of gym today's parents or gymnasts likely envision. My "fancy" new gym was in the basement of a church. I would walk into the church and down a stairwell into the basement. The space was confined, but I was just excited Lakeshore had a vault and uneven bars. This was the first time I could train on either of those apparatuses, even if they were both under less-than-ideal conditions.

It was also the first time I would train with a team and compete in United States Gymnastics Federation (USGF)-sanctioned meets. We competed under Junior Olympic rules, and what we call "levels" today were then called "classes." The classes ranged from class 4 (basic) to class 1 (advanced). Today's gymnasts begin at level 1 and can promote to level 10 before becoming an "elite" gymnast.

While at the Park District, I had learned a class 3 floor routine, and when I tried out at Lakeshore Academy, that's the routine I performed. Having trained in a recreational program, my technique was lacking, but the coaches saw I had potential and had me continue to train class 3 routines even though I might have been better off going down to class 4.

The cramped basement meant there wasn't room for both a men's high bar and the women's uneven bars, so the gym would rotate the two apparatus once a week: one week the uneven bars would be set up and the next week we would utilize the men's high bar. The girls in the gym would practice on both, and occasionally we'd also train on the men's parallel bars too. I was never a strong bars worker and the thing I remember most during that time is that bars hurt. (Yeah, the beam hurts and bars hurt . . . Makes you wonder why I was so in love with gymnastics!)

In the beginning, my Lakeshore coaches supported and encouraged me; they were good people whose dedication to training young gymnasts was focused on the gymnast's success and not their own. Then, in the summer of 1984, Coach Jeremy (not his real name) arrived at our gym. My relationship with gymnastics was about to get complicated.

No matter how hard I tried to please my new coach, nothing was good enough. His arrival also coincided with a huge growth spurt: I grew six inches in three months when I was eleven. Since arriving at Lakeshore, I realized the level of competition was far superior to what I had experienced and I was suddenly faced with not being "the best," even though my tumbling was quite good for someone my age. Unfortunately, my lack of technical training early on began showing up. After my growth spurt, I was suddenly trying to do gymnastics with a body I didn't recognize. As my frame quickly grew, my self-confidence plummeted. I knew I needed to play catch-up with my technique, but my joy began to turn into a sense of failure and rejection—and Jeremy's arrival wasn't helping.

Up to this point, while training was hard and I suffered many bruises and sprains, torn palms, and embarrassing falls, my coaches were always there to support and encourage me. And then all of a sudden that wasn't the case.

Coach Jeremy would make me stay on bars, doing cast handstands for what seemed like an eternity. A cast handstand is when you perch with your hips resting on top of the bar and then you kick your heels behind you while maintaining straight arms into a completely vertical handstand above the bar. Doing this over and over again resulted in bloody hands from the skin on both palms being torn away (known as "rips") and my hip repeatedly banging against the bar to the point that I got so bruised, I could barely sit in school the next day.

This was also the time when the uneven bars were closer together and so gymnasts wouldn't fly between them as they do now as much as they'd "beat" from one to the other. You'd start on the high bar and then swing down directly *onto* the lower bar, "beating" or folding at the hips more than 90 degrees around the low bar before bouncing into another skill. On one occasion I was doing a beat and had meant to twist 180 degrees while swinging down but instead only rotated 90 degrees and crushed the side of my hip on the lower bar. It felt like I had broken my hip. (I hadn't, fortunately.) With tears streaming down my face, I fell to the ground, struggling to stand. Instead of my coach checking on me to see if I was injured, I was scorned for the mistake and was told to keep working.

The floor exercise at Lakeshore had its own unique challenges. Three of the four walls in the basement were concrete and the floor mat snugged right up against the wall, which meant you *really* needed to control your tumbling passes. It's super-scary to run directly at a concrete wall and then start tumbling.

The size of the basement was an issue for the vault too. A typical vault runway is eighty-two feet and we had maybe fifty feet of space available. To maximize our running area, we would start on the stairs that led down into the basement, lunging off the first two steps like a sprinting block and then across the floor to the vault. As you might have guessed, we didn't have a foam pit in the basement of the church, so we landed on stacked-up mats.

When it came to the balance beam, I was excited that it was covered in leather—the opulence!—but the growth spurt I was experiencing and the shift in my center of gravity made everything much harder and scarier. Standing on the balance beam and trying to do skills that required my feet to blindly leave the apparatus—as in a back walkover or back handspring—became much more frightening than they had been. And when I would fall, the distance felt farther, even if the beam height hadn't changed. That's one of the wonderful things about the sport: you are constantly having to face your fears to make your body do impossible feats. You learn body control. You figure out the limits of your strength and flexibility. You get to tap into your expressive side through artistry. And when you finally master a skill and add it to your routine, a fresh challenge awaits for an even harder skill to propel you to new heights. Everyone, if they continue to push themselves, will eventually find out where their limit is. It can be a humbling experience but will help you mature as a person.

Lakeshore was a time of struggle and growth. I don't have a ton of memories of how each practice would unfold, but I distinctly remember how I felt. During one practice I recall being left on a beam rotation for the entire practice because I was afraid to do my back walkover. I was left standing on the beam with my arms up; I wasn't allowed to get off the beam, nor was I allowed to put my arms down. All I kept thinking was *My arms are numb and I'm going to reach back and my head is going to crash on the beam.* Today, when I'm coaching beam, I tell my students not to lift their arms until they are ready to go for the skill.

As the years went on, I remember feeling sadness, disappointment, and fear in that gym. I felt like I was never going to be good enough to earn the approval and praise of my coach. I remember once every couple of weeks we would do this thing they called CD, for "controlled discipline." For the entire practice, we were not allowed to speak—at all. We couldn't talk to the coaches and we couldn't talk to each other. It was very regimented and it's what I imagined the old Soviet athletic system was like. Our coaches thought we lacked discipline as American kids. Remember, this is before the Americans were winning gold medals in gymnastics. The coaches felt that extreme discipline was what we were missing, and the way to develop it was by enforcing silence. I was very, very nervous those days. It's clear to me now that CD was not about teaching self-discipline; it was about obedience.

Even though I exhibited talent, I cried every single day after practice as I got older. My love-hate relationship with gymnastics was akin to loving your job but hating your boss. My mom begged me to quit, but you can't always explain a passion.

I'm sure this must have been excruciating for my mom. She is hypersensitive about feelings and emotions because she has borderline personality disorder (BPD). I can't imagine how tough these years were for her; knowing how worried she was for me just to travel to the gym as a young girl, let alone the emotional pain she regularly saw later with the coaching I was receiving.

My mom is a very rare case of someone with BPD who has not lived through a suicide attempt or died by suicide. I'm thankful she goes to therapy—another tool I was exposed to early on in my life.

It's hard to pin down how this all affected me because my mom always provided not only what I needed but what I wanted. She made a lot of sacrifices. I bring all of this up because later in life as a coach, it would help me understand what the gymnasts were going through, what their parents might be going through, and the tremendous number of sacrifices so many families make to ensure their kids get to participate in the sport they love. It also made me acutely aware of the importance of mental health. When you strip away all the statistics, scholarships, and medals, what we're really talking about is people and families and their choice to participate in an extracurricular activity that hopefully brings them joy.

At Lakeshore, I was pushed to the brink instead of my limits. I was a Goody Two-shoes and thrived on the approval of my peers and coaches. When you love a sport the way I love gymnastics, your coach often feels like the most important person in your life. I wanted more than anything for Coach Jeremy to acknowledge my efforts, but he never would. I desperately wanted his attention, but it was his coaching tactic to completely ignore me—to deprive me of the one thing that motivated me because he thought that I would work *harder* if I wasn't receiving praise or feedback. Well, it backfired. Big-time.

When I was twelve years old, I arrived at the gym early one day. I was working out on my own without a coach, because that was normal in the '80s. In my twelve-year-old mind, I was going to get my coach to like me by showing him how hard I could work. I hopped up on the beam and I casually did a full turn. I was trying to get Jeremy's attention and he was slightly looking over his shoulder, glaring at me. I finished my turn, jumped off the beam, landed straight-legged, and immediately felt a sharp pain. It *really* hurt. But I was a good little soldier and I sucked it up and continued to work out on my leg—unsuccessfully suppressing my discomfort during the regular practice. Coach Jeremy wasn't concerned; he just seemed mad that I hurt my leg and he did the opposite of what I wanted: instead of acknowledging my added efforts, he ignored me throughout the practice. Toward the end of the day, when I went to tumble a front handspring, I landed forward with a ton of pressure on my tibia, and a pain shot through my lower leg. Whatever had been wrong before had just gotten substantially worse.

I told him that I couldn't continue, which of course seemed to make him irate, because we had a competition that weekend. Tears began to roll down my face, and in response Coach Jeremy rolled his eyes.

I went home and told my mom that I had hurt myself, which wasn't a new thing. I'm surprised I don't glow in the dark from all the X-rays I've received over the years. My injuries had never been anything serious, though: usually a rolled ankle or sprained wrist—that sort of thing. The following day I went to school, but it was nearly impossible to walk up and down the stairs. I called my mom from the administration office because I was in so much pain I couldn't take it anymore. She told me we could go to the ER after she got off work. My mom meant for me to take the school bus home and she would then take me to the hospital once she arrived, but I misunderstood her instructions and walked about a mile to her office in excruciating pain.

At the hospital, they x-rayed my leg and wheeled me into the orthopedic room. The super-cute doctor eventually walked in, held up the X-ray, and said, "So . . . Aimee's got a broken leg."

My mom responded, "Is there really something wrong with her this time?"

And we both started giggling as the doctor replied more sternly, "Yes, SHE HAS A BROKEN LEG!"

My mom and I then began laughing hysterically. The doctor thought we were nuts. This wasn't going to be one of our regular ER visits where the doctor told my mom, "Elevate it and put ice on it."

Turns out, I didn't just break my leg; I had fractured the growth plate in my leg—not something you want to do when you're a preteen. And even though we still laugh about our reaction in the ER, my mom tells me she's never forgiven herself for making me go to school and then get to her office on my own before going to the emergency room.

I was in a full leg cast from my thigh to my ankle for ten weeks. And because the fracture was on my growth plate, I couldn't walk or put any weight on my leg. Due to my perpetual need for approval from my coaches, during the months I was healing, I didn't miss a single day of gymnastics. I was there every day to stay in shape with the few exercises I could do and to show my coaches how dedicated I was to the sport. Months passed, and every day my coach ignored me. From the beginning, Coach Jeremy had always been pretty dismissive of me. He had his favorite gymnasts he would regularly dote on; I was not one of his favorites. It's hard to believe that my shunning could get worse, but after I broke my leg, it was as if I didn't exist. I remember how devastated I was.

The day of the injury, I had gotten up on the beam to get my coach to notice me. When I got down, I was nothing. I came in every day in a cast to support my teammates and show my coach how dedicated I was. As far as I could tell, he didn't care—and so why should I? I was emotionally beaten down, feeling useless because I couldn't train, let alone compete. I could see every day that my coach obviously didn't care. That crushed me. After the cast came off, I left the gym.

This was a big deal. Coach Jeremy regularly explained that you didn't change gyms. If you changed gyms, you were going to be worse. More than that, Lakeshore was the only private gymnastics club in the city, and we couldn't get to the suburbs. So I either had to suck it up or quit gymnastics, at least for the time being.

What a trial this was for my mom! It would be difficult for any parent, but especially one with BPD. She was barely able to make ends meet, and more than anything she wanted me to be happy, which meant keeping me in the sport I loved while trying to protect me from the emotional abuse I was experiencing daily. Regularly, on our way home from the gym, when I started crying, my mom would tell me, "You don't have to do this," or she would say she was going to talk to my coach. I would then beg her not to, assuming that it would only make my life more difficult. So my mom would relent and continue paying my tuition. She had sacrificed both her mental health and financial stability to keep me in gymnastics until it was clear that I was ready to move on.

When we decided it was time to leave Lakeshore, I remember my mom calling Coach Jeremy. I couldn't hear what he said, but I definitely heard my mom screaming at him, "You didn't even acknowledge her when she broke her leg—and she broke it at gym!" I remember being happy that she had my back. My mom continued, "You wouldn't even sign her cast!" Being invisible hurt, but my mom saw me, and I will never forget how it felt to be supported like that.

CHAPTER 2

Can't Stay Away

When my cast came off, I noticed my leg had atrophied to about the size of my arm. At that moment I was done with gymnastics. I needed to build back my leg strength and I needed to heal emotionally. A lot of coaches say if you walk away from gymnastics, you'll never come back. I've always felt just the opposite. If you don't like gymnastics, you won't come back, but if you love gymnastics, you *will* be back. Even then I knew that if gymnastics was the real passion I thought it to be, then I would return.

In my eighth-grade year, I started playing volleyball and became a cheerleader. I was growing as an athlete and as a person with these new experiences. This is why I'm such an advocate for young athletes branching out and playing a variety of sports. Expanding my athletic base allowed me to flex different points of athleticism and navigate the unique sports cultures each has to offer. It gave me perspective.

That said, gymnastics was still my number one love, and it kept calling me back. I started bugging my mom to the point where she had to find a new gymnastics facility to keep me from incessantly nagging her.

I didn't just miss doing gymnastics; I missed being in the gym. Even when I wasn't training, I loved being there. I even missed the smell—the mixture of chalk and feet and sweat. It might sound weird, but those scents became comforting for me. It was also easier for my mom to have me at the gym rather than on the streets of Chicago.

So after nine months away, my mom had become more comfortable with me walking farther to be able to catch a bus that would take me north to Evanston after school to a new gym, Crane Plus Crane (CPC). The gym was in a rented space that had everything I needed. I would spend the entire afternoon there. It was impossible for me to train the entire time, so at the age of thirteen I started coaching.

I helped with the preschoolers and some recreational classes. I didn't realize it at the time, but it probably helped me reconnect with gymnastics by spending time with the fresh-faced toddlers who just wanted to bounce around and do somersaults. That kind of joy and play is infectious. It didn't help with my fear of bars, though.

My return to gymnastics after my "gap year" coincided with a change in the uneven bars. The oval-shaped rails were replaced with round rails—which I was convinced were impossible to hold on to—and the closely aligned uneven bars became spread-out. "Beating" the bar became a thing for the archives and old YouTube videos.

During my second year of training at CPC, my mom and I moved from Rogers Park to a neighborhood deeper in the city so I could be closer to my new school, Albert G. Lane Technical High School (now known as Lane Tech College Prep). Lane Tech is a selective public magnet school located on the North Side of Chicago with a long history. It was founded in 1908 and didn't start admitting female students until 1971. I had participated in the International Baccalaureate preparatory program in seventh and eighth grade and had top grades and high scores on state tests, which allowed me to pursue academics at one of the top high schools in the city. All of the schools I qualified for had something different to offer, but, honestly, I picked Lane Tech because of their gymnastics team. My new location made access to public transportation easier, and I was able to compete for both CPC and Lane Tech at the same time.

I loved high school. At sixteen I started running a YMCA gymnastics program in Chicago, where I first learned about scheduling coaches and creating lesson plans. I was very responsible and my mother trusted me. I never had a curfew and the rule was that if I went to a party and there was alcohol, I was not to get in a car with anyone who had been drinking. My mom told me to instead take a cab home and she would pay for it when I arrived. Imagine picking up a landline phone and calling a cab company, figuring out the address of the party you were at, and then staring out the window, waiting for them to show up because there was no such thing as Uber, let alone a push notification alert. (Kids have it so easy today; I'm kind of jealous.) This exercise of procuring a cab was definitely safer than riding with a friend who had been drinking, but that didn't mean I was completely off the hook. Whenever I did this, my mom would always yell at me when I got home, causing me to complain, "That's what you told me to do!" She would appropriately respond, "That's the price you have to pay for not having a curfew and coming home at three A.M." Fair enough. That became our agreement.

My mom understood that, like most typical teenagers, I was going to try new things. She didn't believe that she was going to stop me or any other teenager from drinking, doing drugs, or having sex, so she never put performative constraints on me. Instead, my mom educated me. She taught me how to be safe in all aspects. She respected me and I respected her advice. This really helped forge our bond and provided me with an early insight into the power of respect when building trust in a relationship.

My mom recognized I was being safe and not sneaking around, not regularly staying out late, or even drinking. She also knew I wasn't a liar. This helped when I had a situation in school where a teacher accused me of cheating—not for myself, but in grading a paper for someone else in a way that boosted their score. (I had indeed graded her paper wrong, but it was not intentional.) This girl and I weren't friends, but she happened to sit behind me in two classes. My teacher made an assumption and was going to fail me when my mom went to the school to find out what was going on. The teacher explained that I was cheating for this girl, but I had already explained to my mom that I had simply made an honest mistake. My mom told them, "My daughter does not lie to me." She wasn't in denial: this was the truth.

The teacher wasn't buying it and responded, "All teenagers lie to their parents."

My mom wasn't having it, though, and told the teacher, "Not my daughter." My mom *knew* she could trust me in that situation, and it was a great lesson for me to realize that honesty sometimes comes from allowing those around you to live a bigger life, not barring them from the outside world.

I believe this is one reason why I've had such great relationships with my gymnasts. I followed in my mom's footsteps by understanding that kids will be kids and teenagers will be teenagers. In most instances, it's more productive and healthy to educate them on life than to try and shield them.

This might make it sound like I was a wild child who spent her high school years staying out late every night partying, but that couldn't be further from the truth. In addition to gymnastics, I joined the swim team my sophomore year and added cheerleading my junior year. When it came to swimming, I was a decent sprinter. I liked freestyle and the backstroke. A couple of times I was asked to swim the individual medley, but I didn't know how to swim the butterfly, so I was disqualified both times. Oops. Being an athlete at Lane Tech (a.k.a. the "School of Champions") brought a much-needed sense of excellence to my life, and I was able to earn my varsity letter in all three of the sports I competed in for Lane.

Beyond sports, I was also a member of several different clubs on campus—more involved in some than others. I was a member of the Hawaiian Club. This was mostly jocks who hung out, and every year we'd participate in International Days. This is where different clubs would honor their heritage with food and dance for three days. All the kids in the school would come and watch you perform, and the Hawaiian Club was popular because we'd always do a luau theme. I'm not sure if we had any real Hawaiians in the club, and it basically turned into jocks showing off their bodies during the luau.

I was in German Club too. I enjoyed this club because as a member I got to visit Germany my freshman year. I had only been taking the language for one semester, and so I didn't speak a lick of German, but my first international experience was still amazing. Today, as a parent, I now see how brave my mom was for sending me across the ocean, with people she didn't know, to a country where I didn't speak the language. Since most of the students didn't know much German, our teachers taught us a few "special" words before we left so we would know if others were swearing at us while we were visiting the country. One of the most amazing things about this trip is that it was about six months before the Berlin Wall came down. We went to Schwangau, in Bavaria, to see the Neuschwanstein Castle, which Disney's Sleeping Beauty's Castle is modeled after, and to Oberammergau, also in Bavaria, which I'll never forget because I think it's a cool name and I thought it was a charming little town.

The coolest experience I can remember with cheerleading came during my senior year when our football team advanced to the city championship, which was held at Soldier Field, home of the Chicago Bears. I have been a Bears fan for as long as I knew how to love football. And if you're from Chicago, you don't have a choice but to love Da Bears. I remember standing on the field and looking down, realizing I was standing in the middle of the Bears logo. This was very cool!

Then there was gymnastics. We didn't have our own dedicated space, so we had to share the gymnasium with other sports and PE classes. We would roll out the wrestling mats, tape them together, and use them for our floor exercise mat. We'd also have to take out and put away all the other equipment so that the girls' basketball team could use the space when we weren't occupying it. (The boys' basketball team trained in a larger gym at the school.) So, yeah, we had to set up and break down the gym every day! And once a week we would share the gym with the girls' basketball team, which meant basketballs flying around while you were flipping. Very exciting! What could go wrong?

It was in high school when I really started to love gymnastics again. I honestly don't know if I improved all that much skill-wise, but I definitely grew emotionally. I felt like a natural leader of the team. I no longer needed to prove how good I was or win the approval of a coach. As my confidence grew, I began to give back and I started to choreograph the floor routines of my teammates beginning in my freshman year. By the time I was a senior I was choreographing most of my team's routines, except for a few girls who had come from club programs. So, on top of school and my own training, I was trying to come up with ten different routines for my teammates. Luckily, choreography was natural for me. I have musicality and good sense of tempo, plus I love to dance.

Back then our music was played on tape decks, and often we would take a blank tape and hit "record" when the radio played to capture the parts of a song we wanted. We'd then go back and, using a dual tape deck, cut in the rest of the music. A skill with the shelf life of a fanny pack. But aside from how we get the music, my method of teaching choreography hasn't changed all that much over the years. In fact, what I started doing in high school is the same basic method I used with Simone, whose routines I choreographed all the way up through her first world championship.

I start by having the gymnasts pick three pieces of music they can move or dance to. We then narrow it down to one. I imagine and construct a mental eight count with a theme, and the athlete and I craft a basic "skeleton" routine. I then have the gymnast practice that for a few days to see how it fits and then add more detail. If they have trouble with a certain step—I never try to force them to learn it—we simply change it. My philosophy is, if they're having that much trouble, it's the wrong movement for them. Good choreography exudes confidence, and you won't get confidence with shaky dance moves. We continue to build the routine that way until it's complete. Up until about five years ago, I remembered every routine I had ever choreographed!

Gymnastics was again the love of my life! The other girls on my team weren't great athletes, and the competition we faced wasn't stellar, but it was good, fun competition and I was able to rack up some wins. In my freshman year I won the city championship on the junior varsity team, and after that I placed second every year against a girl from a rival school or to one of my older teammates. It's funny, because as much as I disliked beam and was afraid of it, by my senior year I knew I wasn't likely to win the all-around or the other three events against my rival, but I felt I could win beam. That became my goal my senior year.

To make that happen I went back to Lakeshore to get in some extra training. That's when I bumped into Coach Jeremy again. I was in the gym and I hopped up on the beam right in front of him and did a beautiful series of connect skills. Afterward, I sarcastically asked, "Impressed?"

He looked at me and said, "Aimee, I was always impressed. I just didn't let you know it because I didn't think you would work as hard."

I was floored. My heart and mind flashed back to my adolescence as the pain I felt by Jeremy's constant rejection came flooding back to me. Had he truly thought that his dismissal of my effort was a tactic to help me grow? Most shocking, as I think back, is that this wasn't an involuntary habit or reflex: his complete inattention toward my efforts was intentional. I made a vow to myself right then and there never to forget how sad, small, and insignificant his coaching had made me feel; that included an unspoken promise to my future students that I would do my best not to repeat the errors in coaching that my coach had imposed on me. Coach Jeremy was the meanest coach I ever had and he influenced me the most in how I *would not* do my job in the future.

And in case you were wondering, I did win the beam title my senior year.

CHAPTER 3

Finding My Sisters

I graduated high school in 1991, and by the time I was eighteen years old, my body had endured over a decade of mediocre training on bad equipment. I was ready to retire. I had already been coaching for five years and wanted the summer off before I attended Northern Illinois University. After I moved into the dorms, my mom moved to Vermont, and so I was *really* on my own.

I was excited about college, but I didn't know what I wanted to do. My life was one big open road and so I picked communications as my major because I had to declare something. That first year I was a bit adrift: I did a lot of socializing and not a lot of studying. At the time, I probably would have told you gymnastics was not in my long-term future. I definitely thought I was done coaching.

The summer after my freshman year at NIU, however, I was pulled back to Lakeshore Academy. The gym had moved to a new location, but the atmosphere was familiar. I missed the physicality of training, and I missed helping others achieve new skills and movements.

One hot summer day I was at Lakeshore while the Romanian junior national team was training with their coach, Octavian Bellu. The team was in Chicago on a friendship tour and needed a place to work out on their non-performance days. You have to understand what a huge deal this was. Coach Bellu took over as the Romanian national team coach in 1981 after Martha and Bela Karolyi defected to the United States from Romania after coaching Nadia Comaneci to worldwide fame. Then, at the 1988 Summer Olympics in Seoul, South Korea, the Romanian team won silver and gymnast Daniela Silivaș dominated the games, winning six medals, including three golds. Romania would go on to win five consecutive world titles and back-to-back Olympic team gold medals. Being in the gym with them was a momentous event.

As if an itch needed to be scratched, I hopped up on the beam and performed some basic skills. Coach Bellu, not knowing anything about my gymnastics experience, said to me, "You have it. You have a gift." I looked at him peculiarly as he followed it up with "*You have to coach.*" I'm not sure why he said that. I'd like to think he noticed the pride I took in my technique and believed it should be shared.

Considering I wasn't used to being given any kind of praise in the gym, I responded with a simple "Okay," but his words turned into an epiphany. Those were the words that shaped the rest of my professional adult life.

A simple statement of affirmation unlocked any inhibition I had about my future. Here's where I have to confess that I'm only 90 percent sure it was Octavian who said these words. When I saw him at a competition years later, I was too afraid to confirm my memory in case he didn't have any recollection of what I was talking about. But whether it was Octavian or another Romanian coach, my life was altered. At the time, I had no direction in college, but the next morning I went to the registrar's office and changed my major to sports business. I knew I wanted to own a gym of my own.

I started coaching three to four times a week at a gym called the Northern Illinois Academy of Gymnastics. I coached the compulsory teams, which is a lower level of competition with standardized routines, as well as taught basic classes.

My favorite takeaway from that early part-time coaching job was the conversation I had with a coworker at the time. My coworker shared with me that our boss said I would never amount to anything as a coach: he thought I was *too nice.* Even then I remember thinking, *Fine, I won't be successful, then.* But I already believed that I could—that *everyone* could—pursue a different path than what was standard and expected at the time. I realized then that I had an opportunity to change the narrative.

Even though I had found a purpose, it wasn't as if I dropped everything and dedicated all my remaining time to learning all I could about coaching. When I began my freshman year, I was living in the dorms, and soon decided to pledge a sorority, Delta Phi Epsilon. In my sophomore year I moved into the sorority's newly built house on Annie Glidden Road, which had a magnificent cornfield as our backyard. The house was huge! In total, I lived with forty other women. I was never alone. This might say something about my comfort level of being in a gym with constant commotion. D Phi E is also where I met my dearest friend, Kevi Jackson. We ended up being roommates for a combined five years, between school and our postcollegiate adventures.

For those not familiar with Greek life, once you go through all of your pledge requirements, you become a full, "active" sister. I took a slightly different path. I spent a good portion of my years in college acting like I wanted to be a mixologist and unfortunately my GPA suffered from my lifestyle—and because of my grades, I wasn't allowed to get activated in that first year, making me a "neophyte." In fact, I was probably the longest-living neophyte in my sorority's history, because it took me four semesters to get my GPA high enough to be eligible for activation. While I worked on my grades, I stayed super-involved in the house. Greek life offered a lot of opportunities to compete that I fully embraced. These included swimming, TUGS (an extreme tug-of-war competition), and canoeing in boats handmade from recycled materials, most of which sank. But more important than the competitions and college shenanigans were the bonds I forged with my sisters. Those are everlasting, and the women of D Phi E became the highlight of my college years.

This is where I found my people. I found my team. Even today we can go years without talking with each other, and as soon as we reconnect, it's like we're back in Dekalb, looking out onto the cornfields. To this day I'm still very close with at least a dozen of my sisters, and it's now a running joke to commiserate about having "old" bodies, even though our minds are still free to have fun like college sorority girls.

***

I'm not a morning person. There was only one class I scheduled before 11:00 A.M., and most of my classes were in the late afternoon or evening. While I didn't love all my lectures, I loved my human anatomy class.

Unfortunately, Human Anatomy was only offered at 7:45 A.M., and it was a requirement for my major.

The coolest thing about the class was that the premed students dissected cadavers the night before, so when we would come in—at what seemed to be the crack of dawn—we got to see a new layer of the body each class. I loved it! It was my all-time favorite class.

As the semester went on, I noticed a weird thing starting to happen while I was coaching. I would picture my athletes without skin! Here I was, learning about the skeleton, the belly of a muscle, what the tendons looked like, where the ligaments were attached, and how everything worked together; and then I'd walk into the gym and start offering instructions. Coaching and cadavers collided in my mind. It became obvious where everything went, and the motion of the body became crystal clear to me because I could see it in my mind's eye. When a gymnast performed a skill, it became easy to imagine the muscles contracting under a layer of skin as the ligaments stabilized the joints.

When the semester was over, I had racked up nearly straight As on all my anatomy tests, which was one of the hardest classes I took. I think one reason I did so well in anatomy, aside from my interest in the subject, was because I'm a visual person—so being able to see the muscles in three dimensions, without them being concealed by skin, made it easier for me to learn and retain the information. It might seem like anatomy would be a natural fit for a gymnastics coach, but then again, when I was in high school, my least favorite class was physics. Hello, gymnastics *is* physics!

***

Human Anatomy had sparked an educational desire in me, but it still wasn't enough to keep me in college. After four years at Northern Illinois, and with about half a year left to graduate, I felt like I was just waiting to start my *real life*. I truly felt finishing college wasn't going to further what I wanted to do as a career, and I realized I didn't need a college degree to coach professionally.

Kevi was a couple of months from graduating with a teaching degree, and in March of 1995 she was asked to travel to Houston for an interview for a pre-K special education position in a low-economic-area school. The drive from Northern Illinois was around fifteen hours, so she asked if I wanted to join her. *ROAD TRIP!!!* I was absolutely up for an adventure.

When Kevi went off on her interview, it dawned on me that I had nothing to do. So on a whim, I grabbed a phone book (because we didn't have Google in our pockets) and looked up the nearby gyms. I walked through their doors and said, "Hey, I'm looking to move here from Illinois, and I'd like to coach." I participated in four interviews that day, resulting in three job offers. Kevi received her offer too. We were giddy.

Kevi graduated at the end of May, and the only real thought I had at the time about staying and graduating was considering how the degree might help me with the business side of running a gym—but I was ready to coach professionally now. Since my mom had always advocated for me to follow my passion, she was fully supportive. We both knew that college would be there for me if I decided to go back, making this a surprisingly easy decision.

I've never regretted not finishing the last year. In truth, the only drawback to not completing my degree was being restricted from applying for college coaching opportunities, since most college programs require a bachelor's degree. At the time, I knew I wasn't really happy at school, and except for the few courses that interested me, I wasn't a good college student. I was way more into my sorority than I was into the academics. I needed to stop wasting money and start earning it instead. So in June, right after Kevi graduated, we packed up our stuff and moved to Texas. (And twenty years later I completed my bachelor's degree, summa cum laude, in management while writing this book.)

CHAPTER 4

Coaching

I was standing on top of a ten-meter platform, looking down. The water was crystal clear, making the drop seem twice as far when I stared at the bottom of the pool. This was how my new coworkers at Cypress Academy of Gymnastics initiated me into the program.

Head men's coach, Tom Meadows, and the current Cypress Academy owner Aaron Basham, told me anytime somebody new started at Cypress Academy they had to make this leap. I don't know if it was true or not, but I was game. We climbed a fence to the public pool under the cover of night, and I got ready to dive into my new job—a little scared, but with enthusiasm.

It was then I learned what great motivators the two of them are, because when I expressed concern—"I don't think I can do it"—Aaron reassured me, "Okay, I'm going to hold your hand and we're going to jump on three."

He started his countdown: "All right. One. Two . . ." *Wait, do we do it on three? Or is it one, two, three, and then do it?* Before I had a chance to finish my thought, he jumped while still gripping my palm, which tugged me awkwardly off the edge of the platform—lacking the grace or confidence of a Coast Guard diver jumping from a helicopter, I tumbled into a less-than-elegant position when I hit the water. *Slap!* Always the competitor, I decided I was going to do it again. I climbed back up and I jumped on my own the second time, which I admit was pretty fun. The next morning I woke up with nice petechial bruises speckling the undersides of my arms. (Quick coaching tip: Don't spread your arms out and let them smack the water from ten meters up.)

Aaron's parents started Cypress Academy in Cypress, Texas, in 1982, and Tom was his best friend and college teammate at the University of Oklahoma. We were twenty-three-year-old kids when we jumped off that high dive, ready to make a splash. Within the gymnastics community, Cypress Academy is very well regarded for its men's program; less than two decades later, Tom was named the assistant coach of the United States Men's Olympic Team for the 2012 Olympics in London. We had all dreamed of coaching at the Olympics someday, and when Tom was named a coach for the 2012 USA Team, one thought popped into my head: *Wow, one of us made it!*

Cypress Academy was growing and expanding when I started in 1995, and I got to observe the women's elite program there. There were several national team members in the gym, including Andreé Pickens, who was an alternate on the 1995 U.S. World Championship team, and Eileen Díaz, who competed in the 1996 Atlanta Olympics for Puerto Rico.

Speaking of the '96 Olympics, this was when I participated in my first Olympic photo shoot! *Vanity Fair* was prepping their Olympic preview issue, and they called on the Cypress Academy staff to help with the photo shoot of soon-to-be Olympians Dominique Moceanu and John Roethlisberger. Before the shoot, the photographer, Annie Leibovitz (maybe you've heard of her), needed help to bring in gymnastics equipment, and of course I volunteered. The Cypress staff went to a local hotel ballroom—not the gym—and carried in the equipment. In addition to being movers, we were also there to spot the athletes.

Before the future Olympians arrived, Annie needed someone to pose while she checked the lighting. I hopped up on the beam and did a scale. Annie wound up taking a bunch of shots of me with her little ol' Polaroid camera to check the shadows and whatnot. When she was done, the crew swept up all the pictures on the floor Annie didn't want. I noticed one of the Polaroids she took of me, and I slid it under my foot before reaching down and picking it up to take home. So, yeah, I have a tiny photo of me up on the beam that was taken by Annie Leibowitz. Pretty cool, huh?

When I wasn't posing for *Vanity Fair*, I lived in the gym. Even when I wasn't coaching, I would sit on the steps leading to the coaches' office and watch the elite coaches. There was never anybody else in the gym when the twin sisters coaching duo, Debbie and Deana, were coaching the elites, but they never said, "Get out of here!" so I figured I'd just sit there and quietly observe, knowing at any moment they could ask me to leave the training session. I am forever grateful that they didn't ask me to go. I took a risk and sat there, and I learned a ton from observing these elite coaches. I would watch them instruct for hours and I learned so much about technique just sitting in the background. Even though I had been in the gym weekly for seventeen years, I was never able to observe real sessions with elite athletes. Watching the skill level, form, and self-discipline of these athletes was inspiring. Observing these training sessions made me believe I could coach at the elite level: I could go to the Olympics.

Looking back, I think it's also fair to say the coaches were very hard on their athletes. I heard them speak to their gymnasts in a way that made me, as a bystander, wonder if there was a better way to communicate with their students. Unfortunately, their coaching methods—where intimidation was wielded as a motivator—were commonplace in the 1980s and '90s, and we are now seeing the harm that style of coaching caused. By the time I was being influenced by them, I already understood what kind of coach I wanted to be. When others suggested I was too nice, this is often the style of coaching I was compared to. My philosophy was to take what was useful and throw the rest away.

At Cypress Academy, I was coaching forty hours a week and getting paid $12 per hour. That felt like really good money for that time—the equivalent of almost $24 today. I had been making around $9 an hour in Illinois, so it was a pretty big raise. More importantly, for the first time, I was working under people who had been coaching gymnastics as a full-time career rather than as part-time work. Within months of moving to Texas I was learning more about my profession than I had in all my years in college. If I ever had any apprehension about not finishing my degree, my early experience at Cypress Academy quickly allayed those concerns. However, after a little less than a year, I also realized Cypress Academy wasn't the right environment for me.

At that time, Cypress Academy—from the parents to the staff—was all about winning. Don't get me wrong: winning isn't bad—but when that's the dominant focus, the other great parts of the sport can get lost. The gym had a competitive spirit that I liked, but it was blinding. If they didn't win, the gymnasts were made to feel bad about themselves and their performance. This style never resonated with me. During my time there, the kids were threatened with additional conditioning or demeaned as a form of motivation to accomplish assignments in the gym. They were not allowed to discuss injuries or express fears. They were expected to train without complaints, and making improvements was not enough: they were expected to finish in first place. The training they received from some of the coaches gave me flashbacks to the negative experiences I had with Coach Jeremy. I knew I couldn't be the coach I wanted to be at Cypress. Beyond the culture, there also seemed to be no prospect of upward mobility and little incentive for me to stay.

In the world of gymnastics, there are club environments for everyone. Some gyms will only put you in competition if you show the potential of winning; others wait until you can perform all of the skills safely and without assistance; and some will let the chips fall where they may. Gymnastics in Texas is highly competitive, and becoming a state champion at any level tends to be a driving force for competitors in many clubs. Cypress Academy was a gym that worked hard to be atop the podium.

In the big scheme of things, the gymnastics community is relatively small. So, while attending various competitions with the Cypress Academy kids, I made a few coaching friends at other gyms, which led to another life change.

***

I took my ambition to Bannon's Gymnastix, in Spring, Texas, in the summer of 1996. While I had learned a ton at Cypress Academy from watching professionals in action, Bannon's was my graduate school. Before arriving, I had watched the way the Bannon's coaches interacted with their athletes at competitions, how they talked about their jobs, and how much they loved the kids and their workplace environment. I knew that was the right place for me. I was young; I wanted to grow and be valued. That seems counterintuitive when you consider I went from making $12 an hour to $10 an hour; however, everything at Bannon's was an opportunity.

Martha Bannon was the owner of the gym and also my boss, and she did a great job of finding ways for people to make more money by incentivizing them to be better coaches and gymnastics professionals. If you earned your judging certifications, you got a pay raise. If you received more training, you got a pay raise. If you saw something that was a hazard in the gym that needed to be fixed or replaced, you got a small bonus; you didn't have to be the one to fix it, but you had to fill out the paperwork. So instead of just noticing there was something wrong, like a gap between a mat and the wall, you had to point out the gap, say how it could be fixed, and figure out what it would cost to fix it. Martha would have you do the research for it, and she'd give you a $10 bonus for that. I thought this was a brilliant system, because it upped the level of care and accountability of everyone in the gym, effectively creating a feeling of vested interest in the employees. Not only were we rewarded for our initiative, but our participation in keeping the gym safe and up-to-date gave us a better environment to work in.

Martha's incentives made sure the employees had skin in the game. If I mustered the initiative to take a coaching education class or get a judging certificate, I would have to register and pay for it myself, but doing so would get me a raise, with the level of the judging certificate determining how much my raise was. For example, an entry-level judge's certificate might boost my pay by 15 cents per hour, whereas a more upper-level certificate would increase my pay by 25 cents per hour. Now, these were classes I could get excited about! It didn't take me long to make that $2 an hour back because I studied a lot. The prospect of fast-tracking my income and my knowledge at the same time was all the motivation I needed. It made so much sense from a business perspective, too, because we were not only becoming better coaches; we were becoming more valuable coaches who might garner higher tuition rates for the gym. I always thought that if I ever opened my own gym, I would model a lot of it after what Martha did.

I attended my first USA Gymnastics National Congress while at Cypress Academy and a few more times while at Bannon's. Congress is the annual educational seminar and trade show hosted by USA Gymnastics (USAG), the national governing body. The event typically coincides with the U.S. national championships or Olympic trials and lasts three days, each of which is packed with training on the latest techniques, safety measures, rule changes, and more. On top of that, there's a trade show where you can find the latest equipment, leotard designs, and even insurance policies for your gym. The USAG event is the big one, moving around the country to a new city each year, but many gymnastics regions throughout the country also host their own congress, and Texas, being a huge state geographically and a hotbed of gymnastics, hosts their own. And when I say "hotbed," I'm talking about the best gymnasts in the world going back decades, including Mary Lou Retton (1984 all-around Olympic gold medalist), Dominique Moceanu (1996 Olympic gold medalist), Carly Patterson (2004 all-around Olympic gold medalist), Nastia Liukin (2008 all-around Olympic gold medalist), Madison Kocian (2016 Olympic gold medalist), and of course Simone Biles (GOAT). That's just naming a select few and leaving off many other Olympians and world medalists. People like to talk about football being a big sport in Texas, but the sleeping giant is really gymnastics.

The conference in Texas is called GAT (Gymnastics Association of Texas). Like the USAG Congress, GAT is also a three-day event, and it is bursting with educational opportunities. You show up, get your credential, go to clinics all day, and party all night. It's a *lot* of fun. I went every year and earned every certification I could at GAT.

One of my favorite presenters was Tammy Biggs, an Olympic coach, brevet judge (the highest level in the sport), and educator extraordinaire. Tammy was great at helping me with technical tips on skills I was just learning to teach. In fact, she's probably the clinician I learned the most from when I started becoming an upper-level coach. Maybe it was the way she communicated.

I've always enjoyed the hands-on process of coming up with my own drills in the gym. I think this relates back to my college days of studying cadavers. Tammy is a master of drills. Her sessions at Congress were loaded with innovative ways to break down skills, and her presentations helped me think about how to approach a new skill with a creative and fun maneuver that gymnasts could do without the physical support of a coach.

For example, a glide kip is a skill on bars that is quite standard in gymnastics but is not easy to learn. A glide kip is also one of those core skills everyone celebrates when achieved for the first time. A kip requires you to jump to the bar from the ground and swing your body to the opposite side. Upon reaching the apex of the swing, you have to quickly lift your toes to the bar before your hips swing back past the bottom of the bar, using your body as a pendulum. But there's more: you then have to quickly bring your shoulders up above the bar, so you end perched on top of the bar on your hands.

Now, imagine you're a child at the beginning stages of learning a glide kip. You lack the technical knowledge and strength to execute the skill. So as a coach, I would break it down. I'd have a station set up that teaches the jump to the bar, one that works the extension of the glide, another that reinforces the speed of the leg lift, and, finally, one that fortifies the importance of strength and swing to arrive on top of the bar at the end of the skill. All of these stations would be crafted with tips that resonate with the age group I'm working with. Where a kindergartner might think it's funny to kick a stuffed animal to work on their leg speed, a thirteen-year-old would not. That was the power of going to these conferences. I gained the knowledge of how to make a child of any age feel like the unattainable was achievable by breaking it down into its component parts, no matter how small.

Once, I created a drill for a front handspring layout on the floor. I designed it all on my own and hadn't shown it around. A year later I saw Tammy demonstrating the exact same drill I had crafted. I had absorbed so much methodology from her that I was able to create training exercises like the master. Adding my own personality to the process, I love to include humor into my coaching. When I come up with a really useful drill, I like to joke with the gymnasts, asking, "You know why that works . . . because I'm a genius!" Sometimes they join in on the answer with "because *you're* a genius," usually accompanied by an eye roll.

Using the educational resources at my disposal, I earned every coaching certificate available; so then I decided to take my judging test. I figured, *If I'm more educated on how to judge deductions, and not just read them in the rule book—if I'm actually able to judge—then I'm going to be able to help my kids score better.* Becoming a judge seemed the next logical step in my education.

LEVELING UP TO ELITE

Judging and competition in gymnastics are done by levels, in what was formerly called the Junior Olympic (JO) program. These levels are grouped together into three categories: developmental, compulsory, and optional.

Level 1–3 (developmental): When you take your kid into the gym for the first time and they're doing somersaults, that's level 1. The first three levels in gymnastics are mostly noncompetitive and are considered developmental. (There are some—but very few—gyms that compete at level 1, which is cuteness overload because gymnasts only have to be four years old to participate at this level. Most clubs will have their kids compete in what's called Xcel, an intermediary level before more competition at level 3.)

Levels 4–5 (compulsory): Each athlete will compete with the same skills and routines to demonstrate proficiency. It's "compulsory" because gymnasts don't have a choice on their routines.

Levels 6–10 (optional): This is the competitive gymnastics you're used to seeing, with gymnasts starting to do their own unique skills and composition. It's really not until level 8 that you begin to see original choreography on the balance beam and in the floor exercise.

Elites: These are the gymnasts you see at the Olympics who have worked their way through the JO program. If a gymnast wants to compete internationally, within the U.S. system the gymnast needs to pass compulsory and optional qualifiers to become "elite." The global governing body, the International Gymnastics Federation (FIG, after Fédération Internationale de Gymnastique), doesn't have any such requirement, which is why you can see a wide range of talent competing at a world championship. The FIG elite system is separated into Juniors (ages eleven to fifteen) and Seniors (ages sixteen-plus). In order to compete in the Olympics, you must be sixteen during the year of the games.

I acquired my first compulsory-level judging certificate in 1999 (four years before Simone ever stepped foot in a gym) and immediately started judging. I worked my way up to a level 10–rated judge and I loved it! When I wasn't coaching, I was judging. There are so many competitions in Texas that I didn't need to go far from home to judge. When you are a new judge, you start by judging the lowest levels, so the skills are easier to identify and the judging shorthand (the symbols judges use to identify skills on paper) is very basic. I was paid to sit and watch gymnastics all day. It was more than a win-win. I was training myself to see routines from a judge's perspective and then using that knowledge when I was working with athletes in the gym. I consistently judged throughout the decade until 2011, when my schedule with Simone was so busy, I only had a few weekends free to spend time with my family. In an effort to find balance, I stopped judging for the time being, and I cherished those weekends when I could stay home to be a mom and wife.

So, yeah, I got a *lot* of training while at Bannon's. Throughout all of these conferences and clinics, I learned technique, sports science, and proper periodization—breaking down how you will spend the year training your athletes, incorporating strength and conditioning, learning new skills, constructing routines, competing, and recovery time. I also gained a sense of camaraderie with the gymnastics community. For the first time I felt like I was part of something larger than local sports. I continued going to all of the conferences and classes I could, trying to learn everything I could until around 2014 when I realized I had reached a point in my career where I could be the one giving the lectures. This was a profound moment in my career because I couldn't help but notice the similarities I felt during my last year in college. Was I just wasting money going to these clinics? Had the student become the master? Not yet.

My journey at Bannon's wasn't without conflict. At Cypress Academy, I was the nice coach. At Bannon's, the "nice" label wasn't so easily applied. One day not long after I moved to Bannon's, I said the word "stupid" while coaching. I was coaching a twelve-year-old who was up on the beam, not concentrating and being stubborn. Unsurprisingly, she fell. Then I blurted out, "Well, that was stupid." I didn't call *her* stupid. I was referring to the actions and attitude that led to the fall that were stupid. Either way, I shouldn't have used the word: the kid heard "stupid" and fixated on that, naturally. My choice of words made her feel awful.

Making matters worse (or maybe better, because we had a constructive conversation) was the fact that her mom was a fellow coach in the gym. The gymnast told her mom that I "called her stupid" and my colleague, rightfully, was genuinely upset with me. I explained to her how I hadn't called her daughter stupid, though I was sorry she felt that was what I said. Things eventually calmed down and it was a huge lesson for me about how single words can be very triggering, regardless of the context or even intent.

It's scary to write about this incident because I want this book to be honest while also not wanting anyone on the "gymternet"—the extremely passionate online gymnastics community—to take things out of context or to blow them out of proportion. What I said is not comparable to the time U.S. national champion Vanessa Atler disclosed her eating disorder to a person within USAG and they allegedly replied, "Sometimes you have to do what you have to do." Or when UCLA standout Margzetta Frazier reported her club coach,

Joe Catrambone, for telling her and her sister to "Go kill yourself." Catrambone would later be convicted on child endangerment charges. I've heard other gymnasts share stories of coaches who have been reported for calling gymnasts lazy, fat, useless, retarded, and stupid. (See, there's that word "stupid.")

As a coach who was accused of using it inappropriately, I fully understand how context and recollection matter. I would never call an athlete stupid. That's never constructive language, and I immediately regretted that this was how the young gymnast perceived what I had said.

I'm glad I learned that lesson, because more than anything I wanted the kids to have fun, with winning as a nice bonus if it happened. When I arrived at Bannon's I was now the "mean" coach. In fact, some kids quit because they thought I was too tough. My coaching style didn't change, but the environment sure had. I think what they considered mean was me expecting effort in their execution of skills and accountability. I didn't yell and I didn't put gymnasts down, but I did expect a certain level of discipline. Although the gym may have looked like a playground, this wasn't recess.

In general, Bannon's had some talented gymnasts who could win at competitions, but when I started working there, in competition we weren't very strong. My philosophy was "You're only as good as your worst gymnast." So if your worst athlete is out there not looking like they know how to do gymnastics at all, you need to work harder and become a better coach: Figure out how to communicate with the gymnast and bring the very best out of that struggling kid. In short order, the ones who didn't quit did win—and these weren't exceptional gymnasts; they were just kids who were able to balance fun and technique. I think before I arrived there was a lot of fun and not a lot of technique.

The other thing that was somewhat unique about Bannon's was that while other gyms pick the gymnasts who compete on their teams, at Bannon's we weren't selective. If you could do the skills, you made the team. It wasn't about whether a kid had the right body type, or was the right age, or had the right physical fitness, or what their parents looked like, or how much they paid for extra coaching through private lessons.

We had all makes and models of kids in the gym, which made it much more challenging to coach a large group of diverse athletes.

As a coach, I think it's important to treat every kid the same. I have the same expectations in regard to work ethic with each athlete I coach, and every kid gets taught the same techniques. Of course, that will require flexibility (no pun intended) every once in a while. For example, if a kid can't physically do a technique you need to make an adjustment and come up with something different. You get creative.

Have you ever heard of a gymnast "throwing" or "chucking" a skill? That's when they attempt a skill without any technical training, throwing caution to the wind. Some coaches allow this, and this is a process (or lack of one) that I do not agree with. Coaches have to *teach* technique. Throwing skills without proper technique is how gymnasts get hurt. In general, however, everybody under my leadership gets the same assignment, everybody gets the same praise, and everyone is expected to have the same self-discipline and show the same respect. That's how you form a team.

What was also striking to me, when I changed gyms, wasn't just the gymnasts and my fellow coaches but the parents. At Cypress Academy, parents expected their kids to win. With winning came confirmation of their child's status and the seriousness of the training. The parents were always nice to me during my time at Cypress, but I had to stand by and watch parents burden their children with high expectations of success. At Bannon's, parents were definitely less intense and would get excited when their kids would win. Instead of being the standard expectation, winning was more of a thrill, a welcome surprise, something to celebrate.

Over time, we started doing more of that: winning. When I started at Bannon's, there were maybe a total of five level 9s and 10s, with some gymnasts testing elite—and through the years those numbers improved. One of my proudest moments at Bannon's was coaching a really good bunch of kids whom I had started working with when they were at level 4 and continued to coach through levels 8 and 9. Effectively coaching them from the introductory compulsory level to become very capable, competitive mid- to upper-level gymnasts. That group did a lot of winning. I didn't have to change my philosophy to get them to perform at their peak. I believe what took them to that next level of competitiveness was a step up in expectations with regard to how they practiced and performed while keeping their time in the gym fun. They were just kids, after all . . . and it was just gymnastics.

***

How did I step up my expectations? We started doing skills testing four times a year. The gymnasts and parents knew what skill sets were required to be able to move up to train at a new level and eventually be competitive at that level. It made everybody accountable, and it worked wonders. There were no surprises when you had to decide what level a child was going to go into. The parents knew where their child was supposed to be even if they didn't always like it. Their daughters' level placement was justified, and both parents and athletes understood. This saved countless hours of conversation with parents.

Accountability also came in the form of making good choices about fueling their bodies. A gymnast and her parents were in control of her diet and education. I was her gymnastics coach. I could teach her how to be an amazing gymnast, but I didn't want to sit and lecture her (or her parents) about what they should or shouldn't be feeding her.

Is that to say I never had any opinion on food? No. I would mention to my athletes how food is the fuel source for their machines, and the type of food they consume would determine how their machine was going to run. So if Simone chose to have Cinnabon every night, her machine wasn't going to run at its optimum level. I didn't want the discussion of her diet and nutrition to become part of our relationship.

The most frequent conversation I had with the girls about food involved reminding them that it was important they *did not* skip meals. Since practice was in the late afternoon, some days the gymnasts would become lethargic, and I'd ask, "What did you eat for breakfast and lunch today?" Shockingly, they would admit that they hadn't eaten anything that day.

"No wonder you're struggling in practice," I'd emphasize. My experience was that most of the girls weren't overeating; rather, they were not nourishing themselves enough, and therefore their bodies weren't performing. Whenever I discovered a girl's tank didn't have any fuel in it, I'd make her stop and go eat something during practice.

Later in my career, when I was running my own program, I had a rule that if practice lasted more than three hours, there was a mandatory snack break for everybody, including the coaches. The fifteen-minute break was perfect for the three R's: relieving themselves, refueling, and rest.

I think sometimes coaches and parents forget just how stretched the days are for many of these kids. It makes sense, because parents are running errands, working full days, and feeling tired, too, but coaches need to take into consideration the gymnasts' time. Many of these kids are up at 5:30 in the morning, complete a full day of school; then they come to the gym for three to five hours, not finishing their workout until 8:00 or 9:00 at night. Then they still have to go home and do all of their homework, sometimes not getting to bed until midnight before repeating the process the next day.

When do these kids ever just sit and rest? As coaches, we need to offer the gymnasts time. Time to rest, time to recover, time to eat. If we don't allow them time to eat something decent, they're just going to grab fast food on the way home because that might be all they have time for. This is all a recipe for their minds and bodies to break down. I would sometimes get ridiculed by coaches from other gyms when I argued that their kids shouldn't be going nonstop for five hours straight.

A lot of attention is put on the fuel that the gymnasts consume, which is important, but people forget that coaches need to keep their energy up too. At the end of a three-hour afternoon practice, most coaches have already been in the gym for six hours. The fifteen-minute break that we put on the schedule was not just for the athletes but for the coaches as well. Getting "hangry" is a real thing, and often we need a mental time-out, too—an opportunity for us to go into our offices and close the doors for fifteen minutes so we can finish the last two hours of practice strong.

There were days when I could tell my athletes were stressed about something other than their training. If they felt like they were overwhelmed with schoolwork, I suggested that they go home an hour early so they could study. Or instead of having a fifteen-minute break, they needed to take a thirty-minute break to prepare for a test they might have the next day. Some days it was as simple as "Come in later" or "Stay home tomorrow."

My goal was to be flexible about their training. I didn't want them to feel like there would be repercussions for them if they missed gym because of school. I always set the order of priorities as family, school, and then gymnastics. I wanted them to put gymnastics before any other sport they might be doing, but family and school needed to come first.

So, if Grandpa's having an eightieth birthday party, you skip the gym. Grandpa might not be around much longer. It's your best friend's birthday? Go to the party. You're not going to forget how to do gymnastics in one day, plain and simple; heck, we learned through the pandemic that gymnasts didn't lose their skills even after weeks or months away. (Conditioning, however, is a different story.) I believe it's important to take that time to live life because you won't get that time back.

You can make up the hours in the gym, but you can't relive an event that won't happen again. I know a lot of coaches who think just the opposite. They believe you'll never get the training time back. Well, yeah, you actually can, but your family isn't going to celebrate Grandpa's eightieth birthday again just for you. Once these moments are gone, they're gone. And it's not just those singular moments. If I had stayed in Chicago to train each summer, I would never have gotten to see my dad when I was growing up. Each year, I took a two-month hiatus from the gym to see the rest of my family in Vermont, and each time I returned to Chicago, I was happier, healthier, and more eager to improve—and I never forgot how to do my skills while on vacation.

Family . . . school . . . gymnastics. In that order.

In the summer of 1996, my mom decided she wasn't going to miss any more moments with me. Shortly after I had settled at Bannon's, she moved to Texas. In hindsight, without her presence, I'm not sure my upcoming journey with Simone would have been possible.

CHAPTER 5

Puppy Love

In 1998, I was working at Bannon's and living in an apartment with my dog, Deohgee, a Rottweiler/German shepherd mix. Directly below my apartment lived a handsome landscape architect named James and his Weimaraner, Tucker. When I was at the gym, my mom would take my dog on walks, and soon Deohgee fell in love with Tucker. It got to the point that when I opened my front door Deohgee would sprint downstairs and sit in front of James's door.

I understood the attraction of our dogs. Deohgee was really smart and a bit intimidating, and Tucker was much calmer and even a little dopey, which balanced the pair out. I'm not going to say the dog personalities matched the owners, but there were definite similarities.

On October 4, 1998, James and I went on our first date to the Texas Renaissance Festival, and we instantly clicked. James was chill and endlessly fascinating. He was a Navy brat and had lived all over the world. He was born in Morocco and lived in Hawaii and the Philippines before his family settled at Naval Air Station Corpus Christi in Texas.

James's family has an esteemed naval history. His great-grandfather Norman Schwien was captain of the light cruiser USS *Raleigh*, and his grandfather James Albert Boorman II was a rear admiral of the USS *Oklahoma*. On the evening of December 6, 1941, James's grandmother was rushed to the hospital, causing James II to leave his command to be with his wife, who was suffering a miscarriage. Early on December 7, 1941, the *Oklahoma* was torpedoed in Pearl Harbor in the infamous surprise attack by Japan. The ship sank during the attack. The replacement officer, sadly, went down with the *Oklahoma*. The tragic loss of the baby, which forced James II off the ship, saved the Boorman family lineage.

The next child born was James's father, James Albert "Skip" Boorman III, who was a bit of a prodigy. He graduated from high school a couple of months after turning seventeen and graduated from the University of Texas Business School at nineteen. He added a law degree from University of Texas School of Law at twenty-three and by twenty-six he was a member of the Navy Judge Advocate General's Corps. While in JAG he received a master's in international law from George Washington University. He also served as a general courts-martial military judge. Skip married Bonnie Crenshaw, of the prominent Crenshaws of Austin, Texas, in 1968. Their first son was James Albert Boorman IV, born in April 1971.

James chose not to follow in the family's footsteps and did not enlist in the Navy, becoming the black sheep of his family. Perhaps more sacrilegious, he passed over the family school, the University of Texas, for Texas A&M. At the time, James was interested in aerospace engineering, and A&M offered a highly ranked program. He is an amazing artist, and we still have an incredibly detailed space shuttle image hanging up in our home that he drew by hand while still in high school. When the dust settled in College Station—and after James changed his major six times—he discovered the school had another high-quality program that better suited his interests: landscape architecture.

When I met James, he was designing golf courses. James likes to say, "Anything inside the walls is the job of the standard architect; anything outside of the walls is the job of the landscape architect." It turns out that designing golf courses was more in line with the family business than outsiders might assume. James's uncle is the two-time Masters golf champion Ben Crenshaw. I remember being invited to Ben's house for Thanksgiving dinner. My grandparents were huge fans of Ben's, but, having never watched golf in my life, I had no idea who he was.

Beyond designing golf courses, James has done everything from grading and drainage to designing hills, lakes, community gates, and landscape placement. Basically, if nature didn't put it there, James intentionally designed it that way.

James and I were engaged the year after we started dating and married on February 11, 2000—the only weekend on my calendar without a competition scheduled. For the record, James knew exactly what he was signing up for when it came to my career and schedule. The fact that he met my mom before me—she was walking Deohgee—was his first clue that being a coach meant I wasn't operating on a nine-to-five workday.

On the day of the big event, we had a modest wedding party of three bridesmaids and three groomsmen, but if you viewed our wedding photos, you might think it was a royal engagement. We cared a lot about the team I was coaching and it was important for us that they were all there together, so, along with our official attendants dressed in all black, we had a grander party of thirteen flower girls and thirteen junior bridesmaids. Dressed in white-and-black dresses, accessorized by floral headbands made by my mother, the flower girls gracefully sprinkled the aisle with petals, followed by the junior bridesmaids, who proudly illuminated my path with a procession of candles. (Admittedly, I was terrified that with the amount of hairspray in the room, someone's hair would catch on fire!) Finally, steering away from traditional norms, my mother escorted me to my soon-to-be husband.

Unfortunately, I wasn't there to coach the youngest members of my wedding party the following weekend. I missed my first meet ever as a coach because I was still on my honeymoon in Ocho Rios, Jamaica. Nine months later, James Albert Boorman VII (a.k.a. Jamie) joined our family. I had worked up to my due date, but Jamie wasn't quite ready. He was born a week later, on November 18, and within three days he was already in the gym with me. Before Jamie was a week old, he was at his first gymnastics meet. James was busy with work, so my mom would come to the meets and hold Jamie while I was coaching, and in between the sessions I would nurse him. It took a village. I didn't take my official maternity leave with Jamie until he was six months old. I wanted to get through the fall and spring seasons before I felt comfortable taking a break from coaching.

This pattern repeated itself with the births of our second and third sons. Chris was born in March 2004 and Ben was born on October 4, 2008—exactly ten years to the day from our first date at the Texas Renaissance Festival. I worked up to my due date again with Chris but then took the following week off. I concede my pregnancy with Ben was a little bit different. We were still in competition season when Hurricane Ike ripped through Texas. The Category 4 hurricane knocked out the power at the gym, which enabled me to stay home for two weeks before Ben was born. I'll be honest: being a little older, my pregnancy with Ben was the toughest. Simone was a level 9 at that time, and so the schedule was still manageable. I had cut back on some of my hours before Ben's due date, but I was still actively coaching; and when the hurricane hit, I wished I had gone into labor because I was *so over* being pregnant. Even in my discomfort, though, it still took an act of God to keep me out of the gym.

My mom lived with us almost the whole time I was coaching in Texas. She wanted to be Grandma, but she was almost more of a parent to them because I was away so much. For several years, a normal workday would consist of me waking up as late as 11:00 A.M. I would go to the gym to do administrative work around 1:00 P.M. and then coach until 9:00 P.M. After talking with gym parents and wrapping up the day, I usually would not leave the gym until about 9:30. James was the one who would wake the kids at six in the morning and get them fed and ready for school. James and my mom also split dinner duties, although my mom did most of the cooking. This is where her grandparent nature kicked in. She regularly served a kid-friendly menu of hot dogs, hamburgers, fish sticks, and pizza. My mom went above and beyond, though. She would make organic chicken patties and nuggets from scratch, plus organic bread, baked fresh every day, and organic hot dog and hamburger buns. Most nights, dinner also included peas, because that was a tolerable vegetable for my kids. When I wanted my kids to eat more veggies, they went on a mini hunger strike in protest and we compromised for more fruit. (If they read this, they'll find out that I also added veggies to their smoothies.) Even though I walked through the door well past dinnertime, every night James would wait to eat with me.

Having been all over the world himself, James was comfortable when I began traveling the country—and then the world—with Simone. The fact that my mom lived with us and helped us out made the entire process feasible; I honestly don't know what our lives would have looked like without her. The life of a mom and coach is filled with compromise, sacrifice, and understanding from those around you. In all the years I've been coaching, James has never expressed an issue with the hours I spent at the gym or on the road. If anything, I would apologize about being gone and he would wave my apology away, reminding me that this was my career. But the time you put in with other people's children you can't get back and give to your own kids, who have no choice in the matter—and over time it can get to you.

I wouldn't have been able to stay in this career if I hadn't had a great support system—people who will be there for you, through the good times and the bad. I found one of those people in my dear friend Rebekah Ma. Rebekah and I met at Bannon's in 1998. She was a young coach with a toddler. Like me, she had been in the gym her whole life. Rebekah and I clicked on coaching philosophies almost immediately, and as each year passed, our bond as friends grew stronger. She became my rock. Rebekah has been by my side for twenty-five years. Our combined eight children were neatly staggered in age, so they always had a "cousin" to hang out with. When my mom wasn't coaching or cooking for my kids, she could be found at Bannon's, watching *all* of the coaches' kids. The reality is that great coaches put in more than they ever get back, so it's great to have people to rely on and even better to have a friend by your side through it all.

PART TWO
Simone

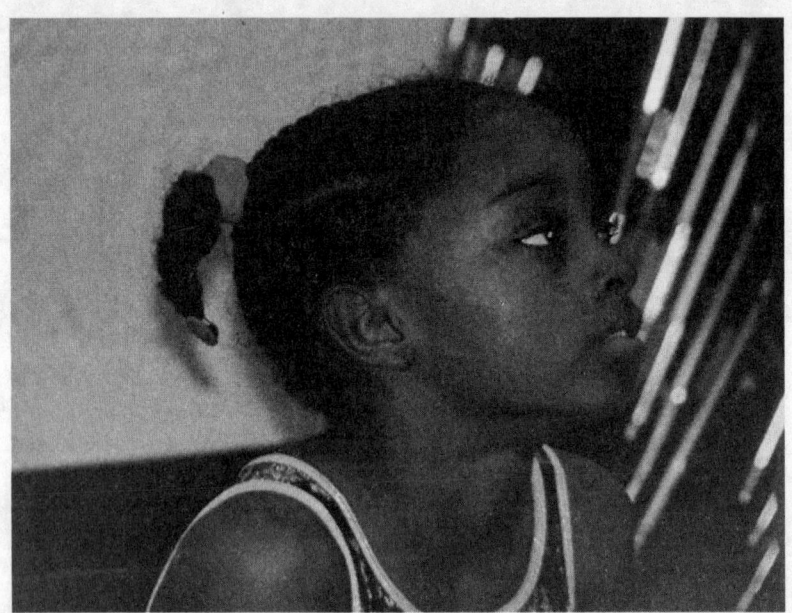
Simone waiting for practice. Courtesy Teresa Remmert.

CHAPTER 6

Young Simone

In addition to helping around the house, my mom also took a position at Bannon's, doing mostly administrative work. Over the years my mom has spent a lot of time in gymnastics gyms and has seen three decades of gymnastics in person. Then, one serendipitous day at Bannon's, my mom recognized something special in a six-year-old little girl who had just arrived on a field trip: Simone Biles.

Simone first arrived at Bannon's in 2003 because it was raining outside and a planned excursion to an oil ranch needed to be rerouted indoors. Typically, during one of these field trips, the kids will explore the gym and bounce around a bit, and then we'll send them off with some paperwork to sign up for classes if they are interested. During her visit, Simone was bouncing all over the place, and it was obvious to my mom that she had something special, so much so that she came over to me in an attempt to get me to watch Simone.

"Sure, Mom," I remarked, then went off to do something I deemed more important at the time. No additional conversation. I completely blew her off.

Fortunately, Simone's parents, Nellie and Ron Biles, signed her up for classes. That same year they also adopted her; Ron is Simone's biological grandfather, and Simone had been put in foster care at age three along with her siblings because her biological mother struggled with drug and alcohol abuse. (I didn't know Ron and Nellie were Simone and her sister Adria's adoptive parents until Ron mentioned adoption in a casual conversation several years later. Two of their siblings, sister Ashley and brother Tevin, were adopted by Ron's sister.)

Soon after Simone started at Bannon's, I was walking through the gym one day and I noticed this little, tiny, muscly kid bouncing around. She just couldn't stand still. She would drop on her bottom and bounce back up to her feet like she was on a trampoline . . . but she wasn't. She wasn't even on the spring floor: she was on a four-inch cushion base mat, which is only slightly softer than a tire. Next, I was strolling past her while she was sitting on the floor with her legs out in front of her. Without standing up Simone pressed down with her arms and lifted her bottom up off the ground, giving her legs room to slide under her body as if she were weightless. She pulled her legs between her arms all the way behind her until she was lying on her stomach. That's something normal people just don't do!

So I went over to my mom to tell her about this amazing kid who had caught my eye and whom I had just "discovered."

And she remarked with annoyance, "That's the kid I was telling you about!" But I foolishly had not listened to her the first time she approached me. Life lesson: Listen to your mom!

Simone participated in maybe three or four classes at the very most; then we moved her up from level 3 to the competitive program on the level 4 team. She was just learning everything so easily and so quickly.

One day Simone was watching some cheerleaders doing standing backflips. Simone had just turned seven. She said, "I can do that." To which she got a response of "No, you can't: you just started gymnastics." And then she stood up and she did it!

Then one of the coaches said, "Hey, can you do it on the beam?"

And so what did Simone do? Because she's fearless, she sprinted over and jumped up on the high beam. The high beam is four feet off the ground, so imagine little three-foot-tall Simone hopping on top of it. Collectively the coaches shouted, "Get down!" Thankfully she did. Blindly challenging a gifted and adventurous athlete was probably not the best example of what great coaching was, since a backflip on the high beam was way too risky for a completely new gymnast to attempt.

But we were still curious. "Could you try it on the low beam?" Pointing to a training balance beam that sits directly on the floor. Simone stepped onto the low beam and did a standing back tuck. She had just started in gymnastics and she was doing standing back tucks on a beam when she should have been learning how to do basic elements like handstand, cartwheels, and walkovers. This was similar to a young kid grabbing a baseball bat for the first time and not only making contact but hitting the ball deep into the outfield of Wrigley Field.

Many people might think that Simone immediately started winning everything from the moment she entered the gym. It wasn't that way at all. For one thing, she was terrified of bars. She was so small, she was afraid to jump to the high bar from the low bar because it was a *long* eight feet off the ground for her pint-sized body. On the other hand, Simone was a very powerful tumbler, and we knew she had the ability to learn quickly.

In 2004, Simone spent a full season with the level 4 team winning the state vault title before we moved her into the level 5 group. Simone then competed a full season at level 5.

While Simone is now considered one of the greatest vaulters of all time, many young gymnasts may be encouraged to know that Simone's vault score at her second state meet was a *zero*. She was joking

Early competition. Courtesy Teresa Remmert.

around a little bit before she saluted, and on her first run she sprinted down the runway but tried to stop herself at the last second, threw her hands in front of her body, belly slid on the vault, but didn't actually go over the vault table. Zero. Then, on her second attempt, she completely overcompensated. To make sure she got over the table, she punched the springboard like she was trying to catapult herself into the stratosphere, causing her to fly way over the apparatus without ever touching it. Another zero.

By November of that first year, when she was seven years old, we moved her up to train at level 6. This was the lowest-level team I was coaching at the time, and it was when I officially began training Simone.

In those days level 6 was a compulsory level; today it's an optional level. Even though Simone didn't do well at level 5 due to her lack of experience, flexibility, and consistency, everyone could see that she had raw ability, and we wanted her to start training with the higher-level girls. Her teammates were always four or five years older than she was, making them twelve and thirteen when she was just seven and eight. This trend continued throughout her progression. In a fun reversal, as of this writing Simone is the oldest on the national team, but she's still one of the shortest in the lineup at camp and competitions.

During this process, Simone's parents were very supportive of her coming into the gym and rapidly moving up in level. It was a great place for Simone and her sister Adria, who is two years younger, to spend time after school. It kept them both occupied, out of trouble, and burning energy. When Simone started in the gym, she was in a recreational class for only one hour per week. As we saw her true talents emerging, she gradually went to nine hours a week, slowly increasing to twenty hours per week. Our trainings were well planned out and I needed to run them efficiently while still allowing the gymnasts time for a snack break and a proper warm-up and cooldown within a four-hour session before sending them home.

I quickly learned that coaching Simone was going to take some finesse. When somebody is super-talented, they generally don't need to work very hard to become competent because things come so easily to

Simone flexing with Teresa. Courtesy Teresa Remmert.

them. For example, I would ask the team to do a conditioning exercise and Simone would do maybe two-thirds of the amount she was supposed to do: she would start when the girl next to her started and stop when she stopped, regardless of how many repetitions she had actually completed. I don't think Simone was shirking her assignment on purpose, but this was a very regular occurrence. I felt hoodwinked. I started counting her repetitions for her and then, if she was short on the count, I would tell her she had more to do: "Simone, you have ten more." Then she would start crying because she didn't want to keep going. When she was young, Simone cried a lot. In this, she reminded me of myself. We both cried a lot, but we always came back to gym the next day.

It was still undeniable: Simone had a lot of talent. We considered fast-tracking her. That would mean moving her quickly through the competitive levels, sometimes two or three levels in one season. At that time, the USAG had the pre-elite program, which helped identify potential elites. (Today they have the HOPES program, which has a category for twelve- and thirteen-year-olds—the program Simone would have fallen into.) We decided to follow the pre-elite path, which required lower qualifying scores than regular elite before a gymnast could move up a level.

In the complete hierarchy, a gymnast's level progression finishes by moving to junior elite and then senior elite. It's not uncommon for coaches to spot a little bit of talent and immediately want to advance the gymnast as quickly as possible. I didn't even talk with Simone's parents about her doing elite until after she was a level 10. I felt it was important for Simone to take each step to learn how to compete, how to lose, and how to win. Advancing her into elite before she could grasp those concepts could stunt her personal growth. Why rush it?

Even though Simone had proven herself to be incredibly gifted, I was hesitant about moving her up too quickly. I didn't want to pull her out of compulsories. I knew her gymnastics would benefit from the foundational repetitions. I had never coached a gymnast with Simone's raw talent, but I recalled my own experience of being promoted to the next level before I was ready; I know I would have been a better gymnast had my coaches taken more time, slowed down, and helped me to develop better techniques. I thought about this as we navigated through the system with this vivacious kid who had an immense capacity to grasp the challenges we were asking her to meet in the gym. I was comfortable advancing Simone more quickly than her teammates through the levels until it became obvious to me that it was time to slow things down to allow the precision of her gymnastics to catch up to her dynamism. It became a tricky balance, because developing pristine execution was paramount; on the other hand, I recognized that Simone would get bored working on the elementary skills. I could also see her becoming frustrated because she had knobby knees and low flexibility and she wasn't scoring very well on the compulsory routines. I figured that, once we could get Simone into the optional levels, we could harness all that energy she had and she could concentrate on more complex skills that played to her strengths. I also knew we had time on our side to work on her flexibility and refine the precision she would need to become a champion.

Whenever I debated whether to hold Simone back for the sake of the process, improving her form and body positions in skills, I remember all the times when an unchallenged Simone would simply stop participating if the activity wasn't fun or exciting. During one testing session for TOPs (Talent Opportunity Program, used to identify gifted young gymnasts), Simone just stopped doing chin-ups. It wasn't because she was tired, but because she was bored. There was no challenge or progression with chin-ups. So I figured I'd make it a little more interesting as we headed to the rope climb. I told her, "Simone, don't stop until you get to the very top of the rope." I wanted her to climb beyond the line near the top, which was the mark of a full rope climb test, to the end of the braid where the rope connected to the ceiling with a U-bolt. Simone started climbing and quickly passed the line, reaching what appeared to be the top of the rope. However, the rope was connected to an I-beam surrounded by ceiling tiles. Simone then *kept going*. I watched as this tiny gymnast disappeared *into the ceiling*. Everyone started yelling for her to stop, but because I had told her to keep going, she just kept going. Even at nine years old, the ceiling wasn't high enough for Simone: she wanted to break through and no one could stop her. It was a sign of things to come.

To move through the levels, a gymnast needs to "test out" by achieving a minimum score set by USAG at a sanctioned competition. Simone had to attempt her testing twice at level 6 because she had some trouble staying on the equipment during her routines. Actually, she fell four times. Thankfully, tackling level 7 took only one attempt. Simone was already learning skills that were well above her competitive level, but those skills were rough and often carried a lot of deductions.

Another challenge we faced had to do with Simone's stature. Because Simone was so small, she had a hard time wrapping her hands around the uneven bars. For a sense of perspective on her size, I have a picture of when she was around nine years old and she's comfortably modeling a pair of shorts for a Build-A-Bear doll!

Once, when she was learning to do giants—a basic move where you swing around the bar through a handstand position—she tried to rotate around the rail and slipped right off because she couldn't maintain her grip. Nichole, the coach working with Simone on bars, knew that it was safe for her to repeat the skill, so she lifted her back on the bars to give it another try. With her teammates cheering her on and coach Nichole spotting her, Simone fought through her tears and did it.

That's the thing about Simone's progression: it wasn't linear and she didn't excel at everything she tried. She could do a standing back tuck on the high beam but struggled with her splits. She could do a straddle back—a backward swinging release move from the high bar to the low bar—but was afraid to jump from the low bar to the high bar without having someone there to spot her in case she slipped. Simone was never afraid to go backward. I recall asking her, "Are you looking at the equipment when you're in the air?" She responded that looking would be way too scary.

What makes Simone so exceptional is that she's an air-sense savant. One of her greatest gifts is that she trusts her instincts more than her own sight. Even when she was very young, she always seemed to know exactly where she was in relation to the ground, so she would never crash when attempting a new skill. I had to learn to trust her. Over the years and many thousands of hours we spent together, I saw her get lost in the air only twice. No matter what we were doing, Simone would always bail in a safe way, which meant we could try new things and it was never frightening for me as a coach. I knew she could push herself and that the risks would be limited.

While Simone was getting her bearings in the sport, the sport was recalibrating itself. In 2006, when Simone was not yet nine years old, the FIG issued their new Code of Points, abandoning the famous 10.0 system, under which gymnasts were simply deducted for errors they made in the execution of skills. Instead, the sport's governing body replaced the capped system with an open-ended scoring structure that combined two scores, one for execution (E score, out of 10.0 possible points) and one for difficulty (D score, unlimited, although 5.0 to 7.0 points are considered medal caliber, if not insane). While I believe Simone would have thrived in either scoring system, since she would go on to have impeccable form, the open-ended D score meant we could take advantage of her ability to master the hardest skills in the world, ones that would push her and the sport beyond what other gymnasts believed was possible.

In 2007, Simone began competing at level 8 and did well. She finished in first place on vault, eighth on bars, tenth on floor, and eleventh on balance beam, with a fall at the state championships. She finished the all-around competition in sixth place, but did not qualify for the regionals. That was really tough for her. She was in the youngest age division, which also turned out to be a super-tough group.

The next season, Simone moved up to level 9. At that time it was common for coaches to move their talented gymnasts from level 8 into the elite world—skipping levels 9 and 10 and having their athletes start training for junior elite, which involved a completely different set of rules and expectations, in the hopes that it would put them on the fast track to the national team. I and my coaching partner, Luis Brasesco, were not fans of this tactic because it could put too much pressure on gymnasts at a young age. I believed that gymnastics should remain fun, and the elite program was grueling. It was also incredibly important that Simone was part of a team. Luis and I shared a few of our coaching responsibilities, but he would primarily coach Simone and her teammates on bars, while I would coach them on beam and floor; vault training would be split between the two of us. I wanted to make sure Simone got the skills, confidence, and camaraderie that would serve her well in the future. We were advancing Simone rapidly through the various levels—and she was starting to place and win in competitions— but at the same time we didn't want to push her to go too fast and do too much, which could lead to physical injury and/or mental burnout.

To reach our goal, small steps had to be taken. We needed to break down the larger tasks into smaller, achievable objectives and then steadily work toward them. It was about staying focused and not getting overwhelmed. Simone had to work through her own trepidation when on occasion fear would creep in and she would not attempt a skill. Most athletes experience fear of failure in sports, but if a basketball player airballs a three-point shot, they can try again on another possession, knowing that no one shoots 100 percent from deep. But if a gymnast slips during a skill, they can seriously injure themselves and never get another shot. We had to attack those fears. For example, I remember she had a mental block on her beam series. After she stretched at the beginning of practice, she had to attempt the skill three times. She could take as long as she wanted and use as many mats as she wanted, but she had to at least attempt the skill three times before she could move on to her regular workout. Some days, this would take coaxing, a few tears, and long delays before we could move on. What I wouldn't do was keep her on the beam for an inordinate amount of time like I had experienced with my coach when I was growing up. That kind of coaching, to exhaustion, can be dangerous. I wanted to teach a lesson and show Simone there was nothing to fear; I did not want to punish her.

I want people to understand that although Simone was obviously athletically gifted, she was just like our other athletes: another young girl growing up in the gym. It was easier for her to learn certain skills compared to the other gymnasts, but the fears, the mental blocks, and the distaste for conditioning were all the same. Admittedly, Simone was the object of a lot of envy because some things came so easy to her, but she was a good teammate, and she was very well-liked. Simone was bubbly, funny, and had a lot of friends.

Later that spring, Simone competed against the top-level 9 gymnasts from most of the states west of the Mississippi River at the Western National Championship, placing first on the floor and second in the all-around competition just shortly after her eleventh birthday. For the hard-core gymnastics fans reading this who could give their own seminar on gymnastics history, Simone's beam dismount at the time was a flic,

Forever by each other's side, Simone and sister Adria.
Courtesy Teresa Remmert.

connected to a one-arm flic, and a one-and-a-half twist. For the casual fan, this means that she jumped backward, passing through a handstand on two hands on her first skill, then onto one arm on the second skill before dismounting the balance beam with a flip with one and a half twists. However, back at Bannon's, she had been training the same flic series into a double pike (two flips backward with her legs straight)—and, yes, she did her double pike from one arm, which required a tremendous amount of strength and speed. (To date, I can't think of another gymnast I've ever seen do this. Simone was doing it when she was eleven.) Simone was feeling strong in the warm-up gym at the Western Championship and decided to give the more difficult dismount a try. She was successful. After she landed, I looked around the room and noticed some of the other coaches in the gym scrambling to pick their jaws up off the mat. Most coaches didn't know who Simone was at the time, but I'd venture to bet that they never forgot the moment they saw a tiny-but-mighty level 9 gymnast perform an elite dismount from only one arm.

As Simone competed and moved up in competition, my goals for her were always to just do the best she could, to try her hardest, and to shake off any adversity. We never talked about scores or performances during a meet because we had to keep moving and focus on the next event. Winning was never the focus. Becoming "the best version of Simone," as her mom used to say, was the ultimate goal.

Around January 2009, Simone started getting asked for autographs, and my conversation with her was shaped by an encounter I had with Mary Lou Retton from my childhood. I remember being a young teenager when an elite meet rolled through Chicago and with it Mary Lou Retton, the first American woman ever to win the all-around gold medal at the Olympics. Once the meet finished, when I excitedly approached Mary Lou for her autograph, she didn't come across as the cheerful, friendly gymnast I was expecting. She wasn't mean—she was more dismissive than anything—but I sensed a bit of a snotty attitude. The encounter made me feel horrible. I'm sure Mary Lou was just a tired teenager ready to go home after a long day's competition, but the feeling I had after that interaction really made a huge impression on me. I later told Simone she should always be nice when engaging with fans and signing autographs. I added that when she was tired and ready to leave, she just needed to let me know so I could shut things down and take the brunt of disappointment from the fans so that she could stay the hero for the kids. (I'm sure this was quite a lot to take in when Simone was very much a kid herself.)

Since Simone's potential skill level was well above the average level 9 gymnast, she naturally transitioned to level 10 the following year. Not surprisingly, Simone started the season with a bang, winning the Mary Lou Retton Invitational in Houston. This was a relatively small competition, but Simone's floor routine captivated the judges and the crowd through her explosive amplitude, which was not expected from such a tiny package.

Next up was the Alamo Classic in San Antonio, Texas, where Simone was spectacular on three events but showed her struggles on bars. Simone was still fearful of jumping to the high bar, and her size and inexperience made it difficult for her to excel in that event. So being asked to do skills that required her to swing, release with both hands, flip, and then regrasp the bar was just a step too far for her at that point. She still placed fourth on uneven bars and in the all-around.

Our competition schedule then took us back home to the Houston National Invitational. This meet was held at the massive George R. Brown Convention Center in downtown Houston. Participants came from all over the world, but when Simone competed, all eyes were on her. Even though she was just a twinkle in the universe of stardom, people couldn't help but gravitate toward her when she was performing. Everything she did was a little bigger, higher, and faster than what her peers did. Her small size and beaming smile bounced around the convention floor like a bundle of joy ready to explode.

As the season continued, Simone showed steady improvements in her placements, winning first in the all-around and becoming the vault and floor champion at the Rose City Classic in Tyler, Texas, in March before heading into the Texas state championships. The promise of her becoming one of the Texas greats was increasing, and she rose to those expectations, easily qualifying for the regional championships with her fourth-place finish in the all-around.

At the regional championships, even though Simone dazzled on vault and floor, her bar routine got the best of her, and she scored only an 8.10. She ended the day as the regional floor exercise champion, but a fourteenth-place finish in the all-around eliminated her hopes of qualifying for the national championship. Her season was over.

Simone's placement at meets never upset me and I never used the outcome to punish her or push her harder to meet the needs of my ego. Simone had shown amazing potential and did extremely well that season. Despite her season coming to an end one meet early, she kept her charming smile throughout 2009 and was ready to get back into the gym to once again challenge her own beliefs about her limitations.

Simone was about to become a teenager as we entered the new decade. She continued to compete as a level 10 and was starting to rack up several wins in a row, dominating the all-around in the Ricky Deci

Simone always flashing her brilliant smile. Courtesy Teresa Remmert.

International Invitational as well as taking first in the Space City Classic, both local Houston competitions. Her first big test outside of Texas would be at the Arizona Sunrays' Classic Rock Invitational, where more than 1,000 athletes at various levels would compete.

When you think of Arizona, you don't typically think of it being cold, but in February 2010 it was really cold. The Sunrays meet took place in the NFL's Cardinals Stadium in Glendale, where the temperature was in the upper 50s and heated to a not-so-warm-feeling mid-60s. It was cold enough that the organizers thought it was a good idea to give blankets as the athletes' gifts. I say all this not to make my Chicago friends laugh at my description of "cold" weather but because that temperature made the mats, designed to protect gymnasts from hard landings, feel as hard as wood. I was concerned about Simone getting injured, so I made sure she was careful with her tumbling passes, ensuring that she felt safe with all of her landings during the warm-up period. Her health and safety were always on my mind. Simone handled the cold just fine by setting the place on fire. She won the competition with a 37.60 and even scored a 9.0 on bars, an improved fourth-place finish in her division. Simone did so well at the Classic Rock invite that, if she had been competing in their division, her score would have bested all but four of the gymnasts in the senior age group out of the one hundred–plus juniors and seniors in the meet.

Our trip out west was strategically planned to coincide with an elite qualifier at Arizona State University the day before the Classic Rock Invitational. That year, junior age group athletes needed to score a 49.0 to be invited to compete in the American Classic, the first qualifying competition on the road to making the U.S. national team. Simone was twelve, and inevitably she got bit by the bars "stink bug" again. She was disappointed in her performance, and when she walked away from the apparatus after her dismount, she threw her grips on the ground. I gave her a calm yet strong reprimand for her behavior and was overheard by famous LSU coach D-D Breaux, who simply nodded at me and said, "Get her." Simone knew from that moment on that how she conducted herself was just as important as how she performed her skills. Interestingly, even though D-D didn't like Simone's action that day, she must have liked her tenacity, because a few weeks later Simone received an informational letter from the LSU gymnastics team—at twelve years old!

Gymnastics as a whole is very time-consuming, but for an elite-level athlete time takes on a whole new construct. One weekend of travel frequently bleeds into the next; we often only have time to get home to wash some laundry and pack our suitcases again. Family life and school can sometimes suffer, which is why most elite gymnasts are homeschooled. During this stretch, Simone competed in four states in four weeks. Not the typical schedule for a twelve-year-old.

After we thawed out from Arizona, we headed to Ohio for the Buckeye Classic. This was Simone's second elite qualifying meet. She did well, but a fall off the beam brought her score down to 46.70 overall. Once again, one major error prevented Simone from achieving the requisite qualifying score. Nevertheless, there were some standout moments from that weekend—one being Simone's bar dismount, in which her double back finished both rotations completely above the high bar (most gymnasts finish their rotation right before hitting the ground) and her seemingly choreographed wedgie pick during her floor routine after her leotard had slipped up her backside. Also on the competition floor in a bright orange and white leotard was Simone's future Olympic teammate, Laurie Hernandez. Laurie had started her elite journey in the youngest HOPES division, was only nine years old, and was already a force to be reckoned with.

After a long weekend in the cold of Columbus, we were ready to go somewhere warm for the next weekend. A week later we landed at the New Orleans Jazz Invitational, where Simone would compete as a level 10. Moving back and forth between levels is allowed before you compete at a U.S. Classic meet; this allows gymnasts to try to qualify to elite without giving up the level 10 status. New Orleans is one of my favorite places to visit, so admittedly I remember more about the city than I do about the gymnastics, but I do remember that Simone almost had a sweep on all four events at that competition.

We were on the road a lot, and at each one of these meets Simone would travel with her parents. The following week we were back in Texas for the Houston National Invitational. Simone had drawn attention the year before, but now she was starting to acquire a fan base that was eagerly anticipating her performance. When she was on the floor, her supporters erupted with enthusiasm.

Simone took the title of champion on vault and floor and placed third in the all-around. During the awards ceremony, she was presented with a giant cardboard check for $5,000. When I saw the check, I went over to her and told her she couldn't accept it. At that time, if a gymnast took any kind of prize money or endorsement, she would be considered a professional athlete, making her ineligible to compete in NCAA gymnastics—something that was still a high priority for Simone at the time. I could see a moment of panic in her eyes upon hearing this news. Simone and I had talked about her desire to compete in college, and she was certainly not going to let this check ruin her chances. If you thought Simone ran fast down the vault runway, you should have seen her take off when the organizers tried to hand her the check for a picture. The organizers kept telling Simone to hold the check for a photo and she kept squirming away from them, not wanting to even touch it. Eventually, she let the check lean against her leg. It was hilarious!

After Simone's stellar performance, I sent a video of her routines to the U.S. national team coordinator, Martha Karolyi. In addition to being the leader for the U.S. team, Martha was responsible for selecting aspiring elites and their coaches to attend developmental training camps. At these camps, coaches and gymnasts are mentored by experts in the sport, guiding them on what it takes to be an international elite athlete. It was clear that Simone could win at level 10, but the jump to elite is bigger than just adding a few more difficult skills to your existing level 10 routines. This camp could give us more training to adjust to the differences between the age group program that most gymnasts are involved in and the elite world. Without much explanation besides "she's not ready," Martha rejected our request.

Following one more competition, Simone advanced to the level 10 national championships. This was the one time a year that all of the best level 10s converged for a single competition. USAG broke down the country into eight regions. There were eight age groups and each region would qualify eight gymnasts per age group. Simone would compete in the youngest age group, Junior A. The venue for the event was a typical convention center with two sets of equipment and two age groups competing at the same time. If you're doing the math, that was eight regions, times two age groups, plus an average of one coach per athlete, which comes out to around 250 people on the competition floor at the same time, which didn't include judges and volunteers.

When you are at the nationals, you are part of your regional team. Everyone in the region wears the same attire, and even though our athletes are all vying for the lone spot atop the podium, coaches are still working together, looking like ants scurrying around while exhibiting the efficiency of a NASCAR pit crew, moving mats and setting up equipment to make sure that their region comes out on top.

On the lead-up to this event, Luis and I were very excited because we felt like we had finally figured out the perfect bar routine for Simone, the one event that seemed to be her nemesis. But the universe had other plans on that day. It started with Simone not completing a skill, which led to her making up part of her bar routine on the fly. I'll say this much: she didn't give up. Simone is no quitter, so she just kept swinging until she felt it was time to dismount.

Making it through a stressful bar rotation, we moved on to the beam, where Simone proceeded to fall twice in an otherwise very nice routine. Had she stayed on the beam, she could have won the event. Simone was resilient and finished second on the vault and persevered to become the national champion on the floor. If you search her floor routine online, you'll notice that just about everyone in the shot—coaches, other gymnasts, and even judges on other events—is watching her routine. There was no doubt she was on her way to being a major player in our sport. Unfortunately, the first two events threw off her all-around placement, tying her for forty-fourth. Now it was time for us to focus solely on the final showing for her pre-elite season, the CoverGirl Classic, a little more than a month away.

In a three-steps-forward, half-a-step-back kind of way, Simone was improving with every passing day. However, despite her best efforts, she still hadn't achieved the compulsory (where all the gymnasts perform the same routines) or optional elite scores she needed to move up. So when the time came to compete in Chicago at the CoverGirl Classic in July 2010, her competition classification was HOPES pre-elite, which felt more like a consolation prize to her after all the work she had put in over the season. Simone did not let it get her down and she stepped up to the challenge and ended the season as the all-around champ.

Simone was still just thirteen years old. Knowing that she wouldn't be old enough to compete at the 2012 Olympics in London—you need to be sixteen the year of the Olympics and she'd be only fifteen—there was no benefit to pushing her into the elite system right away; so when the new season began, we never considered the move. I also knew what a jump in skill and competition awaited at the next level. Simone had done well at level 10, but she wasn't competing at an elite level yet and could still benefit from some refinement.

Simone's parents were not happy about this decision. They wanted to know what benefit repeating competitions at level 10 would provide their daughter. Having been around gymnastics my entire life, I recognized the deficiencies in Simone's gymnastics. She needed to polish her basic elements. She had to improve her form and her posture. Every angle that is off in elite gymnastics is a deduction. Yes, you're scored for connecting skills and sticking landings, but gold medal excellence requires precision in every position. Fortunately, the Bileses trusted me enough to go along with the decision. Simone could already do some big skills, but she was also going to incur some big deductions. I had seen so many talented gymnasts move into elite at a young age and watched them struggle, never finding success. In the face of that frustration, eventually they would leave the sport before their potential was ever achieved. I did not want to see that happen to Simone. When she made the move to elite, I wanted to be sure she would be a contender, and I didn't believe she was there just yet.

One final point I considered was the time ahead of us. Even though I hadn't really started thinking about Simone competing at the Olympics, I understood that the stretch from 2010 until the first games where she'd be eligible to compete was six years away. Six years is an *eternity* in elite gymnastics. There was even a saying regarding gymnasts being born in the "wrong year," meaning they were going to be only fifteen when the Olympic Games rolled around. At the time, many gymnasts would not continue to train at the elite level for an additional four years to try to make the team for the next Games, instead opting to move into the world of NCAA. You've probably calculated by now that Simone was born in the "wrong" year as well. I had seen too many amazing gymnasts suffer injuries and burnout before they were able to peak when it mattered most. Ultimately, I didn't see the benefit of pushing Simone early into a full-time elite training regimen. It wasn't necessary to add the hours in the gym, the expense, the pressure, and the homeschooling if we were trying to pace her to make the Rio Olympics in 2016.

Instead, Simone started a third season at level 10. I believe holding her back actually motivated her because she didn't want to be a level 10 gymnast anymore. Every event we went to she would dominate, getting near-perfect scores. It was as if she was saying, "See, Coach Aimee, I'm too good to be a level 10!" After Simone turned fourteen in the spring of 2011, we finally made the official leap to elite. With this shift in levels, our commitment to the daily grind would also increase. Simone and I would meet at Bannon's at 7:30 A.M. to get our first workout in before school. Early mornings and late evenings became our norm.

She hasn't looked back since.

CHAPTER 7

The Progression of a Legend

In gymnastics, there are a few skills that have become a rite of passage—skills that put you on the map as a serious contender. The Amanar vault (named for Romanian Simona Amanar) is one of those skills. It's like a pitcher clocking a fastball at more than 100 miles per hour: a sign that a player is truly elite. In the Amanar the gymnast sprints down the runway into a round-off onto the springboard, performs a back handspring onto the vault table, and launches into a two-and-a-half twisting laid-out back flip. Simone, at age fourteen, performed her first Amanar in competition on February 19, 2012, at the WOGA Classic as a junior elite. We had started developing the Amanar in training about a year earlier, but knowing that it was no use to her at level 10—it had the same difficulty value as a full twist—we waited until she was an elite to showcase the new vault. To be clear, she didn't just show up and perform the skill; she smashed it, getting so much distance, she almost flew off the end of the landing area, scoring a 16.150 and earning her a first-place finish. Not only was this the top junior vault score of the meet, but it outscored the top senior vault of 14.050. Simone also placed first on the floor and third overall. Katelyn Ohashi, whom you might know as the UCLA gymnast who went viral with her perfect 10.0 college floor routine years later, placed first overall, and future Olympic teammate Madison Kocian took second in the all-around. Simone had officially caught Martha's attention and was invited to some developmental camps at the Karolyi Ranch.

The "Ranch," located in a heavily wooded pine forest an hour north of Houston, was home to Bela and Martha, but it also acted as a summer camp for eager young gymnasts and a national training center for the U.S. women's gymnastics team. There were cabins for the campers who visited during the summer, but during the developmental and national team camps, the coaches and athletes stayed in motel-style rooms, each named after an Olympic Games (Athens, London, and so on). The rooms were basic, with a couple of beds (the gymnasts had bunk beds in their rooms), a mini-fridge, a small bathroom, and an open wardrobe to hang a few items.

The knowledge we gained at these camps was invaluable. We quickly learned the ins and outs of the U.S. elite program, what to do, and what not to do. In the end, however, no one could stop Simone from being Simone. She was giggly, loved to play, and still didn't like conditioning.

At the beginning of each camp, the staff held a physical abilities test. This was designed to monitor progress and deficiencies in each athlete by testing strength, flexibility, and speed. The person who performed the best in this challenge was recognized and awarded. It was kind of a big deal. This was Simone's least favorite day of camp. One time, while testing leg lifts (where the gymnast hangs from the high bar in an L shape and lifts their toes to touch the bar), Simone became bored, which she tended to do during conditioning—she wasn't tired, just bored—so she jumped down. Martha swiftly walked over to confront her, wondering why she had stopped. Simone responded that she just didn't feel like doing any more of the exercise. Martha quickly understood what she was in for with Simone. Even though I could see that there might be a conflict in personalities between them, Martha could not help but be entranced by Simone's raw talent. At one camp, Martha remarked on how Simone "floated like a butterfly" but followed up with how she needed to figure out how to get her knees straight.

Once again dialing into my need for acceptance, I sought out people to help me improve my coaching so I could guide Simone to her peak. I remember asking Katelyn's coach, Valeri Liukin, in 2011 if he had any advice on how to fix Simone's press handstands, because she could only ever do a few in a row during her physical abilities testing. As a seasoned veteran, Valeri told me not to worry about it. He continued that his daughter, Nastia, was always at the bottom of the physical abilities rankings and still ended up as the 2008 all-around Olympic champion.

By late 2011 we had become regular attendees at the training camp at the Ranch, and during one of our early visits, Simone received praise from nearly the entire national staff. The exception was Martha. During that visit, the day-to-day training had been going great. Simone was eager to improve and please the national staff, especially Martha. Instead, the national program leader ripped into Simone, telling her she looked sloppy and lazy and shredding the confidence she had built up during the camp. The attack was undeserved. Simone didn't need to be broken down to be motivated to excel; she just needed time and supportive guidance. When Martha invited us back three weeks later, I declined. I had seen how Martha's admonishment had affected Simone and didn't want her to get verbally torn down again. Simone agreed with the decision—she didn't want to go back either. Why would she? This was the first time I stood up to Martha, and it wouldn't be the last.

The following month, when a national team camp opened for the selection of the team that would represent the United States at the annual City of Jesolo Trophy meet in Italy, it appeared that Simone had been blackballed. Martha wouldn't invite her, nor would she consider allowing her to compete at the meet. I believe this was in direct retaliation for our declining the camp invite a few weeks earlier. It was if Martha wanted to prove that Simone couldn't succeed without the Karolyi touch.

Instead, Simone stayed home and watched as some of her friends whom she had been outscoring at recent competitions were awarded coveted places on the national team roster. Those girls went to Italy and performed spectacularly well, and even though Simone should have been with them, she kept her head down and continued working. We didn't change any of our training. We went back to Bannon's, chalked up, and kept elevating the quality of her skills. Although not being invited to the selection camp stung at the time, I have never regretted my decision to keep Simone home from camp when I knew, deep down, that it would have damaged her spirit.

***

In May, we finally returned to the Ranch—not to train but instead to compete at the American Classic meet. This is a competition usually for non–national team members to post a qualifying score for the national championships. The returning world team members are already qualified and others typically earn their qualifying score either at camp (which we declined) or at international competitions, like the City of Jesolo Trophy (from which we were excluded). Having been to the Ranch multiple times for camp, this was a very comfortable environment for both me and Simone. Under the judgmental eye of Martha, performing at camp could be very stressful, and this had become very normal to us. As she had done the last time she was there, Simone killed it, placing first in the all-around. Unfortunately, it still didn't release the tension with Martha.

At the end of the month, we arrived at the Secret U.S. Classic in Chicago. Being able to return to my hometown as an elite-level coach felt amazing. So many family members and friends came out in full force to support us, and it was validating for my local community to see the progression I had made. There was one person there whom I had not expected to see: my former boss from when I coached during college, the one who said I was too nice to amount to anything.

The Secret U.S. Classic is typically the first domestic meet that the national team members compete in. The competition is held on a podium where all of the equipment is lifted about three feet off the ground to give the spectators a better view of the action. Competing on podium typically happens during the larger meets and in larger venues. The consequence of being on podium is that all the equipment is bouncier and less stable—which means when you jump on the balance beam, it may actually wiggle a bit.

While I was stretching Simone before the competition, Martha came up to us and inquired about how training had been going. I told her that Simone was doing amazingly. I remember Martha being dismissive, responding with "Well, isn't that a bit optimistic?" I simply said, "Aren't we supposed to be optimistic for our athletes?" Martha shrugged and said, "We shall see," then walked away.

It seemed like Martha was expecting Simone to fail because we hadn't been at her camp to train with the rest of the team. Our goal was to show that Simone could excel whether she trained with the national team at camp or not. With calm anticipation and utilizing the extra bounce produced from the podium, Simone soared in her gymnastics—and to a first-place all-around finish—highlighted by a nearly stuck Amanar vault. This was the first time that the fans got to see Simone in action on the big stage, and they were awestruck by her power and charisma.

Two weeks later Simone competed in the 2012 U.S. national championships in St. Louis, Missouri. The itinerary for this two-day championships required us to be in St. Louis for a week. Amid the daily trips to the practice gym and podium training, we were able to enjoy the beautiful weather and even visit the Gateway Arch. I think it's important to step away from the gym when you can and explore when you have the opportunity. However, ultimately we were there for a purpose, not to sightsee. Simone wanted to do more than just show up; she wanted to stand out—and stand out she did. During her floor exercise on the second day of competition, Simone completed her first tumbling pass, which included a double layout right into a stag jump—a jump with one knee bent and the other leg extended behind her in a split position. Simone bounced so high on her jump, she didn't look so much like a stag as she did a reindeer floating off into the sky on a mission to deliver us a gift. The crowd gasped as she sailed into the air, probably worried that she wouldn't come down safely. But Simone was very cat-like and didn't require the use of any one of her nine lives on that day. Her competition ended with the glory of becoming the junior elite national vault champion and a third-place all-around finish, bested only by two then-current national team members. According to the directives of the national championship, the top six all-around finishers in the junior age division would become national team members. Simone had officially earned her spot. Martha's approval wasn't required.

***

In elite gymnastics, your division is determined by your age as of December 31 of that year. In March of 2013, less than two weeks before her sixteenth birthday, Simone traveled to Worcester, Massachusetts, to the American Cup as a senior elite gymnast for the very first time. The American Cup boasted an international roster of athletes and judges from Canada, Great Britain, Germany, Italy, and the United States. The only American women selected to compete were Simone and Katelyn Ohashi, with Kyla Ross there as an exhibition athlete. In truth, I think Kyla had a more important purpose for being there. Coming off her gold medal–winning performance as a member of the "Fierce Five" team at the London Olympics, I believe Kyla was there to mentor Simone and Katelyn as they navigated through their rookie competition as senior international athletes. And since this was our first time representing the United States, Jenny Liang, Kyla's coach, also helped to show me the ropes.

At this specific competition, men's events alternated with women's events. Everyone warmed up at the same time. Since the men had six events, they started off the meet with their first two apparatuses while the women would rest in the caverns under the seating, some even taking a nap. After a short rest, the U.S. women ran through a light stretch and some basic tumbling elements on thin panel mats before walking out into the arena to perform in front of the judges and the fans.

At large events, each athlete was allowed only one credentialed coach on the competition floor. For her comfort, Luis and I let Simone decide whom she wanted by her side. Per her decision, I was on the arena floor, trying to hold it together, and Luis sat in the stands with his wife, Stephanie. I'm not usually nervous at competitions, but this was Simone's first opportunity to face international competition—even though we were still on American soil—and I was a wreck. As the houselights dropped and the spotlights came up for the introduction of the athletes presented with their countries' flags, my anxiety spiked. I recall turning to Valeri, a 1988 Olympic champion, and telling him, "I'm freaking out right now!" Valeri tried to calm my nerves and said, "Don't even worry about this." He told me that the American Cup was so much easier than any U.S. national championship we were ever going to be at. It doesn't sound like much, but that pep talk helped calm my nerves . . . a little bit. Even so, my heart was pounding out of my chest: I was almost in a panic and thought I was going to vomit. I suddenly found myself envying Luis's position as a spectator in the stands.

Simone started off great, putting up top scores in the competition on both vault and uneven bars (yes, bars!), but she got a little nervous and fell off the balance beam on a two-foot layout, a backflip with an extended body. After she fell, I could see tears forming in the corners of her eyes. It was the first time I had ever seen that from her at a meet. Worrying more about Simone and less about the competition standings, I gave Simone a reassuring smile, trying to convey that she was fine and to finish up strong, making sure she understood I was not disappointed in her. After the routine I was also grateful that Kyla, despite being only five months older than Simone, was also there to act as an encouraging big sister. Simone recovered from the beam breakdown and performed a solid floor routine, securing a second-place all-around finish next to Katelyn at the top of the podium. Bouncing back on the floor was important for Simone because she added a lot of skill upgrades into this routine, including a double-double in her first tumbling pass (two flips with two twists) and a one-and-a-half step-out through to a double pike on her third pass. She had a couple of crazy landings that showed up in deductions on the scorecard, but just as the addition of the Amanar vault at the U.S. Classic turned heads, successfully performing these upgrades started to make Simone a real domestic and international threat.

Simone had proven she could handle the challenge of foreign competitors, but she still hadn't faced the pressure of traveling outside of the United States as a national team member. Following the American Cup, we trekked back to Huntsville with our bags packed for the much-anticipated trip to Jesolo, Italy, a seaside resort town about a forty-minute drive from Venice. This would be the first of many international trips Simone and I took together. When we arrived at our hotel in Jesolo and got settled in our rooms, I felt my nervous anxiety kick in once again. I knew Simone and I had both done our jobs in the gym and she was prepared to compete. The root of the nerves wasn't gymnastics; it was a card game called canasta. I had recently learned how to play the game at the Ranch, and I remembered that it is played with four people, two sets of partners. Then it hit me: What if I ended up with Martha as a partner? Sure enough, when we sat down to play, my fear became a reality. Martha had chosen me as her partner. I was more nervous about that card game than I was at the American Cup. My hands were dripping (and I'm not a sweater) because I was so worried about screwing up the game and letting Martha down. She did not like to lose, and our relationship hadn't settled into a comfort zone just yet. It was a small taste of what the girls must have felt emotionally all the time as they worried about pleasing Martha.

I held my own during our games and I admit our relationship strengthened after that experience. It felt like a rite of passage for me—and, as predicted, Simone won the all-around title in Jesolo, beating athletes from Italy, Japan, and Switzerland. She again stunned the crowd and judges with a near-perfect stuck Amanar. Additionally, Simone qualified for all four event finals, but she and I decided to pull her from the uneven bar finals. This was one of two competitions during this two-week trip, and it was my job to pace her.

I knew Simone was going to have to compete in the all-around just a few days later, during the second half of our European journey in Germany. I wanted to give her a little rest. Even though she had improved tremendously on bars, it was still the event that took the most out of her both physically and mentally. With Simone's withdrawal from bar finals, Brenna Dowell, an amazing bars worker, stepped into her spot. Brenna seized the opportunity and captured the bronze.

You might be wondering why Brenna wasn't already in the bars final if she is so amazing. Blame the rule implemented by the FIG in 2004 that limits the number of competitors from a single country who are allowed to compete in the finals to two. That means if a country's four gymnasts place first through fourth overall in the prelims, only the first two get to compete in the finals for a medal. Perhaps the most famous example of a gymnast getting "two-per-countried" (or "two-per'd"—yes, it's now used as a verb) happened to Jordyn Wieber in the 2012 Olympics. Jordyn was the reigning world champion and qualified in fourth place in the prelims behind teammates Aly Raisman and Gabby Douglas (and Russia's Viktoria Komova) and therefore wasn't allowed to compete in the all-around final. That meant twenty other competitors who posted lower qualifying scores were given a shot at an all-around medal and the reigning world champion wasn't! Jordyn rebounded like a champion two days later to set aside her individual medal ambitions and helped the team capture gold.

In Jesolo, Kyla—who was the other top American qualifier—ended up winning bars, while Simone swept the other three events. Simone got her first taste of being internationally famous as the team signed autographs for fans after the competition.

Once the final awards were given out and autographs scribbled, we had a moment of leisure. The weather was terrible, but we persevered through sleet and cold and made a trip to Venice and the famous glass factories on the islands of Murano, known for their exquisite craftsmanship. We had to take a ferry to reach Murano, and as the girls huddled under the sturdy canopy of the ferry, I stood on the steps leading outside and let the sleet pelt my face. Even though our coats were not warm enough and the girls seemed miserable, I wanted to soak in every moment that I could. By the time we reached Murano, the sleet had turned to a lovely, light snowfall. The coaches were frolicking around, catching snowflakes on their tongues, as the gymnasts showed their obvious disdain for our silliness. They were cold and wanted to get out of the damp air. Luckily, in the factory, the furnaces needed to be set at over 2,000 degrees, providing a toasty warm respite, but it was too little too late. Our time outside had turned our clothes soggy, and even though we tried to lift their spirits, the girls remained grumpy throughout the experience. After the glass blowing, we headed to dinner in our sodden shoes. It was a tiny seafood restaurant that seemed like it could accommodate only our small delegation of people. We were seated at our table and, seeing our diminished enthusiasm and saturated clothes, the maître d' quickly brought over space heaters and told us to set our shoes in front of them and to hang our socks. This might seem unsanitary in a restaurant, but it provided much-needed relief for our cold, wet feet.

Sticking with my "keep the positive and throw the rest away" attitude, the entire Italian adventure was a positive one. Although we were already feeling blessed and grateful, Martha and the national staff had a surprise for Sarah Jantzi (Maggie Nichols's coach), Jenny, and me. All of us had birthdays that week—Sarah and I actually share a birthday—and the staff brought out a birthday cake for each of us. Yes, three cakes, which was plenty for all of the staff, coaches, and gymnasts to share. Although we were away from our families for our birthdays, it was such a nice treat to be able to celebrate with the team, whom we were all growing close with. I felt as if I had found my new tribe.

The next day we headed north to Chemnitz, Germany, roughly 250 miles north of Munich. Chemnitz is located near the Czech border, known for its textile production and machine construction back in the early 1900s. Germany has always felt like home to me—I can't explain why (being of German descent, it must just be in my blood)—so I was a little sad that we were there for such a short time and we wouldn't get to explore. Martha would always remind us that we were there on a business trip, not to sightsee, and she felt our icy one-day visit to Venice was enough downtime for us.

These team competitions allowed us to pick in which order the gymnasts would be performing in front of the judges. Historically, the best person in the event went last—the theory being that, when the judges score an early routine, it sets a baseline, forcing the later ("better") routines to score higher—so coaches often fought for a spot near the end of the lineup. In the middle of our meeting to select the lineup order, one of the coaches, Al Fong, turned to me and said, "Well, Aimee, you don't have to worry about it because you have the 'Golden Child.'" It was really snarky, and, to be honest, it pissed me off. Several of the other coaches were struck by the comment as well and gave subtle disapproving head shakes. "Golden Child" sounded more like a slight than a prediction of success. I wanted to reply, "You have no idea what you're talking about!" but I didn't say anything. It wouldn't be the last time that type of comment was thrown my way either. The reality is Martha didn't always believe Simone was the Golden Child. What Al and the other coaches didn't know was how Simone and I had been retaliated against when we declined the camp invite the previous year.

Chemnitz turned out to be the last time that anyone beat Simone in the all-around standings while I was her coach. Due to a fall on bars by Simone, Kyla was able to move ahead of her, outscoring her by 1.30 points.

***

Heading into the U.S. Classic, Luis and I knew Simone's practices hadn't been great. We were hoping our return to Chicago would see Simone continue her climb in the standings. But as the meet approached, it was hard to be optimistic, since Simone was being confrontational in the gym. She wanted to show us, at sixteen years of age, how she could be in charge of her own training. Simone would make only half an effort or skip parts of her assignments she didn't want to do. These were the toughest days coaching Simone. At the same time Simone transitioned into Senior elite, she also transformed from a child into a manipulative teenager. I don't say this in a disparaging manner. She was what I would consider a very typical teenager exhibiting very normal behavior. As her coaches, we needed to figure out how we were going to outsmart a hormonal young adult to make sure she was as prepared as possible.

I knew what kind of day it was going to be when Simone started falling off the apparatus. It wasn't because Simone couldn't execute the skills; it was because she didn't feel like training that day. Simone would randomly jump off the beam, fall over on cast handstands, and sit down on her tumbling passes. Even on her magnificent Amanar vault, a skill she had been practicing and competing for years with pristine technique, she would let herself fall. I saw all this as Simone's way of controlling her environment when she didn't want to do the work. Our goal was to make sure she didn't hurt herself in practice. This would sometimes include

Simone expressing a little attitude. I used to say to her all the time, "Why are you being so mean to me? I'm just trying to help you." In response I would get Simone's infamous eye roll as she walked away.

When this dynamic materialized in the gym, I was reminded of a GAT clinic I attended as a young coach. The presenter brought an attendee to the front of the room and had them face her and press their hands against hers. She then asked them to push—hard. This prompted the presenter to push just as hard in return to maintain balance. Then she asked a question: "What if I stop pushing?" The presenter then dropped her hands, and instead of the coach falling over because there was no resistance, she also dropped her hands, almost as a reflex. When you take away the fight, they will stop fighting you. As a coach, it's important to remember you have the ability to shift the point of balance in the environment.

This exercise had a profound impact on me. When Simone would start falling, I knew it was time to move to the next event. I didn't see the need for fighting. I saw it as wasting time. Yes, in a way Simone got what she wanted, but what was the point of keeping her on the apparatus if she was determined to fail? I told her that I would not let her trash her gymnastics. Without hesitation a lot of coaches would have forced their gymnast to complete the assignment, no matter how indignant the gymnast might be. This would keep the gymnast in an antagonistic mood and begin to erode their love of the sport. It might also break them. I understood I was never going to get Simone's best through force. This process wasn't always easy for me, but I needed to practice what I preach—it's just gymnastics.

This testing of boundaries repeated itself over and over again, and when we were wrapping up, I would often say, "Tomorrow's a new day." I thought it was important to turn the page and encourage Simone to hit the reset button. This was something Martha was also very good at. I regularly heard her say the same thing. When the next morning arrived, I would greet Simone with "Good morning! How are you? Let's have a good day." Usually in the mornings, practices were good, but the afternoons were sometimes a different story.

These days were much harder for Luis, and he had a hard time letting go. Luis would express his annoyance about Simone's not completing the assignment from the day before, and I would remind him that today was a new day.

I shared some of the frustration, but I also recognized this might be an educational opportunity. I would be lying if I didn't admit I carried a little fear of being judged by other coaches. My logical brains knew their judgment didn't matter, but I wondered if other coaches thought we were ruining an incredibly talented gymnast.

I was fine letting her go out and not perform well. I thought it was important for her to learn that her lack of good preparation would result in poor competition performance—that is, until it looked like she might get hurt.

I had never seen her fall so many times in a competition: Simone fell off bars, wobbled throughout her beam routine, and fell again on floor. When she started warming up on vault, her last event, I watched with concern as she took a really scary fall. She completely got lost in the air. This was the first time I had ever seen her do that! After witnessing her discombobulation, I decided it wasn't safe for her to finish the competition, and we scratched her from vault. We knew she didn't have a chance of winning the all-around: she had a self-defeating attitude, and I was afraid Simone might seriously hurt herself if she attempted her difficult vaults when I could tell her head wasn't in it. I didn't care about saving face or about our reputations; I needed to pull her to protect her health. I hadn't yet figured out what was wrong, but I knew she wasn't mentally in it that night.

Too often, grit and mental toughness are hoisted up as reasons to keep pushing, particularly in sports. That's fine if you're tossing a ball into a hoop, but not if you're hurling your body through the air. With the danger of flipping and twisting as part of her daily routine, I wasn't willing to risk her safety. Forcing Simone to finish the competition, knowing a loss of focus could not only end her career in sports but also end her life, was never a consideration. The only lesson to be learned would be negligence.

Though the Secret U.S. Classic competition didn't end as we had hoped, there was a true highlight. Simone debuted her first eponymous skill, the "Biles," on the floor exercise. After a rough start on bars and a shaky beam routine, Simone had to muster everything within her to showcase this new skill to the world. Her huge smile gleamed as she started her routine and approached her first pass—a double twisting-double back—with confidence, followed by a dance series that included sky-high leaps. As she prepared for her next tumbling pass, the look in her eyes changed. Simone was determined to show the crowd the new skill she had worked so hard to perfect. From the corner of the floor, she began her sprint and then effortlessly rotated into a back hand-spring before punching her feet into the floor to catapult her body. Into the arena spotlight her body soared, weightless and laid out for two complete flips. On her way back down to earth, she quickly twisted 180 degrees to face forward as she planted her feet into the carpet like a stuck dart. The crowd erupted. The noise from the stands was deafening. She had accomplished her goal . . . but the routine wasn't over. Simone had put everything into that skill and given little regard to reserving anything in the tank to finish her routine. In that one moment she was a shooting star. Sadly, her routine finished with a full-twisting double back that ended with her landing on her hands, knees, and head. As quickly as her star had risen, it came crashing down. In that moment, in front of a large crowd, Simone learned the hard way that conditioning wasn't something she could magically manifest. To be great, she needed to do the work.

The first Biles was Luis's brainchild. Simone had been complaining about pain in the fronts of her ankles when she was landing backward skills, so instead of just telling her she had to keep landing in the direction that was causing her discomfort, Luis offered up a solution: "Well, let's just land forward." And because it was Simone, why not add an extra 180-degree turn right before the landing like it was always meant to be that way? As the saying goes, "Necessity is the mother of invention." We discovered a few months later that the reason the landing was so painful was that Simone had a bone spur at the bottom of her tibia.

Simone finished third from last at that Secret U.S. Classic in 2013, but it might have been the competition where we learned the most. When we returned to the gym, I remember asking Simone, "You didn't like the way that felt, right? How would you like to move forward?"

Heading into the previous meet, Simone was able to test the limits of her talent without the work. The freedom of that experience was humbling and inspiring. I can't say for certain what it triggered in her, but somewhere in that moment she made a choice. When it came to getting ready for this competition, the old adage "failing to prepare is preparing to fail" held strong. After her experiences in Chicago, I believe, Simone decided to be great. She had always demonstrated superior ability, but now she was ready to become a champion.

Simone only had a few weeks to adjust her game. In August we were set to travel to the 2013 national championships in Hartford, Connecticut. When we arrived at the XL Center, all eyes were on Simone stepping onto the floor. At that point in her young career, her only all-around victory as a senior elite was at Jesolo. To this day I wonder if she was the favorite because the fans thought she was going to win, if they just wanted to be wowed by her gymnastics, or if they wanted to see if she would fail spectacularly.

Simone had become known for her high-difficulty scores on vault and floor, while Kyla was renowned for her impeccable execution, which was reflected in her scores. But Kyla and Simone were not only fierce rivals: they were also fierce friends, each cheering the other on during the competition. After the first night of the two-day event, Simone had posted the top all-around score, edging out Kyla by 0.75 points. On the second night, Kyla matched Simone's night one score, while Simone faltered, dropping her bar score by 0.5. In the end, however, Kyla's comeback wasn't enough to close the overall gap when the two-day score was added up. Simone had won her first national championship all-around title by a mere 0.2 points. She was solid across the board and swept silver in each of the four individual events, giving up only the event titles to Kyla and her fellow Olympic champion McKayla Maroney.

We had trained hard, we had improved our communication, and we had believed in each other. It all came together in this weekend. Congratulations and praise came from all around us. The moment felt natural and unbelievable at the same time. The girl who had to be pulled from the meet three weeks earlier had decided to excel and not watch others pass her by. Any question of whether she would flame out after her junior competitions, as so many talented athletes who had come before her had done, had been extinguished. Simone was the 2013 senior national champion. That evening she was also awarded the Gymnast of the Year (voted on by the gymnasts competing at the championships) and I received my first Coach of the Year award (voted on by the coaches). It was an honor, but the season wasn't over just yet, and Simone's unprecedented run was just getting started.

CHAPTER 8

The World Is Yours

Luis was concerned that Simone, coming off of the high of the win at the national championships, was progressing too quickly. Too many times we had seen athletes peak before the Olympic year only to have their dreams dashed when they didn't make the team. The curse of turning fifteen in an Olympic year was something we had to face. The Rio Olympics were still three years away. We didn't want Simone to flame out, but I couldn't help but ask myself, *What if this is the only chance she gets? What if she becomes one of the greatest ever?* We never know what the future holds, but I knew then and there that what I was seeing was greatness. I didn't want to tame that. We proceeded with her training as if she were right on track even if elite gymnast years passed like dog years.

I was confident Simone, as the reigning national champion, was going to be a member of the World Championship team. It had been only a couple of weeks since she was victorious in Hartford, but we still had to show up at the selection camp in Huntsville and prove her readiness. As expected, Simone showed the judges and national staff that she had the goods to take on the world. We were off to Antwerp, Belgium, along with Brenna Dowell, McKayla Maroney, Kyla Ross, and their respective coaches, adding another stamp to our passports.

Antwerp was beautiful. With so many days of competition, I didn't get a lot of time to explore the city, but the bits I was able to take in were striking. Wandering the city, sampling the amazing food, and seeing the Old World architecture, the quaint streets, and the beautiful flower gardens filled my soul and sparked my lust for adventure. But as I had learned the last time I traveled to Europe with Team USA, this was a business trip.

Simone had a lot of eyes on her as she headed into the world championship. She had shown loads of potential and captured a national championship title, but she had not yet fully proven herself on the international stage and was not the favorite to win. Both Kyla Ross and McKayla Maroney were front-runners, just a year removed from their 2012 Olympic gold medals, along with 2010 all-around world champion and Olympic gold medalist Aliya Mustafina from Russia.

Most years, world championships include a team competition, but the format changes the year following the Olympic Games. Every fourth year, awards are given out only to individual events and all-around winners.

World championship competition involves a much higher level of intensity, not just because of the exceptional level of performance, but also due to the lengthy format. Participants from most countries arrive in the host city a week or two early to get acclimated to the time change and climate. About a week before the competition was scheduled to begin, our team traveled first to the Netherlands for a few days of training at Flik-Flak, a facility about an hour south of Amsterdam. Practice was going great until we went to vault. The vault runway was set up so the athletes had to sprint toward a brick wall. All of the American athletes were *big* vaulters and could get extreme distance while they were flying through the air, so running toward the brick wall was intimidating. Their fears of going too far on their repulsion were legitimate. All of the gymnasts started holding back on their power, making sure they didn't collide with the wall. This was obviously causing the quality in the vaults to go down, with most of the athletes under-rotating and sitting down (winding up on their butts). Brenna was having a particularly hard time and wasn't able to complete any of the vault assignment. Martha was incensed. Instead of telling Brenna that she would be fine when we got to the official practice gym in Belgium, she decided in that moment to make her a reserve athlete. Up until that point in time, nobody knew who was officially in the lineup. Brenna ended up not competing at all.

We left the Netherlands all feeling down about what had happened to Brenna and fearing Martha could easily make the same decision about any of the team members. The next stop was our destination city of Antwerp, where the practice facilities had opened up. Teams from all over the world started training on the official equipment, in a separate venue from where the competition was going to be held. In the training facility, the equipment is a little stiffer and a little more stable, with everything mounted directly on a concrete floor. Brenna was expected to train full routines alongside her teammates, just in case someone became injured or ill. I can only imagine how crushing this was for her, but she was a great teammate despite her disappointment.

Once the tournament began, each country went through podium training inside the competition arena. For the safety and performance of the athletes, they were allowed one session, approximately an hour and thirty minutes long, to train all of their routines on the elevated surface. A day or two after podium training, the qualification rounds began. During those rounds, athletes were ranked by score, placing the top scorers in the finals. To reach an individual event final, an athlete had to rank in the top eight—this competition had more than 130 gymnasts competing—as well as hold one of the top two scores from their country. Being the third-highest score from your country would get you "two-per'd." To qualify for the individual all-around final, a gymnast needed to place in the top twenty-four to advance. The finals start with all-around, then proceed with two events per day until all of the titles for women and men have been awarded.

Simone was exceptional in the preliminary round and secured her spot in every single event final and the all-around final. That meant that she was (at worst) top eight in the world on every apparatus—and, for comparison, no other gymnast in the world qualified for every event final. This was a phenomenal result of the qualification round, but for Simone it became somewhat normal going forward. Kyla ranked second and McKayla finished sixth, so she was left out of the all-around competition—another amazing gymnast who fell victim to the two-per-country rule.

Before she'd won a single medal, the trip was already a major success. Simone stepped onto the floor during the prelims, wearing a powerful red leotard with silver accents. She was officially introducing the "Biles" to the international gymnastics community. Skills in gymnastics—like the Amanar vault, as noted earlier—are named after athletes. To get a skill named after you, you must be the first person to perform the element at a qualified competition, the skill must hold a high difficulty rating, and you cannot fall on the attempt. In short, it's incredibly difficult and the stars must align. Simone's routine started out pretty flawlessly, but the crowd was oddly quiet. The educated spectators seemed to be holding their collective breath, wondering if she would make the skill. As she danced her way into the corner, preparing for her second tumbling line, you could sense the white-knuckled hold she had on the arena. Simone exhaled as she started her approach, turning herself through her round-off and into her back handspring, propelling herself into the air: One . . . two . . . turn. It was as if time stopped as her feet hit the floor, her knees bending deeply. The crowd exploded with excitement, virtually willing Simone to stay on her feet. They had just witnessed history being made. She had done it. The "Biles" was born and etched into the Code of Points. Simone had always expressed joy in her floor routines, but the radiant smile on her face after landing her newly named skill was an awe-inspiring mix of joy and relief. As of that moment, she would forever be a part of gymnastics legend.

The first final for Simone was the big one, the all-around. She had been adding difficulty to her routines and polishing her execution, so we knew a world championship title was possible. This was the first meet where Simone demonstrated she could hit when the pressure was highest. Even better, Simone did what are now known as "Simone things" (an effusive phrase by the gymternet to highlight a dominant performance): she hit all four routines, this time nearly sticking her newly solidified eponymous skill, comfortably winning the title of world champion! On top of that, she began to separate herself from all of the other competition in a manner that put her on a completely different level, even if she was standing only slightly higher on the award podium. Kyla finished second and Aliya finished third. In just two months Simone's margin of victory grew from 0.2 to nearly a full point.

During the award presentation, the coaches were not allowed on the floor. We were forced to stand behind a curtain, and I realized the athlete I had coached for a decade was being crowned world champion and I wasn't going to be able to watch it! I approached the event organizers, asking where I could get a better view, and they pointed up to the nosebleed section. The ceremony was about to start, so I sprinted up the stairs, breathing heavily and gasping for air—again, highlighting that I'm not much of a runner. Just as I arrived at a clearing in the stands, I turned around to see Simone getting her medal. She was just a speck from that distance, but it was breathtaking—which had nothing to do with the shape I was in; it came from the satisfaction of witnessing an amazing goal achieved. With a lump in my throat, I stood proudly as Simone faced the American flag and they played our national anthem.

When the ceremony concluded, I was making my way back downstairs to meet up with Simone and the other coaches but was stopped by security. Before sprinting up the bleachers, I had taken off my coach's badge and hung it on my backpack because the day's competition was over. In my haste to see Simone get her medal, I had carelessly left my backpack and badge behind, and now security wasn't going to let me back into the restricted area on the floor. And since I didn't have a ticket, they weren't going to let me back in the stands either. I was stuck in arena purgatory. All I wanted to do in that moment was hug Simone and congratulate her on her huge accomplishment. Luckily, I had my phone, so I called Luan Peszek, mother of Olympic silver medalist Samantha Peszek and vice president of development for USAG, who was still in the field of play. She quickly grabbed my badge and rushed it over to me. Feeling grateful although irritated by the inconvenience at the same time, I flashed my badge at the security guards, who then allowed me to rejoin our delegation. But the ordeal had taken too long, and by the time I met up with the group, Simone had already been whisked away and was heavily involved with media interviews, people calling her name, and snapping photos. I would have to wait. So I stood in the wings while she embraced her moment.

There were still two more days of event finals for Simone, so she couldn't bask in the glory for too long. At that point in her career, the international gymnastics world still didn't know who she was, and the announcer in the arena kept introducing her in a singsong accent as "See-money." The next day she needed to compete in the vault and bar finals. After missing out on the all-around final, McKayla, one of the greatest vaulters of all time, showed her resilience by topping Simone's vault score by a slim 0.129 points, making the Americans the gold and silver medal winners on the apparatus. That same night "See-money" also competed on uneven bars. After so many years of toiling on bars, we were thrilled she had qualified for the finals. Even more remarkably, she almost won a medal, placing fourth in the overall standings.

On the last night of the competition, Simone was up for medals on beam and floor. The first was beam. Before jumping on the beam, Simone approached the apparatus and drew her dismount line. To distinguish her mark from the others on the beam, Simone scribbled an S over the line. This unintentional dollar sign has been a ritual of Simone since she was a level 8 and has since become a signature.

Simone mounted the beam and moved aggressively up and down the apparatus. It wasn't a flawless routine—she lost her balance on her front tuck and under-rotated her dismount—but I noticed something was off when her difficulty score was shown on the scoreboard. Simone wasn't awarded full credit on a bonus connection in her routine, so, following protocol, I submitted an inquiry for a score change. (This type of check within the system typically happens a few times in the course of a competition). The judges reviewed the video of Simone's routine and agreed that they had undervalued her efforts by 0.2, changing the total to 14.333. This change bumped Vanessa Ferrari of Italy out of the bronze medal position into fourth with a 14.300. The fifth-place finisher on the balance beam was Vanessa's teammate Carlotta Ferlito. The judges had made an error, it was corrected, and that should have been the end of it. Unfortunately, it wasn't.

Next was floor. Simone won gold, again one place above Vanessa. Simone was the world all-around champion, won a gold medal on floor, silver on vault, bronze on beam, plus a fourth-place finish on bars. We were ready to celebrate until we saw a video from one of the Italian athletes. After the competition, Carlotta told a reporter, "I told [teammate Vanessa Ferrari] that next time we should also paint our skin black so then we can win too."

Whoa!

This racist comment pissed me off, but I typically stayed in my lane and let Simone's family handle stuff like this, and they did. Ron gave some comments to the press and Nellie had a conversation with Simone.

I wasn't the target of these comments, but they affected me a lot because I don't deal well with racism at all. I'm an inner-city Chicago kid, growing up surrounded by a multitude of colors and races. I don't treat people differently because of their race or religion. After so many years working with Simone, she is like my fourth child, and I felt very protective of her. I found myself in an awkward and uncomfortable position, recognizing that because I'm white, it wasn't my place to be more enraged than Simone or her family, nor should I project how she should feel about Carlotta's comments. I didn't have to: Simone's parents were furious.

Carlotta later offered a nice apology, but it was diminished by an inflammatory Facebook post from David Ciarelli, an Italian Gymnastics Federation official. According to Philip Hersh of the *Chicago Tribune*, "[Ciarelli stated that] 'Carlotta was referring to a trend in gymnastics at this moment, which is going towards a technique that opens up new chances to athletes of color (well-known for power)' while penalizing the more artistic Eastern European style that allowed Russians and Romanians to dominate the sport for years. 'Why aren't there blacks in swimming?' Ciarelli wrote. 'Because the sport doesn't suit their physical characteristics. Is gymnastics becoming the same thing, to the point of wanting to be colored?'"

This came after Gabby Douglas won the all-around Olympic title in 2012 and now Simone had just become the world champion in 2013. Ironically three years later Simone Manuel, the African American swimmer, set an Olympic record in the 100-meter freestyle to win

Olympic gold, becoming the first Black woman ever to win an Olympic gold individual swimming medal. I should mention there are many reasons Black athletes, at least in America, haven't excelled in swimming until recently. Most glaring has been the historic lack of access to public swimming pools. Even after the passing of the 1964 Civil Rights Act, which granted equal access to public pools, the battle to prevent access continued. Instead of sharing public facilities, some were sabotaged, such as with bleach or acid being poured into the water, or the pool would get filled in to prevent a desegregated environment with concrete. This would then get exacerbated by housing discrimination laws that kept African American families out of the more affluent neighborhoods with private pools in backyards.

In another moment of great parenting, Ron and Nellie helped Simone navigate this instance of racism, helping her understand that the remarks were reflective of those making the comments, not a reflection on her. They didn't want those comments to take away from Simone's joy just days after becoming the first-ever Black all-around gymnastics world champion.

It had been a busy few weeks since we had left the States. In total, Simone competed four days in a week's span—three days in a row to close out the competition. By the time the event was over, Simone had amassed four medals and had gotten her name officially in the gymnastics history books forever with her new skill. She was a champion, she was *exhausted*, and she was understandably ready to go home.

CHAPTER 9

A New Beginning

In January 2014, I knew my time at Bannon's was coming to an end. Martha Bannon had moved out of the state a few years earlier, leaving Luis as manager to handle the daily operations. Luis eventually purchased the business, and some aspects of the gym started to change. From my vantage point, the commitment to excellence and to some degree the professionalism I was used to with Martha at the helm were fading away.

We still had some of the old perks and procedures in place, such as bonuses for winning meets, but these quickly became sources of aggravation rather than incentives. Before, you would just turn in an official copy of the results and collect the bonus on your next paycheck. Now you had to submit the results and then follow up . . . and follow up . . . and follow up. Before, we had staff shirts that were different colors for the days of the week. Did I love them? No. The shirts were scratchy and pinched when we tried to coach in them, but they made the staff very identifiable to our clients, and we looked sharp. Luis didn't seem to care about the appearance of the staff, and we were quickly losing the patina of professionalism.

I can't tell you how many times I would offer suggestions on things we could do to help the business grow, and Luis would dismiss them out of a lack of interest. And when it came to running an elite program, Luis always responded with some kind of gripe, like "We're not cut out for this." I'd try to reassure him that I was confident enough to take the lead, saying, "Well, you might not be, but I am. I got this under control." It made no difference: Luis remained unmoved.

Once Simone turned elite, we were participating at a new level of the sport and Luis didn't seem to be as interested in it as much as I was. I became more unhappy as every new step became a struggle.

I was surprised: Luis was a true gym nerd, and yet he didn't grasp the opportunities this new level of competition offered. For example, once you're on the national team, the gymnastics club would receive an annual allowance from USAG to upgrade equipment so the gymnasts could train and get a feel for the apparatus they'd be competing on at international competitions. Luis was resistant to upgrading the equipment and was very slow to place an order. When I started traveling with Simone to training camps at the Karolyi Ranch, there was an additional stipend allocated to the club by USAG so that an extra coach could come to Bannon's and substitute for my classes. Even though the funds were provided, Luis wouldn't bring anyone in to help out. In fact, he seemed unwilling to alter his gym program to accommodate Simone's needs, including opening the gym earlier. I was working more hours without extra pay, becoming burned out and frustrated. I seemed to be a thorn in Luis's side with my requests, and I felt his lack of interest in trying to build an elite system was making the process more difficult than it needed to be.

One of the most mind-boggling incidents happened after Simone won her first world championship. I suggested we get a banner printed to hang outside the gym that read, "Home of National and World Champion Simone Biles." Talk about cheap and easy promotion! Luis responded with befuddlement: *Why would he spend money to advertise for her?* I saw it as such an obvious opportunity to promote the gym— and besides, Simone was already more famous than the gym. [Head explode emoji]

I was loyal to the gym, which had shrunk from roughly 1,200 students when I started in 1996 to around 300 by 2014. Luis didn't seem to care because the remaining gymnasts were enough to pay the bills. I was also loyal to Luis: he was my "work husband" and despite my frustrations with his management style he was still a great coach and good friend. I had just gotten enough little signs and gripes that I didn't need a banner to get the message: it was time for me to go. There was a problem, though: I wanted to leave, but I didn't want to leave Simone.

I needed to take a step, and so I reached out to Nellie. This was three months after we returned from Antwerp and I was ambitious about the future, but now the environment at Bannon's was stifling. I met with Nellie and disclosed that I had become miserable at Bannon's and felt it was no longer the company it used to be. I had grown increasingly unhappy since Martha had moved to New Mexico. I loved Luis but not in this new role. I also shared that I didn't think Simone was being treated the way she should have been or given the opportunities she deserved and had earned.

Nellie listened as I divulged that I wanted to leave and go to another gym. I then asked if her family would follow me. I know this may sound unethical, but I had dedicated my life to coaching, sacrificed much of my personal and family time, and knew I could shepherd Simone to the next level. I clearly remember what I said next: "If you won't, I will just bury my head in the sand for the next three years. I'll get her through Rio, but then I'm leaving." I was nervous about how Nellie would answer, because I felt desperate to leave Bannon's, a place I had called home for seventeen years, but I wouldn't go if it meant leaving Simone.

Nellie paused, and her response set me on my heels. She mentioned wanting to build a gym of their own. Apparently, she and Ron had been looking for an investment opportunity, and this might be it.

Simone didn't know just yet about the new gym her family was thinking about building, and she definitely didn't know about my discontent with Bannon's. Being such a loyal person has been a blessing and a curse. People know they can count on me, but, on the flip side, it can lead to situations where I feel like I get taken advantage of.

Shortly after my conversation with Nellie, she confirmed that she and Ron wanted to proceed with building a facility and creating a legacy for their family. It was time to tell Luis I would be leaving. Even though it is what my head and heart wanted and needed, it wasn't an easy conversation. Bannon's was home, and Luis was my family. My chest was pounding throughout the entire conversation, but when it was over, I felt a sense of relief and believed that Luis and I would be all right.

Next, I had to tell my cherished friend and coworker Selinda about my move. She said that if I was leaving, she was out of there, too, because there was no way she was staying without me. Selinda had been at Bannon's since she was a child—and Luis had been her coach—but she felt the same way about the deterioration of the program. She was also ready to move on.

It didn't take long for rumors about my departure to swirl among the staff. I found out another coach had told Luis that I had been trying to recruit her to start a cheer program at the new gym. That never happened. Naturally, when Luis heard this, he wasn't happy. He called me while I was on my way to the gym and confronted me about the rumor.

I was flabbergasted. I had known Luis for nearly two decades. He knew I was leaving, so why would I try to recruit people from right under his nose? Honestly, the fact that he had believed this other coach sent me over the edge. I was angry and sad when I arrived at the gym that day. Knowing that the trust between us was gone, I walked over to Luis, handed him my company credit card, and told him, "I can't do this." I knew that I couldn't walk into work every day wondering if people were accusing me of being disloyal. I was an easy target of gossip because the staff knew I was leaving. I had to remove myself from that situation.

I wasn't planning on leaving Bannon's that day in February, but I had hit my limit, and now my integrity was being questioned by someone who had known me for a very, very long time, and it hurt. In my anger I told Luis. "I don't need this shit. I'm done."

So, after seventeen years, in an uncharacteristic move, I just walked out of the gym. I feel terrible that my exit happened so publicly and abruptly. I never planned or wanted it to spill over into the gym. When I walked out, Simone was still in the dark and frantically called Nellie, exclaiming to her that I had just quit and wondering what was going on. Nellie was faced with having to let Simone in on the plans for the future earlier than she wanted to.

The original idea was for me, Simone, and her sister to leave Bannon's at the same time and in an organized manner. Adria was still competing, and her parents wanted both girls to leave together after her season was over. Simone and her sister wound up leaving the following month, in March. Once they left, we were faced with a new problem: the new gym wasn't built yet, and we didn't have anywhere to train. I reached out to Deana and Debbie, the elite coaches who let me observe their practices from my Cypress Academy days, who now owned their own gym, AIM Athletics. When their gymnasts didn't have practice, they let us train at their facility. Knowing it would take a considerable amount of time to build the massive facility that is now World Champions Centre, we searched for a temporary building to train in. During our six-month search for our interim home, the AIM staff and gymnasts graciously hosted us.

About a month after I walked out of the gym, I called Luis. "I miss you," I whimpered into the phone. He shared that he missed me, too, and I started crying as we caught up. Around this same time, Selinda left Bannon's, evoking a different emotion. Before Selinda walked out the door, she wanted to reach out to the parents of her students to inform them she was leaving the gym. Without considering how it might look or the repercussions, Selinda downloaded her team list to make sure she would be able to contact them if she got locked out of the gym's computer system—a standard procedure when you leave. Selinda had no intention of soliciting families to leave Bannon's; not only would that be wrong, but it wouldn't have made sense, because we didn't even have a gym they could practice in.

It didn't matter: the damage was done; Luis took legal action and sent a cease and desist order to both of us. I understand why he did it and why he would be so protective of the information, but it still really saddened me because it broke our relationship. I haven't spoken with Luis since.

When the dust settled, six other kids left Bannon's with us. None of them were recruited.

I didn't realize just how hard the move was going to be. It was tough for me, and it was even more difficult for Simone. She was no longer training in the gym that she had known her entire gymnastics

Claiming the land for the future World Champion Centre.
Courtesy of the author.

life, and, more importantly, she didn't have her teammates. She missed Luis, even though she had fought with him a lot, because he had been her coach for as long as I had and none of this change was her choice. Simone was really sad during this transition.

In the six months when we were training at AIM, missing the normalcy in her day, Simone's emotions would often spill over into tears during our training sessions. I would assure her it was okay to be angry and sad. I understood that the decisions she had to live with were not her choice but my goal was for us to make the best of a less-than-ideal situation. My job at that point was to try and keep her out of a rut. It was life altering for her and we needed to shift gears to get even better, but it was hard. There was a lot of crying and a lot of anger.

This is when being at the national training camps became really important for her. I had to explain to her that even though she was no longer competing alongside her teammates from Bannon's, they were still her friends. I needed to shift her focus to her new group of teammates: the national team. Those were the gymnasts she would be traveling the world with. Those were the people she would be training with for the Olympics. They had a common goal.

I'm sure it didn't feel that way for Simone. We had taken her away from her gym and her friends. I could tell she was bitter, and I understand why. In the gym she could do more than any other human on the planet, and outside of the gym we had made her feel helpless.

CHAPTER 10

Healing Priorities

When the 2014 season rolled around, Simone was starting to have some trouble with her right shoulder. She was scheduled to compete at the American Cup in March, but three days before we were to leave for camp, her shoulder started acting up. I'm not a doctor, but I was confident it would end with a tear or require surgical intervention if she kept training bars; we needed to let her shoulder rest and figure things out. We voluntarily pulled Simone from the competition and Brenna Dowell, the American Cup alternate, filled her spot. Since alternates aren't treated the same when they're not in the starting lineup, we wanted to give Brenna time to prepare as a starter.

Simone now had the space to focus on healing as well as improving her artistry. USAG brought in their national team choreographer, Dominic Zito, to prepare a new floor routine for the 2014 season. Dominic would remain her choreographer through the Rio Olympics. Simone enjoyed working with him but often got frustrated because she struggled with letting herself be one with the music. What she truly wanted to do was flip, but her flipping was limited due to her shoulder ailment.

The U.S. team headed back to the competition in Jesolo, Italy, later that month, but we declined to attend that as well. We needed to take serious time off of bars—which is to say, do no training at all. Instead, we probably went to seven different orthopedists who specialized in shoulders before we finally found one who could help.

The injury—the first and only one that hampered Simone's progress for any amount of time—was a reminder that the sport of gymnastics is hard on the body. Any decision I made as a coach had the ability to help her heal or hamper the process by pushing her to "fight through injury." As a spectator, it can be easy to forget just how superhuman some of the skills being performed are. And the skills aren't just difficult: many of them are dangerous—even life-threatening. However, at the end of the day, gymnastics is still a sport, and, as in all sports, injuries will happen. Some of them happen by accident and some happen from overuse. I knew we had to be careful with our training.

This was brought into devastating focus when, during a few of our doctors' visits, more than one physician confided in me that they would put a gymnast in a cast rather than a brace *even if the gymnast didn't need to be in a cast* because the doctors knew some coaches would tell a gymnast to remove their brace and train through the pain!

Gauging injuries as a coach can be difficult, but it doesn't need to be. Some gymnasts will exaggerate their injuries while others will attempt to hide their pain. There are many reasons for the latter, including not wanting to be taken out of a lineup or fear of being left behind. I have a philosophy that if you have to guess if an athlete is injured, just assume they're injured. If the athlete is claiming an injury as an excuse, that's their prerogative.

I don't care if they're making up an injury. If they're faking it, there's a reason they don't want to do something. And what if they're not faking?! Imagine if a kid is complaining about their back hurting and I make them participate in practice while ignoring their complaints, and it turns out they actually have a broken back! This sounds hyperbolic, but it is shockingly common in gymnastics. Just off the top of my head, I can think of Olympians Jamie Dantzscher, Betty Okino, and Carly Patterson—plus Simone's friend Katelyn Ohashi—who have all competed or trained with fractured backs.

When it comes to those who would rather make an excuse than participate in a drill or exercise, as a coach with some curiosity, you'll eventually figure out why they're making excuses when they're not actually hurt. Some examples could be: they're experiencing a lot of pressure from home; they feel overwhelmed with the amount of time they are spending in the gym; they're missing out on social activities; or they are just experiencing fear—fear of a skill, fear of letting people down, fear of failure, even fear of falling behind in school. Or maybe they are uncomfortable with the sensation of pushing their bodies.

For example, set this book down for a minute and do a wall sit: Press your back against the wall while maintaining a sitting position where your legs are bent at a 90-degree angle as if you're sitting in a chair. Hold that position as long as you can. You'll eventually feel a lot of burning in your legs. This hurts. This pain is not a result of injury but from pushing your body.

I say to the gymnasts, "Are you hurting or are you injured? Because if you're injured, you have to stop. If you're hurting, you can probably keep going. So you have to decide which one it is."

If they really just don't want to participate, it's not my job to force them to do it. None of them have to do gymnastics, and it should be unnecessary to make excuses for not training or performing. It's really that simple. And if they do want to do gymnastics and complain of pain, I feel it's essential to listen to them. This way I protect myself as a coach as well: I never, ever want a child in my care to become injured because I didn't take their complaint seriously, and I never want a parent to confront me and say I made their child do something and now they're hurt because of it.

I also know a lot of coaches who are probably thinking, *If they're not injured, I'm not going to let them get away with it!* Why not? Let them get away with it! They're the ones who will fall behind by not doing their work. They're the ones who won't be prepared when it comes to competition. It's much easier to say, "You are not prepared; therefore, you are not competing." It's honest. The gymnast knows it too. It puts the responsibility of their health in their own hands. It gives the athlete the power to say, "I'm fine. I'm going to keep going," or "I'm actually hurt and I probably shouldn't be preparing for this competition."

I also hear some other coaches say that pushing through pain and injury is what makes them mentally tough—as if, later in life, these kids are going to think back on how they were able to work through that pain. I can't disagree more. Pain is not "weakness leaving the body"; it's your body telling you something is wrong. I have constantly wondered why some coaches insist on punishing their athletes by making them train in pain. Do they feel that a gymnast sitting out is a reflection on them and their coaching ability? If a gymnast wants to do something, they're not going to use pain as an excuse to stop.

Moreover, since my gymnasts don't get in trouble for not doing something—hurt or not—they're less likely to keep pushing themselves (out of fear of punishment or scolding for not participating) when they are injured. This keeps them healthier—and happier—for much longer.

Another example of how I handle injuries is if an athlete wants something—like an ankle—taped, I tell them they get to tape it for two practices. If it still hurts after three days, I need a note from a doctor explaining the injury and offering guidance on how long the injury needs to be braced. Since I deal with a lot of teenagers, another common ailment stems from growing pains in the knees, which can lead to Osgood-Schlatter's disease, an inflammation in the joint between the patellar tendon and the tibia, which can take weeks or months to go away. Trying to force a gymnast to push through that is going to hurt their gymnastics and it's going to hurt their body. Where's the winning in that? How is that teaching them mental strength?

So I never push an athlete if they say something hurts. If it hurts, stop doing what hurts. It's that simple. As a coach, it's important to remember that these athletes are the ones who have to keep their bodies their whole lives. To a certain extent, doing sports at an elite level, no matter how careful, puts a lot of strain on the body. By definition, being at the elite level means you're pushing things to the absolute limit. For younger kids especially, I don't see the need for anyone to make a long-term sacrifice when it's just not necessary.

***

By April, Simone had been doing limited training because of her shoulder, but we felt like it was strong enough for her to go and compete at the Pacific Rim Championships in British Columbia. We knew Simone wasn't in her best shape because we hadn't been doing that many full routines, but we were trying to find a balance between being healthy and being competitive.

While we were training in Vancouver, Canada, before the competition, Simone's shoulder started bothering her again. I remember Martha gesturing to her belly like she was full and puffing out her cheeks to make a plump face to insinuate that Simone had gotten fat and that was why her shoulder wasn't getting better. After Simone had breathlessly finished a floor routine, I asked Martha what she wanted Simone to focus on for the remainder of the floor workout. With an expression of disgust and without ever looking in Simone's direction across the room, Martha told me she didn't care if Simone "crawled under the floor." I told her that Simone was trying her best, but it fell on deaf ears. Martha's revulsion toward the reigning world champion was obvious. So much for Simone being the "Golden Child."

At the completion of that practice, we met with the trainer and decided to withdraw from the competition and head back to the United States. Alternate Peyton Ernst stepped in to fill Simone's spot. I never relayed Martha's comments about her weight to Simone. I know some coaches would have used Martha's remarks as a "motivator." I thought these types of comments were abhorrent and wanted to shield Simone from them as much as I could. Publicly USAG released a statement from Martha saying, "We want to be careful given the upcoming schedule for 2014 because Simone is an important part of the team." In reality, it seemed clear to me that if Simone couldn't win, Martha was done with her.

I think this was the first time Simone saw me tear up. I've always remained on a very even keel when it comes to my coaching style, but this hurt. I was really sad for Simone. She had been trying to heal and wanted to compete, but her body was telling her no. We had traveled to Pacific Rim Championships knowing Simone wouldn't be required to complete a lot of repetitions during practice. What we weren't sure about was the amount of rest she would need between those repetitions, which was something we could control in our gym. For example, at home, she might have had forty-five minutes to do three bar routines, but at a competition training session she would have had less than twenty-five minutes to complete the assignment.

We thought she could do it, but without the longer rests, we learned it wasn't going to happen.

I was disappointed *for* her and I wanted her to know I wasn't disappointed *in* her. Simone was trying and I knew she was hurting. This was her first and only physical injury that resulted in a missed opportunity that I can recall. It was a reminder that you can't control when injuries come along, only how you manage them. These are the truly tough choices a coach has to make—denying opportunity when you know the human spirit is ready to beat the odds.

After we got home, we were on our own in finding a doctor who could specifically diagnose the problem in Simone's shoulder. We finally located a physician who had a history of working with professional athletes with shoulder ailments. He was the specialist for the Houston Astros pitchers, and he gave Simone the diagnosis and treatment she needed. We learned we needed to strengthen her scapular muscles, so we did that.

If Simone had pushed through the pain and trained and competed at full speed, things might have gone differently. She could have injured herself more seriously and needed longer to recover, affecting her progress. Instead, by July Simone was ready to return to competition at the 2014 Secret U.S. Classic. We had figured out how to heal her ailing shoulder.

Even though the competition was in the same venue as the 2013 Classic, we would not let the ghosts of that year's competition, when we had to withdraw Simone from the competition, haunt this day. Looking like a princess in a white, black, and pink leotard and donning the letters of her new club, WCC, Simone showed up in Chicago healthy, determined, and ready to take her place back atop the podium. The highlight of the night was her floor routine. Only a few months after Martha had shown her displeasure at Simone's fitness level in Canada, Simone performed an exquisite routine, virtually sticking all of her incredibly difficult tumbling passes. When the routine was over, Simone bounced up to her feet and enthusiastically waved to the crowd, flashing her signature smile! She was back! Simone finished first in the all-around with gold medals on vault, beam, and floor. Having gotten her shoulder strength up, she finished bars in fourth place.

It would only be one short month before we were in Pennsylvania so Simone could defend her title as national champion. Simone walked into the Consol Energy Center in Pittsburgh as the favorite. Her margin of victory over the competition was beginning to widen. She had just won the U.S. Classic by nearly 2 points over Kyla while the rest of the field stayed grouped within tenths of each other but more than 4 points behind Simone.

Over the two-day competition, Simone was exuding a new kind of confidence. She trusted her training and she trusted her body. Despite an uncharacteristic fall on her side aerial (a cartwheel with no hands) from beam on day 2, Simone bolstered her résumé by repeating as national champion. Simone placed first on vault and floor and fourth on bars, and even with her fall on beam was able to share second place with Alyssa Baumann. Simone's technique was becoming flawless and her difficulty unmatched, overpowering her closest competitor's difficulty score by more than a point. Like the year before, Simone fended off Kyla, who placed second, but this meet was different. Simone had now stretched her lead over Kyla by more than 4 points. Other gymnasts were starting to remark on how "second place was the new first place," implying that there was no way any of them could catch Simone for the all-around title.

For the second year in a row, I was chosen as the USAG Coach of the Year, while Simone received her second consecutive Gymnast of the Year award. Just as in the previous year, it was nice to be recognized for the work I had done. While Simone made things look easy, the goal was only achieved because of the dedicated work we did together. It reminds me of a quote by legendary UCLA basketball coach John Wooden: "Winning takes talent, to repeat takes character."

***

In the summer of 2014, before the national championships, we realized the space we were renting in AIM Athletics was no longer working as more kids wanted to join the yet-to-be-opened World Champions Centre. I guess that should have been expected after Simone won the world title. We knew it wasn't appropriate to take over another gym's space and so the Bileses found a warehouse (which we not-so-affectionately called the Tin Can) that we could quickly convert into a training center while the World Champions Centre was being constructed. This meant we needed to set up the equipment and dig out the concrete in the floor where we would install the "resi-pits" (extra large, very soft landing mats) that you may have seen in the pole vault or high jump in track and field events. Having these soft areas to land on enabled us to train with more repetitions on a safer surface. The space worked, but it was far from ideal. The regulation for the vault runway is a maximum of eighty-two feet plus the length of the apparatus and landing area—a total length of 110 feet. But the building was not nearly that big, so, in order to vault, Simone would back up all the way to the giant metal garage door, while some of the taller girls would need to roll open the massive warehouse door so they could start their run outside. Also, two of the walls touched the edge of the floor exercise, which meant two tumbling passes were straight into the wall. It was reminiscent of when I was a kid first training with Lakeshore in a church basement, except with a little more space—and now with a world champion.

Since this was summer in Texas, the Tin Can was *hot*. We didn't have AC, but we did bring in some large fans to try and cool the place down and prevent the girls from slipping all over the place from sweat. On the opposite end of the weather spectrum, we also contended with a couple of freezes that winter with no heat in the gym. I felt kind of guilty because there was heat in the offices. On really cold mornings, we would bring small space heaters into the gym for the girls to sit in front of before stretching, and they would regularly come into the office to get warm.

Getting the Tin Can operating as a functional gym took quite a bit of work, but there was more going on than just erecting equipment for one gym. Simultaneously, I was writing a plan and organizing the details of the permanent World Champions Centre. This meant I wasn't coaching as much while I focused on operations. The interior gym layout had to be finalized, a ton more equipment had to be ordered, curriculums had to be set up, enrollment portals and payroll systems had to be selected, among other items. Ron and Nellie had never run a gym before, so they relied heavily on my and Selinda's experience. Additionally, I had to consider how I was going to staff a potentially large program. When we moved into the Tin Can, we were focused on the women's program, so I took the opportunity to hire Jason Collins to develop the men's program. Jason has an unusual background himself. He started coaching at fifteen but is also an accomplished opera singer. He attended the Juilliard School in New York and then traveled the world, singing in front of massive crowds in amphitheaters and concert halls. After WCC opened, Jason stuck around for about two months before he had to move back to Florida to care for his father, who had fallen ill.

Even though I'm very good at logistics, I didn't love being out of the gym, but I also didn't think it was a big deal. We had other coaches who could step into my coaching spot while Simone was spending more time rehabbing her shoulder to make sure it would hold strong through the season.

I didn't realize how much my added responsibilities were affecting Simone until one day I stepped onto the floor and approached Simone, whom I noticed was in a somber mood. I asked her what was going on. Simone broke down and started crying. As she recounts in her book, *Courage to Soar*, Simone said, "You never coach me anymore! You're just always in the office! You don't even care!" I was shaken. I gave her a big hug and told her, "Oh, Simone, I'm so sorry. I'm right here. I haven't gone anywhere. I'm always right here."

Simone wasn't wrong, though. I had been in the office more, but Simone was the world champion and I thought she didn't need me to look over her shoulder every second while she worked on her basic skills. While that was true, I also realized that after we had left Bannon's and separated Simone from all her friends and teammates, I was the one stable thing she still had in the gym.

We had chemistry, and—knowing her so well and watching her grow up—I could tell just how much or how little she required each day. That was part of our magic together. I needed to make sure Simone knew she was my priority. There was no point in getting the Tin Can running or working on WCC if Simone wasn't taken care of. I handed off what I could of the administrative tasks I was attending to and made sure I was out on the floor next to Simone from that point forward.

Success doesn't breed comfort; it amplifies everything around you—the good and the bad. The praise can be deafening and the ridicule can be crushing. Self-doubt, apathy, and insecurity will grab your ear to fill the void of a coach who's not there to bat it away. I realized winning was never going to be sustainable if I didn't recalibrate my priorities to put Simone's well-being at the center of my decisions. It wasn't about winning, though; it never has been. Simply put, I never wanted to be the reason her smile disappeared.

CHAPTER 11

The Struggle of Competition

When Team USA traveled to China for the 2014 World Championships, we landed early at the airport for our connecting flight. We were all relieved, knowing we would not have to sprint to get to our connection to our final destination. The delegation was resting comfortably at the gate, finally enjoying a good stretch after leaving the confines of our economy-class airplane seats. About an hour before the flight, we noticed that we were still the only people at the gate. No other passengers were waiting to board. Finally, someone approached the airline agent, who told us that our gate had been changed, but since all of the announcements were in a language we didn't understand, no one had caught it. In a panic, because we were sprawled out while waiting for the next flight, we had to quickly throw everything back in our bags. Looking like a 4 × 100 relay, and having to go through additional security, we sprinted through the airport to make our connection to Nanning, China.

If you've never traveled from the United States to Asia in a large group, let me explain what it's like. Air travel is already exhausting, and when you are traveling with a delegation, everything is magnified. You have to arrive at the airport several hours earlier than even the average two to three hours for an international flight. We do a lot of "hurry up and wait." Unlike in 2013, the 2014 World Championships would include a team competition, which meant more athletes and coaches. Imagine everything you do as a solo traveler or a small family and then add fifteen to twenty people. Everything takes exponentially longer. Just five people forgetting to take something out of their bags at security could delay us twenty minutes. Once you're on board and settled, you realize that you are going to be stuck in the same seat for the next thirteen hours.

The new time zone put us fourteen hours ahead and was doing a number on my internal clock. The gymnasts were struggling too.

Martha made sure that we were always at the first available training, which meant she would often book flights that had us landing in the morning at our destination on the same day the facilities opened. After about eighteen hours of travel, we had to drop our bags off at the hotel and head straight into training. Sensing Martha's constant pressure on her, Simone wanted to try to do everything that was asked of her by the team coordinator while we were in the gym. I reminded her that we had just spent almost an entire day traveling and she needed to listen to her body. This went against Martha's instructions, but I felt it was important for Simone's physical and mental well-being. In fact, I often told Simone to ignore Martha when we were at camp or traveling because I knew what Simone needed and I felt I cared about her health much more than Martha did. We used the first training to get a feel for the equipment and to get Simone's body moving.

The first couple of nights I started waking up at 2:00 A.M. and really struggled to sleep. I needed to get on a better schedule—and fast. On the third or fourth night—who could remember with the foggy state my brain was in?—after the day's training was done and the gymnasts were in their rooms, I went down to the hotel restaurant with a fellow coach for some dim sum. Once inside, we spotted a few friends from the USAG media team and decided to take a trip into town.

We hopped into a cab and rode onto the busy street, landing at a karaoke bar, and a new tradition was born. What happened that night wasn't anything extraordinary, but it became legendary. We laughed, we sang, we had a few drinks, and we laughed some more. It's amazing how comfortable a foreign country can feel when you're cracking up with friends about discoveries like "What do I call the beautifully tiled hole in the floor of the gym to relieve yourself? An opulent 'squatty potty.'"

We stayed out really late, belting out hits. It was a blast! My go-to karaoke song is "The Devil Went Down to Georgia" by the Charlie Daniels Band. The late night worked, and I found a bit of solace. This ridiculous adventure on the town was exactly what I needed to get on a regular sleep schedule. On subsequent trips, a night at the karaoke bar became a ritual for me and "my boys" from USAG.

All those good feelings soon vanished, however. After we finished up training later in the week, back in my hotel room, I sat in front of my laptop and knew something was wrong. My screen was going crazy. I couldn't get anything to work and didn't know what to do. I showed my laptop to my karaoke partner Scott Bregman, director of content and communications for USAG, and he slapped me with a dose of reality: he told me he thought I had been hacked! I spent my days worried about toe point, not digital security. When we traveled with the delegation, we had rules and curfews, but we never received security training or advice on best practices.

I don't know for certain if my computer was hacked, but I definitely provided an opportunity. I had a bad habit of leaving my laptop open and powered on, not really concerned that something might happen to it. Why would anybody care about my life? I was an obscure figure in the world at the time who only had about $100 in my bank account. It could have been the housekeeper just trying to get any information they could. I don't know, but something was definitely screwed up, and it wasn't me who did it. I just knew if someone wanted to steal my identity, they weren't going to get a whole lot out of it. The computer was mine, but it didn't have much personal information on it. When I realized nothing was functioning, I contacted my bank. They told me there was no suspicious activity on my whopping $100 but said they'd keep an eye on things. After that, I unplugged the laptop, which was relatively cheap, and tossed it in the trash when I returned home.

By the time competition day rolled around in Nanning, Simone and I had both adjusted to our surroundings and she was in her element. Team USA was a favorite, but the day wasn't flawless. Simone had a hiccup in her bar routine, struggling on her full pirouette and nearly coming off the bar, causing her to rank in fifty-seventh place on the event in the qualifying round. Luckily, the U.S. team had two amazing bar swingers, Ashton Locklear and Madison Kocian, to pick up the slack. Team USA advanced to the finals and Simone had scored high enough on the other events to secure her spot in the finals on vault, beam, floor, and the all-around.

World Championship, Nanning, China 2014. Courtesy John Cheng.

Qualifications had put Team USA in first place, with a comfortable 4-point margin above the People's Republic of China. The group felt confident and unshakeable on the day of Team Finals when the scores are erased and what you do that day determines the color of your medal. The U.S. women locked in and dominated the field, outscoring second place by more than 6.5 points. Right from the first event, the U.S. team had an advantage of half a point over their closest rival, Russia, in the difficulty alone. Pairing that with their superior execution, the United States came out of the gate with a lead of more than 2 points. Heading into bars, the Chinese team, with their beautiful execution, was the favorite to post a top score, but uncharacteristically two gymnasts came off the bars during competition, placing them in the number three spot heading into the third event, behind the United States and Russia. Knowing they had ground to make up, China moved to the balance beam for redemption, posting the highest execution scores on the event, while the American women fought through a few balance errors and showed their grit by not falling off the apparatus. The U.S. team had maintained a comfortable lead when they started the last event. It was time for them to do their thing on floor—because, in reality, no one could beat the Americans on floor! Once again showing their dominance in their level of difficulty, the United States towered above Italy, the nearest challenger on that apparatus, by almost a point and a half. In the end, the American women boasted the top country score on three out of the four events!

With one gold medal around her neck and only one day of rest, Simone had to move on to the all-around finals. As usual, her vault score gave her a strong start to the meet, but it was feeling like this might not be Simone's year. Showing some nerves about her errors in qualification, her bar routine was a little tentative at the beginning. I was holding my breath and counting the deductions in my head as I watched her perform with a loose body, which meant she wasn't hitting crisp angles in her handstands and pirouettes. Once she got past the part where she had struggled in the previous routine, she was flawless, nailing her dismount as if someone had glued her feet to the floor. As we moved to beam, Simone still looked apprehensive, missing some connections that would have given her bonus points on her score and having uncharacteristic balance errors. It might have been because it was the third day in only five days that she had to perform full routines in front of fans and judges. But the judges don't care how many days you've been competing; all they care about is how you perform your routine, and they would not let a single wobble go undetected. The pressure to repeat as world champion was mounting, with only the floor exercise left. Heading into the final rotation Simone was leading Larisa Iordache of Romania by just over a tenth of a point. Larisa would compete on the floor exercise first. She hit a beautiful routine and posted a very solid score of 14.733. I knew Simone was in a good position, since her high difficulty presented the opportunity to keep her fragile lead, but she needed to hit. With her signature power, Simone flew so high in her first tumbling pass that the cameras had to zoom out just to keep her in the frame. To secure the gold, she would need to be more than just dynamic in her skills; she had to sell this routine to the judges. As she danced in the corner of the floor, Simone looked directly into the camera and made a hand gesture as if to say to all of the viewers at home, *Come with me to my second world championship win.* As she approached the second half of her routine, Simone threw caution to the wind by taking every skill in her routine to the maximum. And even though she was tired, you never would have been able to tell. She started that routine with the intention of winning the all-around—and she did! Simone's score lit up the scoreboard: 15.066. When all the scores were tallied, Simone had outscored Larisa by less than half a point, but one more surprise was in store on the medal stand when an unexpected guest appeared.

During the award ceremony, it was a bee that stole the headlines. After defending her world champion title, Simone was standing atop the podium when Larisa pointed to Simone's bouquet to inform her a bee was residing among the petals. Simone looked down and, having never been stung by a bee before, let out a scream and started jumping around, backing off of the medal stand hoping the bee would not follow. Throwing her flowers on the ground, Simone then ran for protection to Kyla, who was standing on the third-place podium. The bee then made its way to Kyla's bouquet. With her usual poise, Kyla calmly placed her flowers on the stand and led Simone toward Larisa to take pictures.

The faces Simone made as she hopped around were hysterical! But I have a confession: I didn't actually see the incident or realize what was going on. In Antwerp, the coaches hadn't been allowed on the floor during the awards, which was why I had to act like I was on the track team and sprint upstairs. In Nanning, the policy had changed, and the coaches were allowed on the floor to watch the ceremony, but we were staged nowhere close to the athletes. I was standing behind the balance beam podium with Kyla's coach, Jenny, separated by a walkway and far from the floor exercise podium. When Simone jumped off the podium, we thought the award ceremony had ended. It wasn't until I got back in my room that I saw pictures of the incident all over my news feed. I watched the video replay someone had posted online, and I laughed so hard I peed my pants. The dominant two-time world champion had been knocked off the podium by a tiny little bee. *Hilarious!* Simone had dazzled, but the Nanning bee stole the show.

Simone became the first back-to-back all-around women's champion since Svetlana Khorkina of Russia won in 2001 and 2003. I know what you're thinking: *How are those back-to-back? What happened to 2002?* Well, for some reason the federation decided not to have an all-around competition that year (or in 1992). The only other American woman to win back-to-back world titles was Shannon Miller in 1993 and 1994. That pile of flowers Simone left on the ground that day wasn't easy to come by; nor were they the only bouquet Simone would hold on that trip.

The very next day Simone was back inside the venue, ready to take on the vault final. Her performance was stellar. This time the cameras were ready for her and had pulled back far enough to catch her massive flight on her Amanar vault, followed by a stuck Lopez—a complex vault performed with a round-off entry onto the board—followed by a half turn on to the vault table, then lofting into the air while performing a front flip, with half twist in a straight body position. Simone scored a massive 9.60 in execution on both of her vaults; however, she didn't win the gold medal. Hong Un-jong from North Korea had performed slightly more difficult vaults, edging Simone out for the top spot, while American MyKayla Skinner proudly took home the bronze medal.

Happy with adding a silver medal to her haul, Simone was even more excited that she would have that evening off. Since she hadn't qualified for the bar final, she was able to sit in the stands and cheer on her U.S. teammate, Ashton. I'm sure she would have liked to have had more downtime, but there's no rest when destiny calls. The only other female gymnast who competed in three event finals, the all-around final, and the team final was Aliya Mustafina from Russia. Simone was back at it the very next day.

Her morning started with beam finals. I've never been a fan of long speeches or lots of corrections before my athletes compete, but Simone and I did have a routine. She would mark her dismount line with chalk on the top of the beam. I would follow behind her and rub my hand down the length of the beam, making sure it was smooth. I'd then remind her that all she had to do was what she practiced, and with a final fist bump she was ready to salute the judges. Sporting a black asymmetrical leotard with coral sleeves and a ribbon in her hair to match, Simone came out and attacked her beam routine. Abandoning all sense of insecurity, she was as sure-footed and as solid as I had ever seen her as she worked each skill as if she were on the sidewalk. Simone's assured execution resulted in her first world championship balance beam title. After a short intermission, Simone stepped onto the floor exercise mat for one final chance at glory. Knowing it was her last routine of the championships and leaving nothing in the tank, she tantalized the crowd with her charm and athletic prowess, outscoring her closest opponent by half a point.

While an incredibly successful trip, the visit to China was probably the most difficult for me. In total, we were away from home for close to thirty days. By the time the final night rolled around, I was standing in the hallway of the hotel with Steve Rybacki, director of the U.S. elite athlete programs, crying. "I just want to take a shower," I sobbed as the trip came to a close. At this point, I was mentally and physically spent. The time change was difficult, but, even more distressing, I got a real taste of what it felt like when I didn't blend in physically and culturally. When visiting Italy or Germany, it was easy for this white girl to disappear into the crowd. In China, not only did I not understand the language, but it was the first time in my life that people would come up and touch my hair because of how foreign the blond color was. Also, Simone's sister Adria shared with me that when the Biles family was visiting the Great Wall, a little kid walked up to her, touched her arm and screamed, and then ran away. We assume it was because the child had never seen a Black person in real life before.

This is the great thing about traveling around the globe: you get out of your comfort zone and see the world through a different lens. But sometimes, as in China, I felt like that lens needed adjusting. The density of the smog at eleven o'clock in the morning was so thick, you could stare directly into the sun, which was deep red, without the sensation of burning your retina (although this is not advisable). It was really creepy.

I also discovered that the Chinese had a different concept of personal space. I realize standing very close together is culturally more common in China, but I am more at ease with a three-foot perimeter when in a group. This breach of comfort was not malicious, but it's a great reminder that the coaches and staff are surrogate parents for the gymnasts on these trips, and we needed to make sure they were safe— and *felt* safe. At one point when Simone was taking pictures with fans, she turned to me and said sternly, "They need to stop grabbing me," so I intervened.

Most days we would wake up, have breakfast, go to the gym, and come back to the hotel. On this trip I discovered there was no laundry in or near the hotel. This meant my bathtub would have to double as my washing machine. I'd toss my clothes in, fill it up with some water, throw in a Tide Pod (I travel with a few), and then stomp back and forth to slosh the water and clothes around. It was hilarious and ridiculous at the same time. Here we were, in a beautiful hotel with a great tub, and I was stomping around in it like Lucille Ball crushing grapes to make wine. Fortunately for the gymnasts, USAG would send the team members' laundry to a cleaner. Unfortunately, that service didn't extend to coaches and staff, and it was really expensive and not worth it for me.

At least doing the laundry kept my mind occupied during the downtime when the day came to a close. Typically, in the evening, after the girls had eaten and were in their rooms or with medical staff, the coaches and the rest of the USAG staff would go to our rooms. It was easy for some to forget that these are business trips with mostly minors. Parents were not allowed to accompany their children on these trips, leaving the medical staff to act as chaperones when we were back at the hotel. Of course, families still made the trips and watched the competitions, but they didn't fly on the same flights as the team, and if a parent booked a room at the same hotel the team was staying in, Martha would make them find a different hotel. Martha foresaw a bigger picture, and if parents weren't allowed in the Olympic Village, they weren't going to be allowed in our little village during other competitions. Anything that might pierce the cocoon Martha created was verboten.

I would check in on Simone before we separated for the night, but generally, once the gymnasts were in their rooms, the coaches left them in peace to have their own downtime. "Checking in" was really all we were allowed to do. According to the *National Team Handbook*, coaches weren't allowed in the athlete's rooms for their protection, and medical staff weren't allowed in, either; they usually had a suite where the girls could congregate and receive treatment. We foolishly assumed this would keep them safe.

Even though we were in China for several weeks, we weren't given time to visit the Great Wall or go on any other touristy adventures. Our highlight was a short tour of the local shopping mall—a piddling reprieve from the umpteen hours sitting in our hotel rooms, doing nothing. This made the trip exponentially harder. After years of world travel, I have collected a lot of passport stamps, but I haven't seen a lot of the countries that I have visited.

This all brings me back to crying in the hallway. On the evening after our last day of successful competition, we decided to return to the hotel for dinner. There was a banquet later that night; however, we had not eaten since breakfast, and we were unsure what food would be served at the banquet. Unfortunately, when we arrived at the hotel restaurant, we discovered the kitchen was closed. Even though the week had been so successful, this minor delay in acquiring food felt like total defeat. We all headed toward our rooms. With the weight of the world championship expectations removed—and being isolated from most of the team and staff—I allowed my emotions to bubble up. I was hungry, I was tired, I missed my family, and I *really* wanted a shower. The tears came rolling down as if a hose had been pinched for three weeks and the kink suddenly straightened, finally releasing the pressure.

It might be hard for some to believe, but even after two world championship all-around titles, the Olympics were still a distant aspiration for Simone. She is special, but she's not the first of her kind. There are so many unbelievably talented gymnasts who never set foot on a gymnastics floor surrounded by the Olympic rings. She's just the first person of her ability who got through the process and made it to the top healthy, both physically and mentally. Many gymnasts burn out, some get injured, and some have the misfortune in their timing of competing against a deep roster of talent.

One of the worst circumstances I can think of happened to Dianne Durham. In 1983, Dianne won the McDonald's International Invitational inside UCLA's Pauley Pavilion, site of the 1984 Olympic competition. Later that year, Dianne's season peaked when she became the first Black U.S. national champion. Twelve months later Dianne was competing at the U.S. Olympic trials. She entered the final day of competition in sixth place. The top four placers at the trials automatically made the seven-person Olympic team, while the next four finishers would be put on a practice squad to compete for the remaining three spots. Halfway through the competition, the reigning national champion on vault jammed her ankles on her landing. Dianne's coach, Bela Karolyi, told her to scratch the last two events and he would then petition to get her onto the Olympic team. Except Dianne wasn't eligible to petition for the spot. Her only shot was to finish the all-around competition.

Dianne was a trailblazing gymnast, a rising star who helped shepherd in a more powerful style of gymnastics, but those outside of the sport have likely never heard of her. Due to untimely injuries and her coach not understanding the rules to petition, Dianne was left off the 1984 Olympic team. Conversely, her teammate with a similar style would go on to become a household name and the Olympic champion. Her name is Mary Lou Retton.

So while Simone was now the back-to-back world champion, in my mind the Olympics were still only a dream.

CHAPTER 12

Coming into Focus

In March 2015, we were back for another American Cup, this time on the home turf of the NFL's Dallas Cowboys in Arlington, Texas. Most international competitions are held in dark arenas that hold an average of 18,500 people, but the sprawling, glass-ceilinged AT&T Stadium has an outrageous capacity of 100,000 people. With that many people under one roof, you can imagine the size needed for the video screen hovering over the center of the field. It measures 72 feet tall by 160 feet wide. To put things in perspective, the in-stadium monitor screen area measures 11,393 square feet—equivalent to 4,920 52-inch flat-screen TVs. Arlington is only a few hours' drive from Houston, and the Dallas Metroplex is a bit of a mecca for gymnastics, so there were a lot of fans in the building, but still nowhere near the crowd needed to fill a venue that hosted the Super Bowl in 2011. To accommodate the smaller crowd, half of the field was draped off with black curtains and the colossal screen was lowered down to about thirty feet off the ground instead of its usual home ninety feet in the air, making it feel even more imposing.

I remember standing on the floor, marveling at the surroundings. I could immediately tell that this go-around with the American Cup was going to be very different than our visit in 2013. Simone was now a seasoned veteran and a two-time world champion—not an unproven elite stepping onto the international scene for the first time. I was different too. I was more confident, and Martha was sending more respect in my direction. Suddenly, I was teleported back to 2013, to a breakfast at our first American Cup, in Worcester, Massachusetts.

That morning we were at the hotel fueling up, and Simone ordered a three-egg sausage-and-cheese omelet. Even though she didn't finish the entire plate, Martha was appalled she would even order it. Martha fretted to me about how Simone was going to get fat and how she shouldn't eat like that. Martha thought the girls should have half a serving of oatmeal and be done with it. If they wanted more, they could eat a third of a banana but no more, because bananas have a lot of sugar in them. I didn't feel that there was a healthy relationship between food, nutrition, and performance being promoted by the national team.

I had seen glimmers of this fear of food in a brief encounter at camp before the 2013 American Cup. Simone was rooming with Katelyn: the two of them were affectionately known as "double trouble." Simone and Katelyn had come to my room for something after training. When they were there, I asked Simone if would like a caramel. "Sure," she replied without any hesitation. I then inquired, "Katelyn do you want one?" Katelyn just stared at me. Finally, when the shock of the offer sunk in, she asked, "You're offering me candy?" I nodded. "You're the coolest coach ever!" Those words have stuck with me over the years: first, because it was so complimentary, but also because it sent a haunting chill through me when I considered that this tiny sixteen-year-old was apparently afraid to have a single piece of candy.

Looking back, the idea that this tiny gesture was a big deal is absurd. Years later, after Katelyn had gone viral, she began to open up about her disordered eating and the environment that had triggered it. In a BBC article, she's quoted as saying, "I was told I didn't look like a gymnast. I was told I looked like I'd swallowed an elephant, or looked like a pig." In another interview she said, "My friends and I would try to eat 500 calories or less when we were training seven hours a day. At parties, we would go to the bathroom and try to vomit up the food." This response to food isn't innate; it's ingrained.

When Simone started going to the camps at the Ranch and traveling to competitions with the team, I was happy that food was never a point of contention. There were so many other things for us to worry about that food didn't need to be one of them.

I felt good about the fact that I had amicable relationships with several of the girls on the national team, and I got a sense they were relaxed around me. I know a lot of them were worried about eating in front of their coaches and especially in front of Martha. I also know

Simone with her well-earned sundae. Pacific Rim Championship 2016.
Courtesy of the author.

some coaches told their athletes not to talk to me and Simone because we were "bad influences." They felt Simone was undisciplined and had bad eating habits and that I promoted those supposed bad habits. As it turned out, I was a go-to for a few athletes when they were hungry and wanted food, or who needed positive affirmations about their fitness or their abilities. I was never concerned about caloric intake for Simone because I knew how hard she was training. On many occasions I fulfilled Simone's request for a delivery of her favorite candy at the time, Sour Patch Kids.

I'm sure some will be shocked to hear that the greatest athletes on the planet consumed candy while away at a competition. I'll concede it wasn't the most nutritious thing they could put into their bodies, but there's something to be said for a bit of mental comfort provided by those treats. I knew the girls were physically capable of winning gold, and at that point in the competition cycle, it was about staying healthy and mentally sharp. And, to be honest, the girls didn't like a lot of the food available to them when we would travel out of the country, especially when we were in China—and there were only so many days in a row that they were happy eating chicken and rice. So I did what I could to keep those who requested my help happy, understanding how these long trips can wear on you.

At the 2015 World Championships in Glasgow, fellow coach Sarah Jantzi and I smuggled bowls of potatoes, broccoli, chicken, and bananas up to Simone and teammate Maggie Nichols because they didn't want to be judged by Martha or other coaches for what they were eating. There was very much a sense of "Don't eat that in front of so-and-so."

When we traveled abroad, I knew many of the girls, Simone included, would pack a bunch of snacks and treats they couldn't get in another country along with their protein bars. Good or bad, it was stuff I knew they were having at home anyway. The sad part is that they felt they had to hide these treats, which only fostered an unhealthy relationship with food.

***

Back in AT&T Stadium in Arlington, Simone was well rested and hungry to compete. As she began the competition by sprinting down the runway toward the vault, I glanced up to see her tiny, four-foot-eight frame appear gigantic on the $40 million mega-screen. She was no longer metaphorically larger-than-life. Simone dominated the performance with an almost perfect Amanar vault. Her tumultuous relationship with the next event always added an undercurrent of anxiety to competition, but on this day, with an upgraded bar routine, Simone shined. Her beam routine was not quite as flawless as she fought a balance check here and a small wobble there. She looked tentative. Unlike at the world championships, where she attacked the beam, in this routine Simone looked like she was just trying to get through it without giving away too many deductions. After her dismount, she flashed a smile and a salute to the judges, immediately followed by a look of dissatisfaction that she couldn't hide. Great athletes have a short memory in the moment, and Simone wiped the slate clean as she headed to her favorite event to perform. As always, she dazzled on the floor, showing off her newly debuted double layout with a full twist, followed by her signature skill, the Biles. Since she had added a new element, we decided to move her former first pass, the double twisting-double tuck, to her third pass. To keep things in perspective, her third pass contains a skill that only a handful of gymnasts can perform in their first pass when they're fresh in their routine. I know Simone made it look easy, but on more than one occasion she would walk off the floor after completing her routine and tell me how she couldn't feel her legs. Depending on where she landed in the lineup, I needed to make sure when she was heading to vault that she could squeeze every second of recovery time available.

In Arlington, Simone's legs were firing and she once again asserted her supremacy and posted the top score on every event (including bars!) and won the all-around title by almost 4.5 points. This meet showed that Simone's growing difficulty advantage also expanded her margin for error. Even though she clocked an unremarkable balance beam routine, her D score value made it so she couldn't be caught by lesser, cleaner routines. Simone was now competing only against herself.

After the meet, the coaches and gymnasts went to the Fort Worth Stockyards, a rustic and charming historical district that has saloons, restaurants, and live music. After attending a small rodeo we all had a nice meal, then most the athletes went back to the hotel while the rest of the adults stayed out and danced the night away. Oddly, the night concluded with a very atypical and unexpected snowstorm that blew through Dallas. Before retiring for the night, the coaches played in the fluffy snow.

Later that month we were back in the air, heading to Italy for the City of Jesolo Trophy. Gabby Douglas was back on the competition floor to make her push for Rio, which meant this event was the first time since the 1980 Olympics that the reigning women's all-around Olympic champion and the reigning all-around world champion would compete against each other. Of course, Gabby and Simone were teammates and there was no rivalry between the two, but it's amazing to think about how remarkably deep Team USA had become. The participating countries included the United States, Italy, Canada, Australia, and France. Most countries fielded an A and B team; when the dust settled, nine of the ten competitors brought by the United States finished in the top ten. To say they excelled would be an understatement. Team USA bested the competition by nearly 17 points in the team final. That doesn't even account for the outstanding performance of the American juniors who were led by all-around champion Laurie Hernandez.

Simone was spectacular too. She qualified in first place on all four events and won the all-around title by more than 2.5 points. She also went on to win event titles in vault, beam, and floor. To preserve her shoulder, Simone didn't compete in the bars finals. Kyla would go on to place first and American Bailie Key took silver.

The Jesolo trip was particularly important because it was the first international team trip of the season for which Martha strategized to build a team score. She needed to see if the lineups worked. If you didn't make the Jesolo team, it was going to be tough to make the Pacific Rim Championships team that followed. And starting one year out from the Olympics, if you weren't on either of those, your chances were even slimmer (or a statistical anomaly) to be selected for the world or Olympic team after that.

Once the competition was over, the delegation headed south to the Veneto region and Venice. Martha loved traveling to Italy for the team competition. She was treated like a queen there, and, miraculously, Martha found a way to arrange a bit of personal time for us to explore. In Venice, the weather was a little chilly but lovely. Thankful for the blossoming spring weather—unlike the wet and cold in Murano a few years earlier—we enjoyed a few gondola rides and were able to capture much better pictures this time. Squinting through the bright sunshine, we visited Piazza San Marco (St. Mark's Square) before heading to a lovely team lunch on the "floating city." The day ended too soon and the next morning we were traveling home.

Even after so many international experiences, air travel can still be an adventure. Our early morning voyage started without incident, but once we were at the airport, we were informed that our flight to

Amsterdam had been delayed by two hours. All we could do was wait, which was stressful because we had only a three-hour connection to make our flight back to the United States. The weather in Venice was beautiful, so we were perplexed about the delay, but eventually we boarded and were in the air. As we neared Schiphol Airport in Amsterdam, the pilot told us to buckle up and remain seated for the rest of the flight, informing us that there would be extremely high winds on our approach. Schiphol is a sprawling airport with six runways, five of which are designed for jumbo jets. As we drew nearer, the pilot said we'd have to circle: due to the wind, only one runway was open. Finally, when it was our turn to come in for a landing, he warned us that it was "going to get bumpy." Understatement of the year! It felt like every 5,000 feet we descended, the air got more and more turbulent. I was terrified. Then, from a few rows back, I heard an infectious giggle. I didn't have to turn around to know that it was Simone. She may have been terrified as well, but her laughter was contagious, and I couldn't help but join in. The power of laughter is incredible, and instead of being in tears from terror I was in tears of hilarity as the plane and the bodies within it got knocked around.

With our adrenaline high from an hour of circling the airport, then the stimulating landing, we now only had minutes to make our flight back to the United States. Before deplaning, the flight attendant asked the other passengers to stay seated so that our delegation of thirty-five people could make our connection. Inevitably, we landed at the opposite end of the airport from where our departure gate was, so we had to sprint past virtually all 223 gates in the terminal. By the time we reached our gate, I was about to throw up—once again highlighting my lack of cardio training.

Upon our return to the States, I spent the next few months helping Simone refine her skills in anticipation of the national and world championships. After reviewing her recent performances, I could identify areas for improvement even though she was stretching her lead. It was easy to see where she was getting deductions. For example, if Simone wasn't feeling confident while performing on the balance beam, her transitions from one skill to the next were punctuated by little pauses;

these would sometimes cost her a connection bonus. So we worked on increasing the speed of her connections.

Other decisions needed to be made too. Less than twelve months earlier, in the summer of 2014, Simone had committed to attending UCLA and competing for the Bruins. It was a big decision because at that time NCAA athletes were not allowed to profit from their popularity or their success. Simone had to choose between making money as a professional athlete or competing in college. She was in good company: around the same time, 2012 Olympic champion swimmer Missy Franklin refused to accept any prize money or endorsements so that she could maintain her eligibility to compete for the University of California, Berkeley. After winning multiple national championships at Cal in 2014 and 2015, Missy gave up her college eligibility and turned pro while she trained for the Rio Olympics. This was several years before the NCAA's "Name, Image, Likeness" (NIL) rules went into effect. Fortunately for today's athletes, in June of 2021, the NCAA adopted NIL rules: athletes can now profit from their brands while competing in college, and there's been an explosion of elite athletes and Olympians who have benefited. In gymnastics, Sunisa Lee became the first Olympic all-around champion to take advantage of this new opportunity when she attended Auburn in Alabama following the Tokyo Games and could still sign deals with Target, Gatorade, Crocs, and others.

Going to college was always something Simone had in mind, and it was going to be her choice. As a coach, I would help facilitate meetings between athletes and their parents and NCAA coaches, all while staying within the strict NCAA recruitment standards. However, I never got involved in a gymnast's decision-making process. I'd say the same thing to all the gymnasts with college aspirations: it was up to them. Sometimes they would get frustrated with me because I wouldn't advise them on what school to choose. But that wasn't my role. For most of them, it was the first adult decision they would make.

I said the same thing to Simone and her family. I was only a go-between. I met UCLA's head coach, Valorie Kondos Field, for lunch, and the program felt like a good fit to me. The roster at UCLA eventually became filled with Simone's friends, and I thought Simone would like it there too. Yet the only advice I shared with Simone was "It's your decision to make; it isn't your parents'."

Katelyn, who went on a recruiting trip with Simone, and then later Kyla and Madison would all commit to UCLA, helping the school win the national championship in 2018.

But Simone never wore a Bruin leotard.

After her first world championship in 2013, the idea of Simone turning pro and losing college eligibility became an open conversation. After back-to-back world championships under her belt and a third one on the horizon in 2015—plus the Olympics the following year—the calculation for her had started to shift.

I would never try to steer Simone in any direction, but I did ask her questions like "Do you *want* to go to college? Or do you *want* to go pro?" After the Secret U.S. Classic in July 2015, where winning was rote to Simone, she decided to turn pro. The timing of the decision allowed her and her family an opportunity to find an agent—another decision I stayed out of—before the national championships that would take place a couple of weeks later. The Bileses found Janey Miller from Octagon, whom Simone is still with to this day. And while I wasn't part of interviewing or choosing Janey, I think she always has Simone's best interests at heart.

When Simone made the decision to sign on with Octagon, she was worried about telling me because she thought I would be disappointed in her decision to not go to college. I eased her mind by pointing out that I didn't care what her choice was; I just wanted her to be happy. She wanted to attend college to be a part of a team and she wanted to win a championship ring. By the time she made her decision, she had already earned two world championship rings and soon enough she'd have five more rings tattooed on her forearm.

***

By August, Simone was firing on all cylinders. She was entertaining the various endorsement deals being offered while still maintaining focus in the gym. If one of her new professional engagements took her out of the gym longer than forty-eight hours, I would go with her so we could take time out to squeeze in a workout in a local gym.

Inside any gym, Simone was no longer an up-and-comer. She was now famous within the sport and the front-runner at every competition she entered. As she headed to Indianapolis in the middle of the month to defend her national all-around title, a preview article in the *Indianapolis Star* read, "Biles gears up for Olympics" as if the next two national championships and the 2015 world championship had already been won.

From start to finish it was a spectacular national championship for Simone. Her Amanar . . . wow: 🥇 She exploded off the table, kept a straight body, and stuck the landing. NBC commentator and Olympic gold medalist Tim Daggett called for it to be a 10.0 execution, a score that's never been given in the new, open-ended Code of Points. I've watched the replay of that vault innumerable times and the only deduction I can see is that Simone's toes crossed. Seriously, it was that perfect. I guess the judges saw the toes, too, giving her an uncommonly high execution score of 9.9 for a 16.3 total vault score.

Simone cruised to a three-peat national all-around title, outpacing silver medalist Maggie Nichols by nearly 5 points and Aly Raisman by 5.5. In fact, Simone was the only competitor to have an all-around score over 60—and she did it both days with a 61.1 and a 63.0. The win also meant Simone became only the third woman to win three all-around national titles in a row, following Joan Moore (1971–1974: four consecutive years) and Kim Zmeskal (1990–1992: three consecutive years). After the win, I was awarded Coach of the Year by USAG for the third time. Each award seemed less of a surprise, but each came with mounting pressure and expectations.

Once the competition was over and we were back at the hotel, some of the girls went down the hallway to do interviews with the popular gymnastics podcast *GymCastic*. The *GymCastic* crew had turned their hotel room into a makeshift podcast studio with a laptop and a few microphones. Once the girls left, I stepped in with Gabby's coach,

Christian Gallardo. From there it turned into a jovial interview/celebration that went on until about four o'clock in the morning, when we started to get delirious.

After this performance, not only was it clear that Simone was the best gymnast in the world, but she was also the most consistent. We were a year from the Olympics, and while it still wasn't front of mind, if I paused and looked at the horizon, our path to Rio was beginning to come into focus. But first, a trip to Scotland to defend her world title . . .

By this point the pressure was really starting to mount because Simone was beginning to rewrite the record books for women's gymnastics. Heading into this competition, no woman had ever won three world all-around titles in a row. Not only was Simone the favorite to win, but people had begun to expect it.

I knew Simone was ready, but we still needed to do our jobs. We were in Scotland for a full month, which was a long time. On the one hand, it was great to be fully acclimated to our environment by the time the competition rolled around; on the other hand, you begin to go stir-crazy sitting on the bus, caravanning from the gym to the hotel, back to the gym, then returning to the hotel again. As the competition day drew closer, the girls were exhausted and wanted a break from being in the gym. Aly approached me and asked, "Can you talk to Martha about giving us a day off?" Sure.

I approached Martha and made the request. She was gruff. Her old-school mentality was in full force, and she felt like the girls could not take any time off from training. I did my best to explain how exhausted they were and that their routine quality was sliding. They were on the edge of burning out. Simone had started sharing on social media pictures of her fogged-up hotel room window, marking how many consecutive days they had been in training. Martha eventually relented, and although she would not allow them a full day off, she did let them skip one of the two trainings for the day, enough time for a walk to river Clyde, which was a couple of blocks from the hotel. She felt that if they were tired, they should rest in their rooms, which Simone often described as "rotting." What they really needed was some fresh air.

I have a picture of the girls on the walk to the riverfront with their faces pressed against a slatted metal fence, holding the bars next to their heads, all posing with sad faces like they're prisoners. It was obvious they weren't excited about this particular excursion, but they definitely didn't want to be in their rooms or the gym. Martha noted their lack of enthusiasm and remarked that it was apparent to her that they didn't want to be out on a walk anyway, prompting our already short journey to end abruptly.

After two more days of training, the competition was finally underway. Team USA—consisting of Simone, Gabby, Maggie, Aly, Brenna, and Madison—took command of the leaderboard and never looked back. They qualified for the team finals with a ridiculous 5-point lead

World Championship Team in Scotland (from left to right: Aly Raisman, Maggie Nichols, Simone Biles, Madison Kocian, Gabby Douglas).
Courtesy of the author.

over the second qualifier, Russia, and 9 points ahead of Great Britain in the third position.

On the night of the team final, the girls were amazing. The format (known as three-up-three-count) called for three gymnasts to compete in each event and all three scores counted. Team USA had hit all eleven of the twelve routines to be performed by the time Simone walked onto the floor exercise to try and secure the team title. All she needed to do was finish the routine in one piece. In fact, she could have fallen multiple times—a 1.0 deduction for each infraction—and it wouldn't have changed the placement. Her floor routine had been scoring in the high 15s to the low 16s all season long, and she only needed a 10.56 for the team to win the gold. Of course, this was elite gymnastics—which was dangerous and scary—so anything could happen.

Simone performed and finished in her now-famous arching pose on the floor. She ran off the podium and joined her teammates to await the score. The girls all held hands and stared at the scoreboard, looking for the team total to flash across the big screen. I'm sure the girls knew they were going to win, but in a sport where you don't know the score until it's posted, the wait can be a little nerve-racking. I imagine they felt a bit awkward, wanting to celebrate before the score was official while also not wanting to come across as being arrogant. Once Simone's score of 15.733 came up, she screamed with excitement and the girls started jumping around. Maybe because I'm such a fan of sports like football, where you know the winner immediately as the play unfolds, this waiting thing bothered me, especially when everyone in Glasgow knew the outcome. It seemed unfair to the athletes and insulting to the fans, which made the drama of the reveal feel a bit contrived—at least in this instance. Team USA had just won by a historic margin, but an outsider of the sport tuning in for the first time may have sensed feigned uncertainty. Personally, I felt more awkward than nervous or even excited during the wait. Upon returning to the hotel, in a rare moment of generosity, Steve Penny, president of USAG, ordered a mass of pizzas for the gymnasts and surprised the coaches with bottles of Dom Pérignon.

Having accomplished the goal of winning the team gold, Martha allowed the group to go on one real excursion: a half-day visit to Edinburgh. It had been close to thirty days since they had a day off from training, but the girls were still required to do their basics, such as walking through their balance beam routines in the hallway of the hotel before we left. After that, we hopped on a bus from Glasgow to Edinburgh. The whole vibe of the city was amazing, from the men wearing kilts and playing bagpipes to the charming shops, and finishing up with the visit to the Edinburgh Castle that included up-close views of knights' armor and a visit to the dungeon. But the girls seemed a little bored. I remember their general sentiment: "Yeah, we're looking at a castle. This is dumb." They were mostly teenagers, after all. Within hours of arriving back at the hotel the girls would resume complaining about being stuck in their rooms—and who could blame them? The big

Day off. Edinburgh Castle, 2015 (from left to right: Brenna Dowell, Gabby Douglas, Madison Kocian, MyKayla Skinner, Aly Raisman, Maggie Nichols, Simone Biles, Martha Karolyi). Courtesy of the author.

problem was that Martha was still present, which meant the girls didn't feel they could relax. They sensed they were always being *watched* by her . . . because they were!

Still, I thought it was nice to take our minds off gymnastics for a moment, even in imperfect circumstances. Standing inside a thousand-year-old castle, realizing the names of ruling kings over the centuries have been forgotten, you began to get some perspective on the historical feat you're about to embark on. This is the world championships; the greatest athletes in the world competing in rarified air, Simone competing in a stratosphere unto herself. But at the end of the day it's just gymnastics. Simone and Team USA were training to take on the world and they were expected to win, which was oddly reassuring and too brazen to give a second thought to.

Two days later Simone was back in Glasgow's SSE Hydro arena, which glowed a rainbow of colors from the bubbly exterior panels, for the women's all-around final. She started with a huge two and a half twisting vault, taking a lunging step on her landing—a noticeable deduction but still enough to start her off with a half-point lead over any other competitor in the field. Next, she hit a solid bar routine with only a few form breaks. She didn't post the highest score of the rotation among her competitors, but her score was near the top. On the balance beam, Simone performed a very solid routine until about halfway through, when she bounced into her front tuck and found herself bending over, struggling to stay on the beam. She reached down and grabbed the beam with both hands to stay on. She quickly recovered and carried on to finish her routine with a respectable 14.4, even with the major error. (The highest beam score of the night was 14.766 by Romania's Larisa Iordache.) On to the final event, floor. Simone needed a 14.183 to take the lead. On her second pass, while performing the Biles, she had a little trouble controlling the landing and stepped out of bounds. Like the pro she is, Simone gathered herself and kept performing. A lesser gymnast might have easily let things unravel, but not Simone. She was highly confident in the knowledge that one minor error wouldn't threaten her position as the best floor worker in the world. Cool as a cucumber, she finished her routine, arching once again, and you could see the relief begin to wash over her almost instantly. She ran off the floor and we hugged, then she hugged Gabby and went around congratulating the other gymnasts. Then we all waited.

As the arena grew quieter, Simone looked at me and asked, "Did I do it?" Not for the last time, she was about to make history. The score flashed and we embraced. For a moment the cameramen and the crowd disappeared. It was intimate, like standing on the very peak of a mountain where nobody else can reach you. A moment that will forever be etched in my heart.

Simone Biles was now the first woman in the history of the sport to win three consecutive all-around world championship titles.

My second favorite moment of the competition occurred soon after Simone won her all-around title. We had left the competition floor and headed backstage to the warm-up gym. Standing there was Japanese legend Kohei Uchimura—"King Kohei," as he's affectionately known within the gymnastics community. He was the reigning Olympic all-around champion and was twenty-four hours away from winning his mind-boggling sixth consecutive all-around world championship title. Kohei was waiting to take a picture with Simone. To me, it was a moment of the king waiting for the queen.

After a day's rest from competition, Simone was back in the gym to compete in the event finals on vault. Once again she would perform an Amanar, followed by a Lopez. Her second vault wasn't the same level of difficulty as some of the other gymnasts' vaults in the final, so Simone had to perform it beautifully. Despite posting the highest execution scores on both her first and second vaults of anyone in the final, her total score still wasn't enough. Simone placed third. Having observed multiple execution errors by her rivals, I felt the other medalists had been a bit overscored and felt that Simone deserved a different-color medal. But if the judges wanted more difficulty, Simone could bring more difficulty. We were already working on a higher-start-value vault for Rio in order to leave no doubt about Simone being the best vaulter in the world.

The following day Simone competed in balance beam and floor. She was great. On beam she attacked. She moved smoothly between her connections and didn't have any major deductions. Our deliberate intentions to work the fine details in the gym were on full display. She finished her routine with two back handsprings into a massive twist and two flips, planting her feet into the ground. Gold. The floor exercise was the same: although she beamed with confidence after her epoch-making achievement, she wasn't perfect, but she excelled. She overcooked her Biles and took a step out of bounds, a deduction ranging from 0.1 to 0.3. If Simone was competing on the same level as the other athletes, this probably would have pushed her off the podium, but we had built so much difficulty into Simone's routine that she didn't have to be perfect. Throughout Simone's growth and training, I wanted to push her but not stress her. Get her to a level where her gymnastics difficulty was superior to everyone else's but well within her capabilities. Then we polished the skills to ensure her execution score reflected the training we had done. So even though Simone stepped out of bounds, her difficulty score was already at least 0.4 higher than the other contenders' scores in the world championship final. More impressive, she was the only athlete to reach a 9.0 in execution in the final. Simone had another gold medal placed around her neck.

CHAPTER 13

Whirlwind to Rio

After Glasgow, I was exhausted. I had been abroad for a month and I was homesick. So I packed my bags again—along with those of my entire family—and we took a vacation to Punta Cana, a resort town in the Dominican Republic. This beautiful beach escape on the eastern tip of the island offered sugar-white sandy beaches, palm trees, water that looked like it had come out of a bathtub faucet, and a warm sun I hadn't seen in weeks. More than anything, however, I was able to lie around and play with my family. It was the escape I needed. The gymnasts felt like they were constantly being judged and monitored by Martha, and the same feeling applied to coaches. After three world titles in a row, I was confident that Simone just needed to stay healthy to make the Olympic team, but I hadn't always felt that way. It might seem surprising that it took an actual historic feat to find this assurance, but it's true. One thing a coach fears is being responsible for an athlete not getting a shot after pushing them too far, too fast. Luis and I agonized about this when we started on the elite circuit back in 2013. But after Simone's successful run, I knew we were in the best possible position with less than a year to Rio.

Taking a vacation after a long trip may seem simple enough, but for gym owners it means paying an extra coach to take over classes. For weeks, every class I had been coaching had needed a substitute, and now I was extending my absence for one more week to vacation in Punta Cana. This same thing happens at all gyms where coaches take long trips or get invited to train at the national team camp for a week or two. Gym owners have to make provisions for these absences and the parents of other athletes should expect them when they join a program.

When I finally reentered the gym, I was no longer stepping into the Tin Can. Instead, the beautiful World Champions Centre was finally open and ready for business. Located in Spring, Texas, this massive 52,000-square-foot building has everything a coach and gymnast could want. More than anything it was satisfying to finally have a permanent place to train—and unwrapping it in the final stretch for the Olympics seemed like appropriate timing. Concurrent with the building of this extraordinary facility, my family had been building a new house that was within walking distance of the gym. I felt like a stage performer trying to keep several plates spinning in the air.

Still, I knew where my focus needed to be, and I was excited to dig into running the gymnastics program. Getting WCC open was a huge undertaking for the Biles family, and now it was my job to be a manager there. In the best interests of Simone's training, it was decided that I would manage the operations of the gymnastics program while Simone's older brother, Adam, managed the business side.

It wasn't long before I began to get the feeling I wasn't going to be completely satisfied at WCC. Ron and Nellie were growing something from the ground up, and I recognized how each decision could shape the culture both on the floor and behind the glass doors. But after putting so much time and effort into planning to get the gym up and running, I suppose I felt let down. I had my own ideas of how I would run things, and they sometimes differed from the Bileses' vision. All the same, I recognized it wasn't my place to push for my ideals and I respected the Biles family enough to avoid overstepping my boundaries as much as possible. Even though my fantasy was to own my own gym, I didn't have the finances it would require, so I tried to be content in a managerial position at WCC. However, in my heart I knew I didn't want to be *just* an employee of a company anymore. To be fair to Simone's parents, this is not something I ever explicitly expressed to them.

At the same time, James wasn't completely happy with his job. By January 2016 we had begun talking about leaving Houston. I want to be crystal clear: my discontent had nothing to do with Simone or her parents; it was about my own ambitions and a potential lifestyle change that could benefit my family. It's an odd feeling to stand next to someone who you've helped to become literally the greatest person on the planet at their craft, to watch their life change in innumerable ways, while yours was only modified with small perks here and there. I didn't start coaching to become rich and famous (well, maybe now I'd like to be rich), but you can stand next to greatness only for so long before you start to dream bigger for yourself.

In March 2016, Jason, the former director of the men's program at WCC, heard I might not want to stay in Houston, so he reached out to me. He told me that he was partnering with some people to open a new multi-sport facility on the Florida coast, Evo Athletics in Sarasota, and offered me the position of director of the gymnastics program. This offer included an equity partnership in the company. I thought that this opportunity might be exactly what I was looking for as the next step in my career.

Later that evening, I brought up the potential business plan to James. We both knew we had reached a level in our respective careers where the world was our oyster and we were employable anywhere we chose to land.

James and I decided to take a quick weekend trip to Sarasota and meet the three owners at the time: Jason and the founders, the husband-and-wife team of Lydia and Kyle Lawton. We talked about going into a partnership. In all honesty, it wasn't even about the gym, although it was the foundation for a potential move; deep down I had always wanted to live in Florida. After living in the South for two decades, the prospect of living on the beach in Florida was like a dream.

The rhythm of our conversation flowed so naturally, and I liked what this new opportunity offered. James and I decided to take a walk along the beach at sunset. (Sarasota has the most beautiful sunsets.) As we were making marks in our mental ledger of moving to this paradise, our feet sank into the sand with each step. Looking out on the Gulf of Mexico, I noticed two dolphins popping up out of the water. They began swimming alongside us, about a hundred feet from where we were standing. We took it as a sign and we were ready to move right then and there. (Excellent job, dolphins: you closed the deal!)

We still had a lot of things to sort out, but we were getting more comfortable with the idea of leaving Texas. We figured we would give it two years and see how it fit us, and if we hated Florida, we could move on. James wanted a change and he knew I wanted to own a gym as well. It seemed like a good opportunity. We felt we owed it to ourselves to try.

Before we could enjoy more future Florida sunsets, though, we needed to focus on the more present horizon. We were finally in the Olympic year, but it was off to a rocky start.

Simone had developed the twisties. To reemphasize how dangerous this can be and how precise the gymnast's movements are, during the Sydney Olympics the vault table was set too low by five centimeters. This tiny error rocked the sport because it reduced the greatest vaulters in the world to rubble as they came literally crashing down on the biggest stage. When Simone vaults she launches herself ten feet above the vault table into a blind landing—that is, without being able to see the ground before she hits it. Attempting this feat when she was unable to tell where she was in the air was nonnegotiable. This was not how we wanted to start the Olympic year. Simone needed time, support, and reassurance that I believed in her.

Beyond coordinating with her family to seek mental health assistance, I tried to make it a nonissue. For weeks to start 2016, Simone didn't twist in the gym. Everyone knew she could perform the hardest skills in the world when the pressure was on. She had already made history in the sport and was dominating it like nobody before her. Pushing her to perform dangerous skills when her body wasn't cooperating wasn't something we would have ever considered doing. We had to find a way through this. Fortunately, we had time on our side.

The first big meet of the season would have been the City of Jesolo Trophy in March, but we skipped it—not because of the twisties, but because Simone had already proven she was qualified to be on the Olympic team. No one involved—neither the national staff, nor Martha, nor Simone, nor I—wanted her to risk getting injured training for competitions she didn't need to be in.

The next meet was Pacific Rim Championships in April. Thankfully the twisties had passed without injury, and in the process we demonstrated that an elite gymnast can avoid training elements for weeks without losing their skills. And in case anyone thought we were playing it coy about competing in Rio, we left no doubt where our focus had shifted. Simone debuted her new floor routine using the music from "Brazil" by Bellini and bits from the 2011 Twentieth Century Fox Animation feature-length film *Rio*.

"Pac Rims," held in Everett, Washington, north of Seattle, was arguably one of the most fun meets we went to. The five U.S. women who competed in the all-around—Simone, Aly, Laurie, Brenna, and Ragan Smith—qualified one through five respectively. Despite the team's stellar performance, Simone and Aly were the only U.S. gymnasts awarded medals for the all-around due to the two-per-country rule. As expected, Team USA handily won the team competition over our neighbors to the north, Canada, and our friends Down Under, Australia.

In the individual event qualifier, Simone ranked first on the vault, beam, and floor exercise and third on bars behind Ashton and Brenna. During her floor routine, however, Simone overexerted her calf muscle while landing her last tumbling pass, which she stuck. Keeping in mind how close we were to the Olympics, we decided not to risk any further injury and pulled Simone out of the finals. Since she and Laurie, who had a sore knee from the previous day's event, weren't competing, USAG got a suite overlooking the arena for the noncompeting athletes and their coaches. Why a suite? This was only four months before the Olympic Games. Every member of the U.S. Pac Rims team was a true contender for the Olympic team, and the fan frenzy to meet the athletes was very high. Having any of our American athletes sitting in the stands would have caused a huge disruption to the competition. Secluded in the suite, we ordered the girls chicken tenders, fries, and ice cream sundaes to eat while they cheered on their teammates on the competition floor. (You guessed correctly: Martha was not in the suite with us.) Despite our best efforts to provide privacy and security for the athletes, Simone plus sugar equaled a very loud Simone. It was as if Taylor Swift were in the suite: fans started to climb up the rows of seats to get a glimpse of the three-time world champion up close. With security guards keeping them at a safe distance, fans passed posters up to the suite to get a treasured autograph.

After Pac Rims we had a nice break until the next competition, which allowed Simone to rest her calf. This also allowed time for the Olympic hype machine to start ramping up. After three consecutive world titles, Simone became a main topic of conversation leading up to Rio. As time went on, the conversation shifted: it was no longer just about making the team but about talk in the media and among gym fans of how many gold medals Simone might win. But neither Simone nor I could focus on any of that. If Simone competed to her abilities, we were comfortable that things would fall into place. It was a little hard, though, when she was being heralded as a golden girl even before Olympic trials.

On occasion, the stress would bubble up and Simone would express a bit of uncertainty about the lofty expectations. She was starting to worry too much about letting people down, letting her country down. It was my job to keep her mind at ease when it came to the hype, and I would try to comfort her by reminding her of all that she had accomplished so far. I would try and calm her by saying that she wasn't responsible for other people's expectations and that, when all was said and done, she was the only person whom she had to make happy. It was assumed by most people who followed the sport that Simone was a lock to make the team at that time; even Martha wouldn't leave the three-peat world champion home because of some imperfection or minor health issue. Still, each day came with new reminders of how this upcoming competition would be different.

Advertisers were swooning over Simone and she started shooting several Olympic promo pieces for NBC, along with endorsements for sponsors in the early spring of 2016. Simone was becoming the face of the upcoming Olympics before she had even been named to the Olympic team. Almost all of the promotional demands were at the newly completed World Champion Centre, but one commercial shoot took us just outside of Los Angeles. Simone was shooting a safety video for United Airlines, starring potential Olympians, at an old airport, and the next day she attended an event for the Golden Globes called "Gold Meets Golden." I remember being struck by the small size of the banquet hall where such an important awards ceremony was being held. I didn't stick around for the festivities, but Simone and her agent, Janey, stayed.

In June we were focused on Simone's health, refining the small details of her routines and focusing on her consistency. She entered the Secret U.S. Classic in early June in Hartford, Connecticut, which would kick off the final run of elite meets before the Olympics. It wasn't a perfect meet, but it was exactly what Simone needed after several months of carrying a schedule of endorsements and appearances. It's not unusual for the top gymnasts in the country to do only a couple of events at the U.S. Classic that precedes the Olympics. This is a strategic preparation to make sure they don't peak before the Games. Simone chose to compete only on balance beam and uneven bars, since those events not only caused her the most stress and anxiety; they were also the events that were easiest to do a higher number of repetitions on without pounding on the body excessively. Simone took first on beam and performed a solid uneven bars routine. With that performance, she showed that she was ready to take on the rest of the season. Later that month, we headed to St. Louis for the U.S. national championships.

By this point, in nearly every interview, the reporter would ask if Simone was going to win gold in Rio. Internally I'd always think, *If you don't jinx it, yeah!* I'm not a superstitious person, but I found myself becoming one as the Olympics approached and these questions continued to get louder. A few weeks before the national championships, I was asked that question again at a photo shoot with Simone for the *New Yorker.* I told the reporter I needed to find a piece of wood to knock on and started frantically scanning the room for something—anything— that I could use. I later told this story to Kelly McKeown, then vice president of the leotard company GK Elite. Kelly and I laughed, but she also appreciated my conundrum. A few weeks later, while browsing some local shops on vacation in Italy, her daughter stumbled across a solution.

The Thursday before the National Championship competition began, Kelly presented me with a gift that she had picked up in Italy. It was a beautiful dark wooden ring. I could now "knock on wood" whenever and wherever I was. Simone was the perennial favorite on an unprecedented run and I wanted to make sure I crossed all t's and dotted all i's. From that point on I wore the ring all the time. At meets, I would twist it around my finger, wearing the ring to a polish like a rosary bead, and my mind would clear. The new ritual helped direct my focus away from my nerves and anxiety and placed them onto the ring finger of my right hand, like a fidget spinner that was attached to my body.

Simone was in her groove too. She nearly swept the national championships, placing first on vault, beam, and floor. And she cruised to a four-point victory in defending her fourth consecutive all-around national championship title. Everything was falling into place for the Olympics. Just one more stop in early July: the Olympic trials in San Jose, California.

***

In 2016 there was only one way for Simone to guarantee herself a spot on the Olympic team. It didn't matter that she had just won the national championship for the fourth time in a row or won the world championship title less than a year earlier for the third time in a row. Gymnastics is a "What have you done for me lately?" sport. Per the competition directive set forth by USA Gymnastics, the only way for a gymnast to *guarantee* a spot on the Olympic team was to place first in the all-around competition at the Olympic trials. The remaining four slots would be filled by gymnasts who had the best chance of landing on the medal podium when all was said and done. To truly appreciate the power of Martha is to understand that she had authoritarian control. You weren't selected for any team—including the Olympics—without

Martha's approval. In fact, there was no skill being competed on the team that was not first approved by Martha. I recall one day at a training camp, Simone showed her named tumbling pass, but instead of doing her normal jump out of it, she immediately rebounded into a front tuck. Martha's shriek could be heard across the gym: "NO!" We also showed Martha a new dismount off beam Simone had been working on, a double-twisting double-back, that was nearly competition-ready, and again she said, "*No.*" Had Martha approved, the world would have seen the skill three years earlier than when Simone debuted it after Martha retired.

Of course, we figured if Simone could walk, she would be on the team. She had proven at the three previous world championships that she was a medal contender in all four events, but this didn't squash all of the nerves as long as there was any uncertainty about it. After all, Dianne Durham was the U.S. national champion in 1983 and was left off the Olympic team in 1984 when she was injured at the trials.

Everyone reading this knows the same fate would not befall Simone. My memory is that she was flawless, but in reality Simone had a fall on the balance beam on the second night, which was the last event of the competition for her. This might be why it doesn't resonate with me. When the score came up, even with that fall, Simone won the all-around competition by more than 2 points. That meant we needed to pack our bags because we were heading to Rio!

For Simone, the pressure of making the Olympic team was over, but the suspense for the other girls was about to intensify. At the conclusion of the competition, all of the athletes and coaches went to a holding room and waited to hear who else would be on the Olympic team. The selection committee was made up of national team coach Tatiana Perskaia, 2004 Olympic silver medalist and athlete representative Terin Humphrey, and the voice that carried an absurdly disproportionate amount of weight: Martha. There was a general understanding that if Martha wanted you on the team, you were on the team; if Martha didn't, you would be left to watch the Olympic Games from home.

The top ten all-around placement was as follows:

1. Simone Biles
2. Laurie Hernandez
3. Aly Raisman
4. MyKayla Skinner
5. Ragan Smith
6. Maggie Nichols
7. Gabby Douglas
8. Madison Kocian
9. Amelia Hundley
10. Brenna Dowell

The tension in the room was thick. No one was talking except Simone and me, since our anxiety had plummeted knowing we had already punched our ticket to Rio. We were trying to keep things loose and lighten the mood, and I'm sure this annoyed some people. While we chatted, trying to contain our excitement, the other athletes were fixated on their phones, scrolling through social media feeds, and the coaches were staring at the floor. Finally, the selection committee entered the room.

Martha's genius was in putting together the best overall team, knowing the two-per-country rule meant a team consisting exclusively of all-around gymnasts wouldn't have the potential to win as many medals as it would if she included a few specialists. Regardless of who made the team from this group, the Americans were going to be the favorite to win the team gold.

Martha, with tears in her eyes and a lump in her throat, read the names from the small piece of paper she held in her hand: Simone Biles, Gabby Douglas, Laurie Hernandez, Madison Kocian, and Aly Raisman. The reserve athletes, asked to train and step in if any of the team was unable to perform, were MyKayla Skinner, Ragan Smith, and Ashton Locklear. This announcement happened quickly. Ashton wasn't in the top ten all-around, but she ended up posting the second-highest score of the competition on bars and showed she was capable of making the Olympic podium.

The final roster also included Gabby, in seventh place, over alternates MyKayla and Ragan. Maggie was skipped over completely. She had the misfortune of being world-class at everything but not the best on anything—and missing out on the top two on all four events eliminated her from a specialist role.

Gabby was the reigning Olympic all-around champion and demonstrated again that she was competent in all events, but, more importantly, she scored higher on bars than all the other all-around placers ahead of her. Eighth-place finisher Madison was the reigning uneven bars world champion and again posted the highest bars score at trials. Reserve MyKayla had the second-highest vault score in the competition, and Ragan, fifth in the all-around, could fill in on any event if needed.

Almost immediately after Martha announced the team in that intimate setting, the selected athletes and their coaches were whisked out of the room and back onto the arena floor to have their names announced in front of the crowd. Those who didn't qualify were left in the holding area. As the crowd cheered and confetti fell from the ceiling, I remember feeling guilty, wanting to celebrate, but also feeling sorrow for members of my tribe who were not going to be making the trip with us.

CHAPTER 14

The Ranch Before Rio

After the Olympic team had been named and we brushed the tiny pieces of paper out of our hair, I headed to a party being held within the venue to celebrate with the other coaches whose gymnasts had just been named to the team. The girls had already gone off with their families to celebrate, but not before they met Kobe Bryant, who was in attendance. Several of them were very excited about that; my own exciting celebrity encounter would happen later that night.

One of the first things I noticed when I arrived at the party were several historic Olympic torches being handed around the room; then I began noticing the past Olympians and other VIPs socializing among the attendees. Not knowing it was even possible, I had gained even more respect for this group with a fresh understanding of how difficult the journey to becoming an Olympian actually is. However, it wasn't the Olympians I was most excited about seeing at the party, although I did have a blast talking to former champions Jordyn Wieber, Bridget Sloan, and Anna Li. The person I was most psyched to meet was Travis Wall. I had been following Travis's career since he first appeared on one of my favorite shows, *So You Think You Can Dance*—first as a dancer and then as a choreographer. Never one to shy away from an opportunity, I overcame my rare bout of being starstruck and started a conversation with Travis. The little fangirl in me was dancing, and soon we were doing the same in real life. It was special.

After the party, I headed out into the streets of San Jose with a large group. We fueled up at a taco truck (very California), then found a club as it was closing so we could only go in for a quick celebratory drink. Turns out San Jose is a pretty quiet city, even when dreams come to life there.

The next day I was back at home in Texas with one week to pack and get ready for a ten-day training camp at the Ranch before we left for the Olympics. I knew the next couple of weeks were going to be grueling, starting with two-a-days at the national training center. At this point Simone was a heavy favorite in Rio, and keeping her healthy was the top priority. She was also taking care of her mental health with a few calls with her sports therapist, Robert Andrews. Our remaining days in WCC were spent just loosening things up, knowing Simone would benefit from rest. Then off we went to the Ranch.

Going to the Ranch was never easy. The first time I ever visited was in 1995. It wasn't for a training camp; it was for a National Judges Cup competition with compulsory gymnasts I was coaching at Bannon's, and my first impression was: *This place is a shithole! This is where the national team trains?* I was shocked at how unimpressive it was. In the subsequent years, the Karolyis added some newer structures—including updated motel-style rooms, a more modern gym for the artistic women, a gym where the national rhythmic gymnasts trained—alongside the trampoline and tumbling teams, but aside from the new equipment and training building, the living quarters at the Ranch remained an embarrassment rather than the state-of-the-art facility the girls deserved. There was mold all over the bathrooms, the carpets were dirty and stained, and—until the team got sponsored by Hilton—the beds were awful, just painful to lie on, as they provided no support for our worn-down bodies after a long day in the gym. The internet connection was also horrible until around 2014, when they finally got DirecTV, which at least made it serviceable. And then there was the food. "Institutional" is maybe the nicest way to put it. Close your eyes and imagine powdered eggs for breakfast; hard, tasteless bread with processed meat for lunch; and rock-hard steaks, tilapia (one of the worst farmed fish for health), and bland chicken breasts for dinner. The girls usually just ate yogurt and whatever they had snuck into their bags, sitting in their rooms. Since I lived close, about an hour's drive away, I brought my own food that I had cooked at home, as well as my own blankets and pillows.

Despite being out in the country, very few people who traveled to the Ranch wanted to wander around outside because they were afraid they would encounter one of the many peacocks, donkeys, snakes, chickens, camels, or, even more frightening, wild hogs that lived in the area. It wasn't just the rustic nature of the space; the isolation from the modern world was also unsettling. Of course, the remoteness was part of the Karolyis' strategy. They didn't want any distractions. That's fine in theory but terrible in practice. For example, if something went horribly wrong and someone was severely injured or ill, it would require a helicopter to transport them to the nearest hospital. But first, you'd have to cross your fingers that the spotty cellular coverage would let you place the call if you weren't near a landline, which, to my knowledge was available only in the gym and at the Karolyis' house—eating into precious seconds or minutes when these things matter. For comparison, the Dallas Cowboys have a hospital directly across the street from their training facility. Fortunately, I was never there when an emergency called for such action. Still, coming from WCC to the Ranch felt more like a punishment than a reward.

Heading into the Olympics, I understood it wasn't the number of routines we needed to complete in each workout that was the goal; it was the quest for perfection on each attempt, which was exhausting for all involved. Multiple times a day, knowing that the end goal was so close, the girls had to get up on the apparatus and perform, and—particularly for Simone—the expectations were impossibly high. We were going to have to be "on" for nearly five weeks without a real break. I wanted Simone to do as little as necessary before we headed to Rio. To be more accurate, I wanted Simone to train with quality and intention in mind more than hitting an arbitrary quantity of repetitions; we had already fine-tuned her routines for trials. At training camp, this sometimes turned into a cat-and-mouse game of doing what we needed to do rather than what Martha told us or wanted us to do. Martha would sometimes argue with me when I pushed back on her assignments, but, to her credit, she respected that I was Simone's coach and that I knew her best. I had gotten Simone to this point and Martha recognized that. She would relent and walk away or grumble, which prompted a shrug on my part. Every once in a while, Simone would express her own concern about Martha's approval. "Martha's going to be mad," she would fret. I would reassure her: "You let me deal with it." And I would. I'd either ignore Martha's demands or explain how what we were doing was fine and working.

It would always piss me off when other coaches suggested that I could speak to Martha however I wanted to because I "had Simone." I had stood up to Martha long before Simone was a national champion or world champion and we had faced the consequences. In truth, sometimes I was scared to stand up to Martha, but my pushback helped keep Simone in a positive mindset and physically healthy so that she could continue to be the greatest on the planet. In all honesty, I think Martha respected coaches more when they stood up for their athletes, as if it were a test that you had to pass with her.

But here we were, back at the now-familiar Ranch, where we had a morning session that started at 8:00 A.M., a lunch break, then an evening session at 4:00 P.M. before dinner and then bed. I knew Simone was physically in shape and just needed to maintain her focus on doing her best—for herself! Simone's progression had been paced perfectly. In a way, I felt the Olympics would be easier for her than her road to get there. It was always going to be a stressful environment, but she didn't need to do her most difficult skills to win. Part of Simone's confidence in performing came from the fact that I let her decide the difficulty levels of her routines and what skills she would compete in.

In the years leading up to the Games, Simone had been training many upgraded skills. We had to strategically choose what skills would work best for her in her routines, weighing the risk versus reward. Some of the skills that she was training but not yet competing were a Moors (a double twisting, double layout on floor); a Weiler full (a free-hip circle forward around the bar into a handstand into a full pirouette); a Biles dismount off beam, later named for Simone after she landed it at the 2019 World Championships (a double-twisting double-back dismount); a Fabrichnova (a double-double dismount off bars—two flips with a full twist each in tucked position); and an inconsistent Shaposh half (a clear hip circle with a half turn in flight from the low bar to high bar), but it hurt her shoulder to train it, so we nixed it out of the routine.

Her bar mount was a Weiler with a half pirouette: we would always submit the Weiler full as a new "Biles" skill on bars in case she lost her balance after her Weiler half and needed to add an extra half turn to cover her mistake. She's never had this skill named after her because she has never lost her balance in competition. In 2023, Georgia Godwin of Australia intentionally and successfully executed the Weiler full in a World Cup competition and so now it's in the books as a Godwin. In Paris, Simone added another half twist and submitted the Weiler 1.5, but again did not compete it.

Some skills we played with but didn't push toward making competition ready were the Biles II on floor, also competed at 2019 World Championship (a triple twisting double back); the Biles II on vault (a Yurchenko double pike—a round off onto the board, back handspring onto the vault table, two and a half flips backward in pike position); and a Yurchenko triple full (one and a half flips in laid out position with three twists), but we didn't want her to attempt this skill in a vault final because at the time the FIG didn't allow for a warm-up on the podium. Oh . . . there's more! Simone also had a triple full on floor (a single flip with three twists in laid out position) and a double Arabian on floor (a half-turn into two front tuck flips, plus she would sometimes add a full twist on the second flip). She played with that on the rod floor—the floor the power tumblers use (it's extra bouncy)—when she was eleven or twelve years old but never on the hard floor. Of course, there were also the random things she did just for fun, like a standing double back on the rod floor, or a round-off double back *on* the beam pad. Granted, the beam pad is eight inches instead of four inches wide, but the fact that she could do a double back from a standing hurdle was astonishing.

There were so many skills she was capable of including in her routines, but we had to choose the ones she liked performing the most and, from a technical standpoint, the skills she could land the best.

In the beginning we would show up at the Ranch with seven or eight tumbling passes and Martha directed us to focus on only four. It's been fun watching her over the past few years as her current coaches, Cecile and Laurent Landi, have brought some of these skills into her competitive routines, and also adding a half twist on the Cheng vault to get the first "Biles" named after her on that event. If Simone wants, she could have at least one skill on every event named after her in the Code of Points. As of the writing of this book, she is only missing a skill on bars! I always wanted to make competitions as easy as possible for Simone; it's just that her easy is absurdly hard.

When envisioning our participation in the Olympics, I had Simone make the decision on if she wanted everything to be comfortable and routine or if she wanted to blow everyone's mind by showing her new upgrade(s). Since she knew that she would have a lot on her plate with endorsements and appearances heading into Rio, she chose to go the more tested route she knew she could hit.

After the Olympic trials, I was named the head coach of the women's gymnastics team for Rio, a distinguished position awarded to the coach of the highest-placing gymnast. This role came with a few responsibilities along with the title. As the head coach, I was the only coach allowed on the competition floor for the entire meet, which meant I would be responsible for helping with any of the girls' needs: keeping track of their time during touch warm-ups; making sure that start values were correct; submitting inquiries if start values were not given correct credit; and being available to the media after the competitions. Since each athlete had her own personal coach, I became the conduit on the floor.

Back at the Ranch, Martha was definitely in charge. When I look back on how I was able to stand up to Martha, I think a big part of it was that I had never known her when I was an athlete, meaning I didn't carry any of that trauma with me in our interactions together as a subservient competitor needing her approval to be chosen for an assignment. This is not a commentary on any other coach, just a personal reflection on how little historical baggage I brought with me to the Ranch and how that impacted my ability to coach in that environment.

In fact, I had never met either Martha or Bela before I started coaching Simone. And every time we went to the Ranch, I was the buffer between Martha and Simone. By the time we were prepping for Rio, Martha's relationship with Simone had changed—for the better. Martha was still tough, but she understood that she couldn't push Simone the way she might have had I not been there.

Simone didn't always need a buffer, though. Aly Raisman shared a story with me that took place prior to the Olympics. She was in an elevator with Simone and Martha right before a meet. Martha always made sure everything that happened in and around a competition was practiced and prepared for. Simone was well versed in the rituals and thought it would be funny to look at Martha and tell her she had forgotten her grips! I can only imagine the look on Martha's face before Simone burst into giggles.

When on the competition floor, I appreciated that Martha had learned that Simone was at her best when she was relaxed and playful before she saluted the judges. You could often hear Simone talking, laughing, or cheering on her competitors before it was her turn to present. Adding pressure to Simone was not the way to get her to excel.

At the Ranch, the mood was intense but the practices were short. Once a day we would do a full rotation of beam and bars and split a rotation of floor and vault so the pounding on the joints and body was limited. The second practice would be a full practice, running four full rotations instead of three. Every training session we practiced in our official lineup order. This was one of Martha's tricks. She wanted to replicate as much of the process as possible to build comfort in the repetition and routine. As the official team coaches for the U.S. gymnasts, Mihai Brestyan (Aly's coach) and I would be responsible for making sure that all of the equipment and matting was set to each gymnast's liking during each practice. We had to pull boards and be ready to step in to spot every athlete, not just our own. Their personal coaches were not allowed to help us with the settings because they wouldn't be on the competition floor when we were in Rio. Adding further pressure on us, all of this happened while a stopwatch was running in the background. Tending to five athletes was much more strenuous on my body than taking care of just one, so nightly I would have to ice down the swelling in my elbows and heat my back.

The one break we received just before we left for Rio was for a trip to the George R. Brown Convention Center in Houston to get processed and outfitted for the Games. All the U.S. Olympic athletes from around the country made their way to Houston to do this, but for us it was a relatively local trip. That was a fun excursion and took the better part of a day—and the swag was awesome. The girls collected their official Polo opening and closing ceremony attire; more Nike clothes and shoes than anyone could want (although the girls hardly wore them because Under Armor was the official USAG sponsor); beautiful engraved Omega watches (which they probably never wore because they were really big); and Oakley sunglasses (two pairs) . . . and all of their social media accounts got verified because they were now Olympians. The coaches made out pretty well too. We were outfitted with the closing ceremony clothes, some Nike stuff, a pair of sunglasses, and a Swatch watch. Walking out of the convention center with all of the swag was easily the coolest part of the day. Of course, Martha made sure we still got in a morning training session before we left on this pilgrimage.

Then it was back to the Ranch. Before we left for Brazil, the coaches had an Olympic send-off at the Karolyi house, which felt like an initiation into the Olympians' club. Bela cooked us dinner, we socialized, and then we all trooped down to the Karolyis' infamous cellar, which housed Bela's private stock of homemade hooch, *pálenka*. Before Rio, Bela cracked open the really old stuff, a bottle from 1985! This was one of those legendary things you heard about, and to me it felt like a big deal, like I had finally been accepted into the secret society of gymnastics legends.

After our celebration with Bela and Martha, the coaches hung out in our "motel." This was expected to be the last time the Karolyis would host such a send-off. In July of 2016, USAG had agreed to purchase the Ranch for $3 million. It was now time to relax and enjoy each other's company. Thankfully, our first practice wasn't until 4:00 P.M. the next day. After one more day of practice in Texas, we packed our bags and, in a very unceremonious, business-like manner, left for Rio.

CHAPTER 15

Let the Games Begin

We arrived in Brazil on July 27. Simone was riding into the country on an all-around undefeated streak dating back to 2013 and our confidence was high, but this was *the Olympics*. The mystique was still there. We had to endure quite a long bus ride through the streets of Rio. During our drive to the village, we could see the favelas, which was heartbreaking. Here we are, headed to an event that cost billions of dollars to pull off, and we are driving right past people who were literally living on top of each other. It was humbling. And while it made me sad, it also made me grateful for all the luxuries I had in my life.

Pulling up to the Olympic Village was very exciting. This was it, the beginning of the end of our journey. We had officially made it. Upon arrival there was a strong, lingering scent of bug spray in the air because it was the height of the Zika virus scare in South America. The village consisted of thirty-one high-rise–style apartment buildings. Participating nations with large delegations, like the United States and Australia, would have their own buildings, and the smaller delegations shared properties with other countries. Between the structures was a playground area for children, since the village was meant to be repurposed for residential living after the Games. Unabashedly, some of the coaches and staff blew off steam by running around on the playground. There was also a large tent that served as the dining hall for all of the nations. Finally, there was a pop-up McDonald's right next to our building.

Our team shared three apartments: one for the athletes, one for male coaches, and one for female coaches and staff. My apartment mates included Martha; Laurie's coach, Maggie Haney; and Rhonda Faehn, the vice president of the women's program for USA Gymnastics. Maggie and I shared a room that I'm guessing was about ten by twelve feet in size and included two beds and a dresser. Martha was in a room by herself (probably three times the size of mine) and Rhonda had a teeny, tiny room that was probably five by ten. An identical apartment across the hallway housed the athletes and the athletic trainer, Alicia Lysiuk, who stayed in the Rhonda-sized room. There were two therapy tables set up in the living room of the apartment, so the team could easily get treatment and recover after their practices and competitions. In hindsight, Alicia should have stayed in the apartment with the female staff. These accommodations were approved a year after USAG first reported team doctor Larry Nassar to the FBI after they received many credible reports of abuse. I'm not suggesting in any way that Alicia did anything wrong or acted inappropriately, just that with everything we now know about abuse in all sports, athletes, coaches, and trainers—and anyone else attached to the team—should not share personal space in this manner for the protection of everyone.

The first thing Maggie and I did was move our dresser out into the living room to create some more space—a simple procedure, since it was just a flimsy fabric and PVC pipe contraption. The International Olympic Committee (IOC) also hadn't provided any mirrors in the apartments, which is a huge issue, as aesthetics matter in our artistic sport—not to mention the fact that blind makeup application sucks. Thankfully, the U.S. Olympic Committee (USOC) anticipated the issue and supplied us with mirrors.

Our living room included a tiny couch, a TV, and beanbag chairs. There was also an odd utility room that included a small sink and mini fridge. Overall, the apartments were serviceable. Well, mostly. We had to get our toilets unclogged daily because, being from the United States, we weren't used to using the trash bin for our toilet paper. This was apparently a common problem and made headlines in the *Washington Post*, on CNN, and via many other media outlets.

Now that we had settled into our home for the next two and a half weeks, it was back to business. We quickly found comfort in our training, which was no different than it had been for any of the world championships. We had our schedule, we showed up, we got through our routines, and we went back to our apartments before doing it again. Everything was regulated the same way. The only difference I felt was

Arriving at the Olympic Village, Rio de Janeiro, 2016 (from left to right: Aly Raisman, Laurie Hernandez, Gabby Douglas, Madison Kocian, Simone Biles). Courtesy of the author.

perhaps a little more tension between the countries, a mutual understanding that this competition was the pinnacle.

We were in the Olympic Village for over a week before the competition started, and there was a lot of downtime between training sessions. For the first couple of days we explored the village, and it soon became normal to run into people I had seen only on TV. The one person on my bucket list I was most excited to meet—and finally did—was Michael Phelps. I'm a huge fan of the Olympics, and nobody's done it better than Phelps. The American swimmer is the most decorated Olympian of all time, with twenty-eight medals spanning five Olympic games. His sustained success across two decades is truly incredible.

I'd like to have a glamorous story to tell you about meeting Phelps, but it was just the opposite. Early one day I was waiting for the elevator outside my apartment with a bag of dirty clothes, headed down to the laundry room in the ground floor of our building. The doors opened

Meeting the GOAT (Michael Phelps). Courtesy Simone Biles.

and there was a six-foot-four-inch figure standing in front of me. I quickly stepped into the tiny elevator, which must have been no bigger than four feet by four feet. Greeting my fellow passenger, who looked like he was still asleep, I realized that it was the one and only Michael Phelps. I was so thrilled to meet him but had to keep telling myself to "be cool." What I really wanted to do was give him a solid Joey Tribbiani "How you doin'?" Inside, I was buzzing! The U.S. swimmers had just arrived in Rio a few hours earlier, which explained why Michael looked dead tired. We exchanged pleasantries and he asked me how to get to the dining hall. Now, there are memories from my past that are a little foggy, but the fangirl in me remembers all of this very clearly. I had checked meeting my top Olympian off my "athlete bucket list."

Although I had now informally met Michael, I still really wanted a photo with him for my archives. Since we lived in the same building, I bumped into him two more times, but on each occasion he was on his way to be drug tested or to practice, so I didn't want to disturb him by asking for a picture. Knowing Simone had a connection with the U.S. swim team—she shared her agent with swimmer Nathan Adrian—I asked if she would help me get a photo with Michael. When I told her I had seen him three times and didn't ask for a selfie with him, she was less than gentle with me, stating, "You're on your own!" I was embarrassed and thought it was funny at the same time. There I was, forty-three years old, asking a nineteen-year-old to help me with my social game! In the end, I did get my picture with Michael—and superstar swimmer Katie Ledecky—during the *Sport Illustrated* cover shoot a few days later.

Occasionally, we had only one training session a day, allowing some coaches time to sunbathe by the pool. While we were hanging out, Christian braved the ridiculously long McDonald's line for us; then we'd shop in the village store to grab snacks for our apartments, and a few times, since the village is dry, we ventured out to a local hotel that had a bar to wind down after a long day. The girls stayed in their apartments except for meals and training . . . most of the time. There is photo evidence of them venturing out to meet other athletes, but of course that was kept from Martha (though I'm pretty sure Martha knew these excursions were taking place).

On Thursday, August 4, we had our podium training session. This was our last workout before competition and the only time we were allowed to train on the podium equipment we'd use during the games. Similar to the World Championships, many countries worked only particular skills or did light run-through routines. Not Team USA. Like everything else in preparation, Martha wanted us to become comfortable with the routine. This was another ingredient that made the United States so great in competition. Even though scores were not awarded, we held our podium training session as if we were competing. It was a full-dress rehearsal, which meant the girls treated it like the actual competition, styling their hair

Dreams realized. Olympic Village, Rio de Janeiro, 2016 (from left to right: Gabby Douglas, Aly Raisman, Simone Biles, Laurie Hernandez, Madison Kocian). Courtesy of the author.

and makeup and wearing competition leotards adorned with Swarovski crystals. They'd perform their thirty-second, one-touch warm-up before saluting Martha who would serve as the judge for the run-through, then execute full routines. *The girls were on!* In fact, they were on all the time and could have competed the day we landed in Rio. I remember Simone sticking her Amanar vault and wanting the competition to begin right then. She wasn't quite so outspoken at nineteen years old, but I got the impression she wanted to scream, *"Let's go!"* I felt there was a sense of relief in the air, too: after years and years of training and competing, it had all finally culminated in this moment and the window for something bad to derail the dream was closing—for the athletes and the coaches.

On the same day we ran through podium training, the *Indianapolis Star* ran its first story exposing USAG's failure to report and act on sexual abuse complaints. The article named four coaches who allegedly abused gymnasts, but Larry Nassar's name was not among them; that came the following month, weeks after the closing ceremonies. When this first abuse story broke, Steve Penny addressed the coaches and gymnasts, but not much was said about it. It was more of an acknowledgment that the story was circulating. I read the article with concern but didn't recognize the material as anything having to do with what we were trying to accomplish. That original story, while sad and extremely disturbing in its content, felt like a distraction that didn't require our attention at that moment, and we wanted to keep the team focused on what they were in Rio to do.

On Friday, the day of the opening ceremony for the Games, we stayed in our apartments, looking on with envy as the athletes from every nation walked down the winding pathways of the Olympic Village to get on the buses headed to Maracanã Stadium. Our competition started on Sunday, and we didn't want to put any added wear or

Ready to compete the day they arrived. Olympic Training Hall, 2016 (from left to right: Martha Karolyi, Aly Raisman, Gabby Douglas, Madison Kocian, Laurie Hernandez, Simone Biles). Courtesy of the author.

exhaustion on the body, so the gymnasts and their coaches all skipped the march in. (So did the U.S. women's soccer team, among others.) Instead, we watched the parade on television like everyone else back home. Watching it unfold from our apartments in Rio, I remember thinking how similar the pageantry was to my experience of International Days in high school—except it was obviously on a much grander scale. Having eagerly anticipated every Opening Ceremony since 1984, it bothered me that Martha and another coach spent the entire time complaining about the other countries and how "ridiculous" they looked in their traditional garb. It was awful. In truth, Martha did this everywhere we went, and the coaches were constantly apologizing for her rude behavior. Martha was demanding toward all those around her, even people from other delegations and the locals. It was even worse when we entered a training venue. Martha would march through the facility, almost pushing people out of the way, and the coaches would all follow like little soldiers and apologize: *We're sorry. We're so sorry. I'm so sorry. Excuse me.* We did a lot of apologizing to all the other countries. I think some of it—especially in the gyms—was Martha waging a bit of psychological warfare by exuding an attitude of *We're the United States and we came here to kick your ass. You can get out of our way.* Martha was playing a game, and we were her pawns.

Martha had taken something that had always been so magical for me, the Parade of Nations, and ruined it. In Rio, Martha liked to complain about everything, every day, all the time. I couldn't take it anymore, so during the opening ceremonies I got up and went to my room.

Eager to shake off my frustration from the night before, I woke the next morning excited to finally put on the show that the fans had so eagerly been waiting for. We had one more training, and then it was go time.

Sunday arrived, and once the competition started, it felt like other big competitions except for one big difference: the five interconnecting rings that were displayed throughout the arena and on every piece of equipment. One of the welcome things I wasn't expecting was fewer television crews scurrying about on the competition floor. At the world championships, it felt like there was way more media than what I saw in Rio, which made sense because the Olympic video coverage was captured and distributed mostly from a single source: by Olympic Broadcasting Services. NBC, of course, as a premier rights holder did have its own camera crews.

The United States would compete in subdivision four of five. During qualifications, each country was allowed four athletes to compete in each event, with the top three scores counting toward their standing. When we arrived in the arena that Sunday, we could feel the electricity in the air. Wearing navy and red leotards with rhinestone stars and stripes (my favorite), the team went out and hit routine after routine. This was the first day of competition and they were fresh and on fire! The United States started the Olympic games on floor, and the lead-off spot went to the 2012 Olympic all-around champion, Gabby Douglas. She performed as if she was coming to reclaim her crown, tallying a 14.366. Next up was the bubbly new senior, Laurie Hernandez. Despite having never been to a major senior international competition, Laurie performed like a seasoned veteran, expressing herself like a human emoji. As the crowd clapped along, she set the stage for the final two Americans on floor. In the third spot was Simone. And to no one's surprise, she rocked her routine, just as she had done so many times in preparation for this moment, scoring a 15.733. Finally, Aly Raisman was set to take the stage. After striking her opening pose, Aly let out a smooth exhale and started dancing into the corner. Aly was the reigning Olympic floor champion, and she did not disappoint the fans, posting a score of 15.275. The expressions on our athletes were intense that day because they were all business.

Qualifications were incredibly important since, just like at the world championships, the gymnasts were not only qualifying to the team finals but trying to qualify for the individual finals where the medals are awarded. The stakes were high. In gymnastics, the athletes always move through the apparatus in the same order: vault > bars > beam > floor. This is called Olympic order. Since we started on floor, that meant we were moving on to vault next. In 2016, Simone was the only U.S. athlete on the Olympic team performing the requisite two vaults to qualify for a spot in the vault finals.

Young upstart Laurie led the team off on vault with a gorgeous Yurchenko double full, followed by the same vault from Gabby, who had only a small pike down and the tiniest of hops backward. As great as these two vaults were for our team score, our biggest vaulters were yet to come. Aly landed her Amanar with a foot slide so small, if you blinked you would have missed it. At last, Simone was up. Since she was trying to qualify to event finals, she had to perform vaults from two different vault families, which were determined by their entry and exit techniques (e.g., an entry facing forward, then one facing backward). Simone had come to Rio with an upgraded vault. She had added an additional full twist to one of her existing vaults, a Lopez, making it the Cheng. We had been working on upgrading to the Cheng leading up to Rio, but it was difficult while training at the tin can because we didn't have a loose foam pit for Simone to land in. So when we traveled to the national team camp, we had the honor of working with Japanese vault guru Mas Watanabe. Mas wanted Simone to change the entry on her vault to introduce a shortcut so her arms traveled in front of her face and onto the table from the side for the half turn. Simone was so talented and quick twitch—and the technique Luis and I had taught her was so pure—she didn't need the shortcut. Simone's entry was a perfect half turn onto the table where she kept her arms over her head the entire entry. All Simone really needed was a safe place to land so she could get in the repetitions. At home without a pit, we had had to calculate every attempt to preserve her body. Her other vault, the Amanar, she had also learned without a pit. Simone had never competed these two vaults—two of the most difficult vaults in the Code of Points—in the same competition. That night would prove to be the first big test for her. She rose to the challenge, taking only a negligible hop forward on her Amanar and following that with a near perfect Cheng, scoring her a 16.000, the highest score of the entire competition for any female gymnast.

With that under her belt, Simone and the rest of the team moved on to bars, where the team had strong medal contenders in Gabby and Madison—but first the focus was on the team. Aly started off the group with her athletic routine, showing her consistency to hit without incident. Simone was next, beginning her routine with a look of calm in her eyes, but suddenly she got ahead of herself and rushed through her routine. I don't know that I had ever seen her swing so fast through the routine, but having so many repetitions under her belt kept her from making any major errors. The last two routines were from our big hitters. With intricate pirouetting and sky-high release skills, Gabby reminded everyone why she was nicknamed the "flying squirrel" at the London Olympics. She capped off her performance with a stuck double layout dismount. Finally, we got to see Madison in action; she had been put on the team as a bar specialist. Displaying her exquisite technique and form, Madison floated gracefully through her routine, securing her spot as the number one qualifier in the uneven bar finals, which would take place later in the week.

At last, the team moved to their final apparatus: beam. This can be a make-or-break event and the most stressful to end on. The team needed Gabby to set the tone for the event, and that she did, highlighted by her rock-solid standing full twisting backflip. Throughout the routine, she incurred only minor balance errors. The normally unshakable Aly had a large balance check halfway through her routine but demonstrated true grit by continuing as if nothing happened, nailing her Patterson dismount (an Arabian double front, named after U.S. legend and Olympic all-around champion Carly Patterson). Knowing the error would depress the team score, the pressure was on Laurie. The rookie showed no fear during the minute and thirty seconds she was on the beam, earning herself a spot to the balance beam final. Last but not least was Simone. She had a calmness about her as she moved undeterred through her skills. Thanks to the excellent efforts of her teammates, the fate of the team score did not rest in her hands. She took her time, and when her feet contacted the floor after her dismount, the team—and everyone

Arriving in Rio de Janeiro, Brazil, 2016. Courtesy of the author.

in the venue—knew that the United States was the team to beat in the medal rounds.

During the Olympic qualification round, I submitted three inquiries. This is not that uncommon, but it can get costly. Every time you submit an inquiry—which basically means you believe a judge has underscored the difficulty of a routine—it costs money. Yes, actual money. At the Olympics, an initial inquiry set the federation back by $500 and each subsequent challenge increased the fee by an additional $500 ($500, $1,000, and so on). Prior to 2016, the money had to be paid in cash and had to be delivered in an envelope. (The envelope was a new addition to this ritual after Japan challenged a routine during the 2012 Olympics and started waving a handful of cash in the air on live TV. It wasn't a good look.) Obviously, a coach handing money in a discreet envelope to an official doesn't look much better, so today when an inquiry is submitted, the federation is billed for the fee instead of having to post it up front.

With an inquiry, only the difficulty score can be challenged, which is most often underscored because of a missed connection by a judge. If an inquiry is "accepted," the federation doesn't get charged. It's actually pretty stressful. I had only two minutes to submit an inquiry after the routine finished while I also prepared the next girl for her routine.

In Rio, I submitted an inquiry for Aly on floor, one for Gabby on floor, and a third one for Simone on beam. None of them were accepted.

When the event scores were added together Simone had qualified for the individual all-around finals in first place by *more than 2 points!* It was a reminder of how far Simone's gymnastics had come since the first time she stepped inside Bannon's. She had explosive power and could flip on her first day in the gym, but it had been her drive to put in the work to perfect her technique that enabled her to do all of the crazy hard skills she's known for today. Commentators, gym fans, and even other competitors tend to focus on Simone's insane power and skill difficulty, but the true gym nerds know it's her execution that really separates her from the pack. In the FIG Code of Points, even the tiniest of errors cost a gymnast one-tenth of a point, where a large miscalculation can net a half a point in deduction. Additionally, if an athlete comes off the equipment or sits down on an element, it's an entire point taken from their execution score for each fall.

During the first night of competition, Simone earned the highest execution score of any athlete in the Olympic Games, male or female, and she did it twice, scoring a 9.7 on each of her vaults. On the balance beam, Simone posted the second-highest execution score (or "E score"), and on the floor she posted the highest mark to go along with the most difficult. Simone doesn't just chuck skills; she exemplifies them.

During the team final competition two days later, Simone again put up the highest E score of any athlete with her vault, and she had the highest E score on floor. Two days later, Simone continued to show her precision, scoring the highest E score on vault, balance beam, and floor while achieving the second-highest E score on the uneven bars. To wrap things up during the event finals, Simone again posted the top E scores on vault and floor.

It's unquestionable that Simone is a superior athlete, but in order for her name to be forever etched on multiple pages in the Code of Points, she needed superior technique. It's not easy to teach someone with exceptional athleticism to modify what comes naturally to them. When she was younger, Simone struggled on simple execution; we even had to pay special attention to her splits in the beginning. To now hit every position and every angle just right, in and out of skills, required a ton of repetition and coaching, and laser focus on the details. Only with that exceptional technique was Simone able to *safely* attempt sport-redefining skills. The athletic gifts that Simone possessed couldn't be taught, and she was not the first athlete in the sport to showcase them. A good coach enhances talent by teaching athletes the proper technical aspect of the sport, like how to enter a proper hollow position, point her toes, and hit her splits. And then, of course, the athlete needs to put in the sweat to make it routine.

***

After that first day of qualifying, there was really no doubt that Team USA was going to win gold. To be honest, we felt like we knew that before we even got on the plane. Statistically, the team the United States fielded at the Rio Olympics was virtually guaranteed a victory when considering the difficulty of their routines and consistency of their execution. From my observations on training, I felt Russia, as a team, lacked discipline, having witnessed them throwing tantrums in training halls in the recent past: slapping equipment, throwing grips, and arguing with coaches. China was another competitor to keep an eye on, but the numbers didn't add up. Team USA's routines carried such high-difficulty scores that it was hard for others to challenge them. Our cue for the competition was to just relax and do "normal," meaning the team just had to do what they had normally been doing every day in practice. This melded perfectly with a philosophy that I have held tight to with my athletes: Expect nothing more but accept nothing less than how you train.

But team finals differ from qualifications in that, instead of being able to drop the lowest score in each event, one less athlete competes on each apparatus and every score counts. One major error could knock a team out of medal contention—even Team USA.

Two days later we entered the arena for the team finals sporting the Stars and Stripes–bejeweled red, white, and blue leotard. NBC commentator and former Olympic gold medalist Tim Daggett said, "What everybody else in this building is hoping for is that USA has problems, because without problems, it's really not going to be that big of a contest." It was ours to lose, and these young women had no intention of doing so. I wish I could say that there was something spectacular about the ladies' performances, but they were spectacularly uneventful. We did "normal." Their assurance and their belief in each other led them smoothly from one routine to another.

Simone was the final competitor on the floor. From the background, all Russia and China could do was watch their gold medal hopes slip away. One commentator said that Simone had "redefined the combination of power and elegance." When she came off the floor, the team huddled with cameras surrounding them, confident they had done enough to take home the team gold. As the judges tallied Simone's score, the crowd started chanting, "USA, USA, USA." The experience was exhilarating. As they waited for the official results to post on the scoreboard, the team shared sentiments of love and respect for each other. Once the team gold was officially theirs, they jumped up on the podium and waved enthusiastically to the crowd. This was the moment that every little gymnast dreams of. They separated themselves from Russia by more than 8 points to win gold—a historic margin of victory that has yet to be topped.

For the past few Olympic Games, each U.S. team had given themselves a name. The 2012 team was nicknamed the Fierce Five. The 2016 Games was supposed to be the last time that there would be five members on the team (the number dropped to four for Tokyo 2020 but returned to five for Paris 2024), so they lined up in front of the cameras and in unison shouted, "We are the Final Five!"—also paying homage to the fact that it was Martha's last Olympics before she retired.

***

Before, during, and after competition days, Simone was getting tested for performance-enhancing drugs. I imagine the testing is similar for all dominant, high-profile athletes, and I know Phelps, for example, was tested in Rio the day after he arrived, even before he had time to get his first training session in. This was something Simone and I had gotten used to but were definitely not comfortable with. After Simone won her first world championship, she got tested six times in three weeks! What was worse was that at that time Simone was still a minor and an adult needed to be present, which meant I had to be in the bathroom with her for the testing with the United States Anti-Doping Agency (USADA) official. How uncomfortable for her—not that there was anything for her to be embarrassed about. If Simone had just gone to the bathroom before the USADA representatives had arrived, they'd want her to drink a lot of water so she could provide a sample—and Simone wasn't a huge water drinker during practice because it made her feel bloated. The testers would sit, sometimes for hours, in the gym, waiting for Simone to be ready.

When the officials were present to test Simone, they needed to remain within eyeshot of her. On one occasion during practice, one of Simone's teammates got hurt. Simone ran off the floor to get ice—because that's what you do when your teammate gets hurt—and the testers lost sight of her for a second. Simone was reprimanded and almost received an invalid test because she got ice for her injured teammate. If you received two invalid tests, you got suspended. I was outraged.

After that, they started showing up at Simone's house at 5:00 A.M. because they knew she was getting up at 6:00. That meant Simone was waking up an hour earlier than usual to be tested before she left for practice. Honestly, I hated it.

I believe in the anti-doping system and appreciate the job the USADA officials perform, but that doesn't mean it wasn't terribly disruptive. They would show up at her house, they would show up in the gym, and they once showed up two days in a row. The first test hadn't even reached the lab in Switzerland, yet they wanted another sample. I understand that people think Simone is superhuman, but I assure you, she is not. She was tested All. The. Time. It was shocking when she wasn't on their testing list. I remember one time at camp the official walked in and I started to tell Simone to come off the floor because the USADA had arrived. I was surprised when the official stopped me to say they weren't there for Simone that day. I exclaimed, "Hallelujah!"

In Rio, Simone was tested after every single competition.

***

If there was any day of the competition when I felt nervous, it was two nights later, during the individual all-around finals. I have never hinged my emotions on winning a medal because if I stressed about that, I would have gone crazy, but I knew the all-around title meant a lot for Simone. My nerves were always frayed—not from the competition but because I wanted her to come off the floor safely. I didn't worry that she might fall, but because her routines were so difficult, I worried that one bad landing could leave her severely injured. (These are things you don't tell your athlete, by the way.) Her performances that night put my mind at ease. Simone started the afternoon on vault. In training she had been consistently sticking her landings, but on the day of competition her adrenaline kicked in and she took a large step on the landing. I could see the dissatisfaction in her expression. Gymnasts often refer to attacking a routine as being "angry." Then Simone did "angry" bars. She attacked every skill, flying higher on her releases than I had ever seen her perform, causing me to tense up as I anxiously watched for her hands to regrasp the bar. With a stuck dismount and a bright smile, she showed the judges that she was not taking her placement for granted. Although Simone had rocked her routine, Russian Aliya Mustafina, with her spectacular swing on bars, moved ahead of her in the all-around after two rotations. Simone performed her beam routine, gracefully transitioning from one skill to the next, which one of the television commentators described as "smooth as butter." After three events, Mustafina was still leading the all-around, but her margin was decreasing. Also seeking a spot on the award stand, Aly was making her push and would go before Simone on floor. Aly had tied for third place all-around with Mustafina at the 2012 Olympics in London. However, due to a tie-breaking rule, decided by adding each athlete's top three event scores, Aly was knocked off the podium. In Rio, Aly was out for revenge. She stepped into her starting pose for her floor routine and waited for the music to start. With confidence and poise, she soared though her dance and tumbling. When her feet landed on her final pass, her eyes filled with tears, as if she knew this time she would be going home with an individual all-around medal. The whole team was so thrilled for Aly, and as she walked off the floor, Simone and I rushed over to congratulate her on a spectacular performance. We were so caught up in the moment, we almost forgot that Simone was up next to compete.

Aly's floor score moved her into first place, with only Simone from the top group left to compete.

The arena's attention shifted to Simone. As she walked up onto the podium, I moved to my usual spot near the corner of her opening tumbling pass. From there I could communicate with Simone, giving her a last-minute confidence boost. At that point, no matter how nervous I was, I had to make sure that she knew I had full confidence in her ability to achieve her goal.

From the first beat of her music, Simone was dynamic. Through the intensity of her movements, you could tell she wasn't going to let anyone else have that gold medal. Every element was executed far beyond requirement, leaving the judges very little to deduct. Her third tumbling pass, the double double, landed like a javelin, without the slightest movement of her feet. From that moment on, she looked full of joy, like a kindergartner on the playground. Then Simone struck her final pose, her body in a reverse plank, her head dropped back, her face beaming with the biggest smile I'd ever seen. She didn't move. She was soaking in the moment, soaking in the cheers, soaking in the accomplishment.

Upon rising, Simone saluted the judges and jogged off the floor to awaiting hugs from Aly and me. I wanted to hold her up in the air, but the time to shine wasn't mine, it was Simone's, and I wanted all eyes directly on her. We felt that Simone had done enough to pull ahead to the gold medal position, but nothing is guaranteed until the score flashes, so we waited. Aly was holding Simone in the embrace of a big sister, and as the score came up on the video monitors—15.933—Simone could no longer control her emotions and tears flooded into her eyes and mine.

Our moment. Gold medal win. Rio Olympic Games, 2016.
Courtesy of the author.

She had done it! Simone was the 2016 Olympic all-around champion—and she had won by more than 2 points!

***

Three days later the individual apparatus finals started with vault and uneven bars, the only final Simone didn't qualify for. Madison Kocian, the reigning bars world champion, met the occassion and secured a silver medal. Simone was an amazing vaulter, but she had never won gold in the event at a world championships. Her first vault was the Amanar. She sprinted down the vault runway, turning into a back handspring before launching off the table backward, soaring into the air while completing her twists, and landing on her feet with a little side hop. On her second vault, she hit her Cheng and was straight as a board as she appeared to fly high enough to touch the arena lights before heading back down, planting her feet on the mat with a teeny hop. Both of Simone's vault scores were higher than any other competitor's. Simone had done it! She won gold and became the first American woman to ever win Olympic gold on the vault. Not bad for a girl who had scored a zero on vault at her second state meet. Out of all of her accomplishments in Rio, seeing Simone win gold on vault was one of the most special to me. "Always a bridesmaid, never a bride" on vault at three world championships, she had worked so hard to achieve Olympic gold, and all of her efforts had been rewarded. In an ironic twist, when other competitors formulate a plan to try to outscore Simone they typically consider performing cleaner gymnastics because they can't compete with her difficulty. On vault Simone was almost always more polished but needed to increase her D score to win the gold. This seems almost laughable now considering Simone has since been competing the Yurchenko double pike, a vault no other woman on the planet competes and only a few men are willing to attempt. Her generational vaulting prowess is the perfect melding of power and precision. Simone also became the first American gymnast to win three gold medals in a single Olympics—and she still had an opportunity to win two more.

The following night was beam finals. All week we had been in the same training sessions as the Dutch team. They were known for their turns, artistry, and balance beam training. I got to witness this daily up close. They were rock solid on beam, especially Sanne Wevers. In training, standing on one foot on a "wobble board," a round piece of wood with a ball on the underside, used to exaggerate the control needed to hold the board perfectly still, Sanne would close her eyes and go through the motions of her beam routine using only her arms; the board never moved. Yes, Simone had a very high difficulty on beam, but deduction came from balance, and Sanne had that in spades. I had told Martha, "Keep an eye on Sanne," because I felt that she was the one to beat for Olympic gold. I remember Martha scoffed at the notion.

Simone was the third athlete up to compete. She approached the apparatus looking relaxed and focused, then moved swiftly and easily transitioned from skill to skill—but, as the commentators said, "nobody is a sure thing." As Simone went into the punch for her front tuck, she was a little off and under-rotated, causing her to grab the beam to keep from toppling off the equipment. In that moment I was transported back to Glasgow, reliving Simone's save at the world championships in 2015. This error was basically equivalent to falling off, and she knew she had to recover quickly. Simone didn't hesitate through the rest of her routine. When she reached the end, she launched off the beam for her full twisting double back dismount, but I could see the disappointment in her eyes. Coming in as the reigning back-to-back world beam champion, Simone knew she could win the gold in Rio. Now she was done, and all we could do was wait and see how her competition fared, with five competitors to go.

Sanne was the next gymnast up. It had been rumored that she had a 7.0 difficulty beam routine planned (0.5 higher than Simone's difficulty), but when she saw Simone grab the beam, knowing how large the deduction would be, she opted to do a simpler, less risky routine. This time it was Sanne who was looking to even the score after placing second to Simone at the 2015 World Championships. Sanne's skill set was very different from Simone's. Whereas Simone relied on big acrobatic elements to achieve her high difficulty, Sanne demonstrated prowess in her dance element, seamlessly connecting multiple skills in a row. Sanne showed true Dutch elegance throughout her routine, besting Simone's score by 0.7.

Only halfway through the final, and already Simone had been knocked down to a silver position. At this point I was growing nervous. This would be the first time in years that I really had to worry about Simone not medaling in a final. But all I could do was wait and cheer on Laurie, who was coming up to compete. Laurie didn't perform like someone who had just turned sixteen two months earlier. She moved with maturity and tenacity, easing into the silver medal position. Simone cheered unabated for Laurie's accomplishment. Once all eight competitors logged their routines into the records for the day, the final standing was Sanne with gold, Laurie with silver, and Simone going home with the bronze medal.

After the medals had been handed out and the media had gotten their quotes from the athletes, and of course our daily visit with the World Anti-Doping Agency (WADA), we jumped on the bus to the Olympic Village. Before we went back to our apartment, we stopped in the dining hall. We were both so hungry because we had not eaten since breakfast. Simone and I were standing between the tables and the food station in the massive cafeteria when we saw Martha coming toward us, apparently ready to ruin the joy we were feeling about the bronze medal Simone had just won. I knew this interaction was inevitable and I had actually been preparing for it as soon as Simone touched the beam with her hand to catch her balance during the finals, an error that was significant enough to change the color of Simone's medal and apparently Martha's mood. In addition to the pressures of competition, it was really unfortunate that I had to prepare myself and Simone for a moment like this as well.

We knew the meeting was going to be unpleasant when Martha didn't show up at the mixed zone for media interviews. From my recollection and other people's as well, she left *before* the awards ceremony. This was so unfortunate, because Laurie had performed spectacularly well to win the silver, but it seemed that because Martha was so mad at Simone that she didn't stick around. It would have been appropriate if Martha had heaped praise on Laurie and her accomplishment, rather than focus on Simone. Unfortunately, Martha was entirely predictable. As she approached, I could tell she was ready to come down hard on Simone, and I had been rehearsing what I was going to say to prevent that from happening.

Simone had just won a bronze medal and, after a week of competition Simone had competed five times and already accomplished more in a single Olympics than any other female gymnast in United States history—*and* she had the opportunity the next day to expand on that triumph—but Martha wasn't happy with the bronze: she wanted another gold.

Simone knew what was coming too. We stood there, nearly motionless, defiant but also terrified as Martha approached. I could feel the eyes of everyone in the dining hall on us: they could tell there was tension in the air. Martha closed the gap and immediately launched into her critique, charging Simone with acting silly and giggling before she competed, accusing her of being unfocused. I held up my empty food tray to block the room from seeing the looks on our faces. It was getting more uncomfortable, and I glimpsed Simone tensing up.

I told Simone, "Honey, go eat." As she walked away, I reminded Martha that playfulness was how Simone got in the zone. She had to stay relaxed and out of her own head before she competed. I added that it didn't have anything to do with the error.

Martha just replied, "Well, we'll agree to disagree."

"Simone acted as she normally does before every meet, and she just overdid it on one skill on the beam" I said. Up until that point, she was having a pretty flawless routine. She made an error and recuperated from it. Let me reiterate: Simone had to grab the balance beam to prevent herself from falling and she *still* won a medal in the Olympic games for her performance. This is a mistake that sometimes happens in practice, but I'm really proud of Simone for fighting to stay on the beam when the pressure was on. It's a credit to how exceptional Simone is to commit that kind of error and still perform with enough grace and difficulty to earn a place on the medal stand.

I don't remember everything else that was said, but I had practiced a little speech in my head so many times leading up to that moment, I know I ended our conversation with, "If you are not going to congratulate her on her bronze medal, then you have nothing to say to her at all." An outraged look came across Martha's face when I continued my defense of Simone, telling her that if it were anyone else on the team, she would be congratulating them, but since it was Simone and she expected her to win gold, a bronze was a failure. I refused to let Simone or anyone else think that a bronze medal at the Olympics was a failure.

I knew it wasn't our job to make Martha happy. Simone was there to do the best that she could—for herself—and I already knew *she* wasn't satisfied with her bronze. Martha didn't seem to give any thought to helping Simone feel better. With one day of competition left, it was my job to make sure Simone was mentally prepared to close out strong.

Nevertheless, Martha was pissed. If you go back and look at the broadcast footage, you can see her disproportionate response. No doubt we all knew Simone was capable of a gold medal performance—she had matured into an amazing beam worker—but that's sports. Sometimes your foot slips and your opponents seize the opportunity to outscore you.

The next day would mark the final challenge of our Olympic adventure. We traveled to the competition venue to crown the queen of the floor exercise. Once again Simone was the favorite, but as the beam final reminded us, she still needed to hit. Aly was the reigning Olympic champion on floor and had qualified in second place for finals. And honestly, if Aly had beaten Simone on floor, she would have earned it. As it unfolded, Simone again did Simone things. She put up the highest difficulty score (6.900) and the highest execution score (9.066) to post an overall score of 15.966. Aly won silver with a 15.500, only 0.1 lower than her gold medal performance in London four years earlier.

When the competition was over, there was a sense of relief. These amazing women had just become the most decorated American Olympic gymnastics team in history. We were elated . . . and we were tired. All the travel, all the training, the compounding days of competition—it was a lot. Participating in the Olympics is different from dreaming about them. When you're there, it's about getting the job done under enormous pressure. The reality of hard work comes before all dreams.

The moments that really matter. Rio Olympic Games. Courtesy John Cheng.

Now that the nights of the competition were behind us, all the emotions that had been suppressed were finally allowed to spill out in tears of joy, jubilation, and relief. But there was another feeling starting to creep over me, and it was a surprising one: sadness. Simone and I had made it through. She was an Olympic champion and she was healthy, but what now? At that point she was talking very seriously about retiring. Meanwhile, there was a sense of uneasiness growing in the pit of my stomach because I still needed to tell Simone I was going to leave.

CHAPTER 16

The Final Days

We arrived back at our apartment, filled with pride and happy to be done competing. The whirlwind of the post-Olympic media blitz was about to sweep us up, but first I needed to talk with Simone. Her parents and I had spoken about my plans a few months earlier—I wanted them to be able to find my replacement for the gym—and we agreed that I would tell Simone about my departure when she was done competing in Rio. Knowing that Simone was heading out on tour and I was leaving Texas shortly after we landed back in the States, I didn't want to keep putting it off. The longer I kept my plans from her, the longer I felt like I was lying to her. I made my way across the hall to her apartment. I sat on her bed and told her that as soon as we got back to the United States, I was leaving Texas and moving to Florida.

There was silence, and then we both started crying.

It was the end of an unbelievable era. In a way it felt like my daughter had grown up but I was the one moving out of the house and on to the next phase of my life.

Simone sat there, processing the impending change, and then she asked, "What if I decide to come back? Who's going to coach me?"

I softly replied, "Sweetheart, if you decide to come back, anyone in the world would want to coach you." I then tried to reassure her: "I will always be here for you, and you're an important part of my life. It's just time for us to move forward with our lives."

The next couple of weeks felt like we had just finished a thrilling roller coaster ride and we were now coasting back to the platform hopped-up on endorphins while slowly letting the tension relax from our grips. Looking out toward the horizon, we could take pleasure in the gentle turns ahead of us before we finished our crazy ride and moved on to new adventures.

The night after floor finals, Simone was asked to put on her leotard one more time for the gymnastics gala. This was a noncompetitive event that combined a variety of gymnastic disciplines and offered fans and TV viewers a final glimpse at their favorite athletes. It was the first time a gala had been held since Beijing in 2008. I wasn't happy about it, and Simone wasn't excited about having to perform either. We felt like we were done. Simone had just competed for six out of the last ten days—more than any gymnast in Rio—and I thought it was completely unnecessary. Imagine Michael Jordan playing a seven-game series in the NBA finals, achieving a triple double every game and holding that trophy high overhead while being photographed and interviewed, and *then* he is required to perform in a slam dunk competition. We tried to get out of it, but the FIG, the governing body and organizer of the event, said we had to do it. In all honesty, we didn't fight too hard, maybe because we were too exhausted. At least Simone was able to choose her event, a watered-down balance beam routine, because it was the easiest on her body. The only redeeming thing about the gala was that Simone got to wear her white leotard, which she had not done on any of the competition days.

As the head coach, I got to attend all of the post-competition hoopla. That wasn't the original plan, though. I was supposed to head home to the States with the rest of the coaches right after the gala while the gymnasts stayed for the closing ceremonies before traveling to New York City for promotional activities, but Maggie and I convinced Rhonda that she didn't want to chaperone the team on her own. The closing ceremonies were only a few days away, and Simone had been selected by the other Team USA athletes to be the American flag bearer during the Parade of Athletes. I couldn't stomach the thought of missing that! Rhonda got permission for Maggie and me to stay.

While we waited for the closing ceremonies, we moved out of the Olympic Village and visited the private beach in front of the Hilton hotel we were staying at, which was a luxury. Lying in the sun and digging my toes into the sand was nice, but the girls were stalked by paparazzi everywhere they went in Rio, leaving very little space for privacy.

Throughout my time in Rio and the trip to New York, I was fortunate because I was able to experience events the other coaches did not. As the head coach, I was included in the visits to the *Today* show tapings that the team would attend each night after competition. Earlier in the Games—after we won team gold, for example—the girls and I were whisked off to the NBC remote studio while all of the other coaches went back to the apartments. There was no pomp and circumstance, no team gold victory celebration as a staff. If there were still medals to win, we were all business.

Once we finished our media obligations after receiving the team gold medal, I was a little sad that there was no pause to allow everyone involved to revel in the accomplishment. The girls had earned the chance to let loose and bask in the glow of victory. Instead, during the interviews, they were asked to recap the competition and discuss how they were feeling even though nobody had given them the space to really process their emotions. It seemed like even their celebrations were dictated and choreographed. Not that those engagements weren't fun. Famously, Simone's celebrity crush, Zac Efron, flew to Brazil to surprise the team—and specifically Simone—on the set of the *Today* show. It was *adorable*. Zac gave Simone a kiss on the cheek, and she collapsed on the floor with excitement. When Zac walked over to me, he exclaimed, "I recognize you from TV!" I blushed and said, "I recognize you too!" I'm not going to lie: it was a highlight for me, something I didn't realize I should have put on my bucket list. Check!

The girls were in demand and barely had a moment to themselves. One evening we hopped on a bus headed to the Team USA house in Ipanema, which would be full of sponsors' representatives. The girls were starving, having been pulled in a hundred different directions, and excited to have a few minutes to eat their dinner. Just as they settled in, Steve Penny started walking over to the table to interrupt the girls' meal to talk with them about their upcoming interactions with sponsors. I approached him and told him politely to back off. He didn't seem to care about these young ladies. He didn't seem to care that they were hungry and that they needed a mental break, even if it was only a quick meal in a crowded room. It felt to me like Penny was ready to exploit them any way he could, and I wasn't having it. That sure seemed to agitate him, but I didn't care. (The next day we bumped into each other and he told me he wasn't talking to me because he was "mad at me" before walking away. Maybe I should have made him mad earlier!) Once the team had a chance to enjoy their meal, it was time for the Order of Ikkos ceremony. This is when the athletes would speak about how their coaches had nurtured them on their journey to the Olympics and then present them with medals bearing two hands grasping the Olympic torch on it. This was a new tradition started by the U.S. Olympic & Paralympic Committee prior to the 2008 Beijing Olympics, and none of the coaches were aware of this ceremony beforehand. We were all moved by the sentiments our athletes shared about us. In hindsight, I wish I had journaled what the athletes had said about the coaches, but, alas, I was caught up in the moment.

As the weekend closed, so, too, did the Olympic Games in Rio. With Simone's selection as the flag bearer, she became the first U.S. female gymnast to receive that honor. Maggie, Rhonda, and I were allowed to walk in the closing ceremony with the athletes, and I was extremely excited to be able to take part in the ritual. Simone marched out with the other flag bearers, followed by all the other athletes and coaches, who were huddled under the stadium. We entered the arena together in a large wave as rain poured down, adding a final sprinkle of drama to the occasion. Once everyone was on the field, the "Heroes of the Games" portion of the event began, and the athletes started dancing around the perimeter of the field in a conga line. The only problem was Simone was causing a pileup. So many athletes from around the world wanted to take a selfie with her that she literally slowed the closing ceremonies. She had truly become a global star.

I wanted my picture with Simone too. Unlike Glasgow, where we had a moment together on the floor, I didn't feel we had that chance in Rio. We had taken pictures throughout the competition, but there was always more business to be done and it was difficult to fully embrace and appreciate the moment. There were also so many people vying for

Iconic. Rio Olympic Games closing ceremony. Courtesy of the author.

Simone's attention throughout the competition, and now on the day when the Olympic cauldron would be extinguished, I wanted it too. There was something about getting a picture with Simone at the closing ceremony with the American flag that I felt I needed. I was feeling an enormous sense of pride and I wanted to share that with her and bottle it up. It was tough working my way through the crowd, but I was easily able to spot the American flag, which was so massive that when the wind blew, it nearly toppled Simone over. I finally reached her and we had our moment: Simone and me, draped in our transparent rain ponchos, with the American flag. Thank you, Rio! We did the thing!

***

From Rio we flew on the NBC chartered jet back to New York City for more media. Before we departed, the people at NBC asked us if there was anything we wanted to do while we were in New York, and I was, like, "Yeah. Go see *Hamilton!*" So NBC gave us seats in the eighth row, center stage. We were in the Big Apple for one day and left the next morning—and we packed in *a lot*. We went to the *Today* show, where we met 1970s sitcom star Henry Winkler, violinist Lindsey Stirling, and mega recording artist Usher, and then we headed off to our next engagement.

From there, we visited the Hershey store and then went to the top of the Empire State Building. I'm not talking about the observation floor but the very, very top. I was told you had to be a special guest of the owner of the building to go up there. We were standing right below the antenna. It was a perfect day, with a bright blue sky, and all the gymnasts had family members there. I'm not scared of heights, but even I felt a little vertigo kicking in. Aly's brother was a bit freaked out because of the height, and it gave me a good laugh.

We capped off our engagements with a taping at *The Tonight Show Starring Jimmy Fallon.* An interesting thing about *The Tonight Show* is there is no photography allowed in the hallways backstage, only in the greenroom, so as to not bombard the celebrities who were appearing on the show. You could, however, stand in the greenroom and take pictures of people in the hallway. It was also curious to see how everyone responded when Jimmy strolled down the hall. You'd hear, "Jimmy's coming," and everyone would snap to attention; I think this was more of a respect thing than intimidation. Jimmy was super friendly with all of us. Once the cameras were rolling it was a fun show. The girls

Gold Medal Team on the *Today* show with Maria Menounos from E! News (from left to right: Maria Menounos, Aly Raisman, Simone Biles, Madison Kocian, Gabby Douglas, Laurie Hernandez). Courtesy of John Cheng.

stepped onto the stage and the crowd started chanting, *"USA! USA!"* Next, the team participated in a hilarious, gigantic, life-size version of Hungry Hungry Hippos. Even then, you could see the competitiveness of Simone and her teammates. After their appearance, we were out the door and off to Broadway.

We got stuck in traffic for over an hour and we eventually decided to abandon our bus and just walk to the theater. When we arrived, we had to watch the opening song from the lobby because the curtain had already gone up. A minor inconvenience that we quickly forgot because the show was fantastic! I had listened to *Hamilton* multiple times on the flight to Rio, every day in Rio, and on the flight to New York. So seeing it live, with many from the original cast, was very emotional, and the musical will always have a connection in my heart to the Olympics. After the show, we were all invited onstage to meet the phenomenal cast

Hanging out with Jimmy Fallon, *The Tonight Show* (from left to right: Aly Raisman, Simone Biles, Gabby Douglas, Laurie Hernandez, Jimmy Fallon, Madison Kocian). Courtesy John Cheng.

and take pictures. The actors seemed as excited to meet the Olympians as the athletes were to meet the stars of the show.

We were running on fumes, but I still wasn't done with the Big Apple. At two o'clock in the morning, I ventured out with Rhonda and Maggie to a tattoo parlor. Maggie and I both got Olympic ring tattoos on our wrists. Rhonda, an alternate on the 1988 Olympic team, already had the rings and decided to get a small, specially designed tattoo. This was my second tattoo. My first was taken from a photograph of a gymnast doing a split kick with her upper body arching all the way backward. I had gotten this inked on my ankle years earlier. The funny thing is the image was tattooed upside down, so when I look down from my perspective it makes sense. I was nineteen years old and still involved in my college shenanigans when I got the tattoo. Apparently, I still had a lot to learn about the perspectives of others.

The next day I was on a plane heading back to Houston with Simone and Nellie. (Ron and the rest of the family had traveled back home

Late-night Olympic tattoo on my wrist. Courtesy of the author.

directly from Rio.) When we landed, there was a big production setup at the airport. In attendance was the mayor, an alderman, the Houston Texans cheerleaders, the Texans' mascot, news cameras out the wazoo, and a big stage ready for us. I didn't know anything about this but I was excited to roll with it. Then the cameras were turned on and everybody was called up onstage: the politicians, the Biles family, everyone . . . except me. It was very awkward. I felt invisible.

I was hurt, but I was still thrilled that I was going to finally see my family after being away for six weeks. When I arrived home, my boys had made a big sign and hung it across our front porch. It read, "Congratulations Mom! Coach of Olympic Champion Simone Biles." It was so sweet, and I was so delighted to celebrate with them.

The welcoming committee (from left to right): Jamie, Benjamin, and Chris.
Courtesy of the author.

What I didn't know was that about a mile down the street, the neighborhood had scheduled a parade in honor of Simone, and I wasn't included. I would have loved to have been there and participated. I didn't need recognition from the community or even a spot in the parade, but I guess I was stunned that after such a long and amazing journey I wasn't getting the closure I was expecting, and that I quickly realized I wanted.

Our journey together had lasted more than a decade, and my personal journey in gymnastics had spanned over four decades to reach this pinnacle. And while I wasn't looking for global acclaim, I once again felt like that young athlete wanting to hear she had done a good job. Twice during the Olympic Games, Simone had tweeted out appreciation, which meant a lot to me. After Simone won the all-around Olympic title, she tweeted, "I didn't get here alone. Thank you to the world's best coach! I LOVE YOU." Love you back, Simone!

I should be clear: my sadness wasn't about missing out on any financial rewards or even publicity; it was about being seen. It was for the Bileses to acknowledge that Simone's Olympic appearance—let alone the medals—wasn't inevitable, that what we had accomplished together was not as easy as the dominating performances made it look, and how we had gotten there was special. Maybe my experience made this point obvious to me and less clear to them. Nevertheless, I don't have any animosity toward the Bileses—in fact, it's the opposite: I really miss my relationship with the family, and they will always hold a cherished place in my heart.

***

Excited about beginning a new chapter, we left Texas as soon as we could. I had a position waiting for me as executive director of Evo Athletics. Within three weeks of my arrival home, my family packed up our belongings and, after living there for only eleven months, moved from our newly built house in Texas to Sarasota, Florida. It happened so quickly that we hadn't secured a permanent place, so we stayed at the home of Evo's founders, Lydia and Kyle, and their two kids for a month before finding a place of our own. It took us time to find the right house for our family, but we landed on a 1952 midcentury modern, which included a bomb shelter that we repurposed as a master closet. The walls of the bomb shelter were four feet thick on all sides, so we had a safe refuge during hurricanes. Jamie had opted to attend the performing arts high school, while my two younger boys, Chris and Ben, were homeschooled at the gym by another parent while I was coaching.

Several weeks after the Olympics, I sent a message to Martha, thanking her. I wanted her to know I appreciated how she had helped me. Did I admire Martha and look up to her? No, but during the process she did teach me several things. She taught me how to create a proper periodization for an elite gymnast, how to be discriminatory when it came to skill selection, and, most importantly (and inadvertently), how to trust my gut instincts. I respected her knowledge and the impact she had on my coaching acumen, and I thought it was important to express my gratitude. It was also more closure I was seeking as I moved into the next phase of my career.

Halfway across the country, Simone was on the move, too, stuffing her suitcase for a thirty-six-city post-Olympic tour with a huge roster of gymnastics superstars, including her teammates and gymnasts from the men's program. This was the first time I could remember that Simone and I were not talking on a near-daily basis. We had truly started new lives.

Around this same time, on August 29, Rachael Denhollander, a former gymnast, filed a complaint with the Michigan State University police against USAG's former national team doctor, Larry Nassar. In the complaint, she alleged that Nassar sexually assaulted her in 2000 when she was fifteen years old. The following day Nassar was reassigned from all clinical duties at Michigan State University. Two weeks later the *Indianapolis Star*, which had reported the first story of abuse within USAG while we were in Rio, published a shocking story about two gymnasts who accused Nassar of abuse, Rachael and an unnamed Olympian. This was the first time he had been publicly implicated, and the revelation blew the lid off the abuse that had been taking place. On September 20, Michigan State fired Nassar. In the coming days, weeks, and years, we would all learn a lot more. A congressional inquiry along with a cascading series of stories and allegations against Nassar followed. Sadly, the responses from USAG continued to be an insult to the gymnasts. To this day we still don't know who within USAG knew what and when, but we do know that survivors had been sounding the alarm for decades. On more than one occasion Nassar was questioned by police. In 2004, Nassar made a presentation and shared a video to convince the police that his inappropriate touching was a legitimate medical practice. He abused girls with their parents in the same room during appointments. One gymnast shared with an adult the abuse she had suffered and was told she didn't understand what was happening to her and was convinced to apologize to Nassar. She did, and her parents continued to take her to appointments with Nassar. Another survivor told her parents about the abuse and her dad also made her apologize to Nassar. It broke the father-daughter relationship, and when this story exploded, the dad took his own life. USAG, in a statement released in September 2016, said they first learned of the allegations in the summer of 2015, relieved Nassar of his duties, and informed the FBI, but they neglected to inform the coaches of athletes who had received treatments from Nassar. I did notice that Nassar was no longer at camps and competitions starting in mid-2015, but I never thought to ask if he was a serial predator or if we should check with the athletes in our care. I was under the assumption that he had retired from the national team staff because he wanted to spend more time with his family. In November 2016 he ran for a position on the Holt School Board and lost, but despite the horrible allegations against him, he still received over 20 percent of the vote. Less than two weeks later he was charged with three counts of first-degree criminal sexual conduct with a person under thirteen.

After the *Indianapolis Star* report came out, I felt a splinter of anxiety wedged in my heart. I didn't know who the unnamed Olympian was, but I knew a lot of Olympians and had gotten close to many of them, and I feared I might know this survivor. It turns out it was so much worse than I could have imagined. It wasn't just one Olympian, and it wasn't members of just one Olympic team. As the years have passed, it has been documented that Nassar abused well over five hundred girls (and at least one boy), in multiple states, in multiple countries, while working in private practice, for Michigan State, and for USA Gymnastics.

I tried to reach out to Simone several times after the *Indianapolis Star* report was published, but between her post-Olympic tour schedule and my move, it was difficult to connect. When we did finally connect, Simone apologized for not responding sooner and said, "I've just been really sad." That made sense to me: Simone was the "It" girl. She was dealing with a lot of change—even more than I knew at the time. At that point Simone was also very serious about not competing anymore, which meant she was grieving over her gymnastics life. Then there was the severing of our active coach-athlete relationship. Beyond that, our friendship was now long-distance for the first time since we met over a decade earlier.

I still had that splinter in my heart, though. I continued to check in with Simone and never received any information I felt I should be alarmed by. Simone told me no and—for a moment at least—I felt some relief.

PART THREE
Moving Forward

CHAPTER 17

Evo

Evo was the fresh start I was looking for. I invested a small amount of money—giving me a tiny stake in the business—and in return I had full say over the gymnastics program and profit sharing from the gymnastics side of the business. Outside of WCC, it's the best facility I've been in—and that's saying something. It truly is amazing. In addition to gymnastics, Evo also offered programs for volleyball, cheerleading, and ninja warrior training. I wasn't surprised when Evo became the temporary national training center for the U.S. women's program in 2018 after USAG cut ties with the Ranch, where some of the Nassar abuse had taken place.

Simone had returned to training by this time, so I was able to see her when she came to Sarasota. She had matured so much, and it was wonderful to see. I craved spending more time with her, to talk with her about her life, but she was getting adjusted to new coaches and I didn't want to interfere with that process. So I usually kept my distance unless she came over to me to chat. Camps continued at Evo through the world championship selection camp in 2019.

I was happy. I oversaw everything relating to the gymnastics side of the business. I did all of the scheduling and I made sure that the billing was done right. I ran all of the assessments. I handled the coaches' fees and made sure they were doing what they were supposed to. I oversaw the whole program, in a similar manner to WCC, but now I had equity. As far as coaching, I taught gymnasts from level 6 through elite, with an emphasis on levels 9 through elite. There was also a recreational director under me whom I let handle the entry-level students. On the men's gymnastics side, Jason was in charge of the program.

About a month after I arrived, marriage problems between Lydia and Kyle began to boil over. They soon separated and it made things a little awkward in the gym, since Kyle was the CEO and Lydia was the COO. Shortly after their separation, Kyle stepped away from the gym, leaving me, Lydia, and Jason, who was also a part owner, to run things. In reality, Jason and I were the ones doing the day-to-day operations. Lydia built a remarkable facility, but she had never run a youth sports business before: she was a gym mom who thought it would be a great idea to open a gym and she had the resources to make that dream happen. In her vision, she wanted to make Evo a place where parents felt really comfortable—a fantastic concept in theory; unfortunately, in doing so I feel she gave parents too much freedom and too much say. The environment made the parents feel like they could run the program, and every time Jason or I made a decision that any parent didn't like, it became an issue. As far as I'm concerned you can't run a program like that. Half the time I was in the gym, I was dealing with parents, not coaching or managing the facility. This would eventually become untenable.

On the flip side of parents thinking they knew best were parents moving to Florida from around the country to be in my program. When I first left Texas, there were three families and a few coaches who moved to Florida as well. These coaches, parents, and gymnasts knew my program well, and they were excited to venture out with me to this new opportunity. I had a built-in community that wanted to help me create a very nurturing environment for athletes and coaches.

***

About a month after I had started at Evo, I was invited to take one more trip with the Olympic team: to the White House.

We were supposed to arrive at the White House at 7:00 A.M., but at 4:00 A.M. we received a call. There was a change in plans. A bad rainstorm had forced the festivities to move indoors from the East Lawn. Due to the lack of space inside the White House, the meet-and-greet was now going to be only for the Olympic team athletes, not any of the staff or delegation members. Laurie Hernandez had just turned sixteen, and I told the organizers it wasn't acceptable for there not to be an adult chaperone with her during the event. Steve Penny, in perhaps the only instance we agreed on something, backed me up and told the coordinators I needed to be there with the team. The White House staff obliged. We received a tour of the White House and then we were brought into the Map Room, famously named for its use by President Franklin D. Roosevelt as a situation room to track movements of the World War II effort on a wide range of maps.

Soon our first two official hosts arrived—Portuguese water dogs Bo and Sunny—followed by one of their owners, First Lady Michelle Obama. The original plan was for the girls to only meet with the first lady to talk about her healthy eating initiative, part of her Let's Move! campaign. When she entered the room, I was leaning against the wall while a camera crew zipped around. Soon I overheard Michelle asking the girls what they ate. I then heard Simone reply, "My coach doesn't monitor what I eat." Michelle followed up with "Is your coach here?" *Gulp.*

Following that, the first lady and I had a nice conversation and I explained to her my philosophy of not wading into waters too deeply with regard to the food the athletes consume when I heard a voice from behind me: "Hey . . . are we gonna get this show on the road?" Oh my god! The president, Barack Obama, just walked in. For the first time in my life, I began to get truly nervous about meeting someone. I remember thinking, *Say "Mr. President," say "Mr. President." Don't screw this up. He's the leader of the free world and you are just a gymnastics coach.*

Almost as soon as that realization struck me, the nerves I was feeling evaporated. Vice President Joe Biden entered the room as well. A lot of photos were taken and then I struck up a conversation with the president. It was funny, because he introduced himself to me as if I didn't know who he was. *Say "Mr. President," say "Mr. President."* We talked about the girls and how great they had competed in Rio, and then we talked about our mutual hometown of Chicago. It was such a natural, comfortable conversation. During our brief chat, I never felt like I was speaking with the most powerful man on the planet. Eventually it was

Visiting with President Barack Obama, First Lady Michelle Obama, and Vice
President Joe Biden, White House (from left to right: me, Vice President
Joe Biden, Aly Raisman, Laurie Hernandez, First Lady Michelle Obama,
President Barack Obama, Simone Biles, Madison Kocian).
Courtesy of the author.

group picture time, and as I stood waiting in the wings, the president
said, "We can't have a picture without the coach" as he waved me into
the photo. It was nice to be recognized.

***

The move to Florida was amazing. Every morning when I woke up it
felt like I was on a tropical holiday and I kept waiting for reality to drag
me back to Texas or Chicago, but the closest I got to that feeling of my
former life was when I stepped back into Evo to do the job I loved.

Everything at Evo was moving along as I had hoped. The biggest friction points were coming from the parents. Since my notoriety came from being Simone's coach, the expectations from some of the parents were a bit ridiculous. A handful of parents of compulsory gymnasts even sent messages to me stating, "We thought we were going to get Olympic coaching and we're not getting that."

I'm not sure what they thought Olympic coaching meant. I would reply as kindly as I could, pointing out that their child was only a level 4 and at that level they should just be having fun. Also, I was not coaching the lower levels; I was training the coaches for those teams. While I was guiding the coaches, there was only so much I could do. Each coach was their own person. I could give someone my entire business plan and my entire curriculum and they still wouldn't do it exactly the same way I did. And they shouldn't! You have to bring your own personality to something like coaching, which makes it so exciting and unique.

The thing I realized was that these Olympic dreams were never something we promoted, but they had definitely become the expectation for some. To be fair, I understand why. After all, Evo wasn't making it a secret about who I was and what I had accomplished as a coach. I think some parents believed that, because I had nurtured an Olympian, I could make every child in the gym into an Olympic athlete—and that was just not realistic. All I could promise was that I was willing to give each gymnast the same knowledge and attention I had given every other gymnast I had ever coached, including Simone. Unfortunately for some, that was never going to be enough.

I think many parents expected a more regimented style than what I offered. They saw Simone's consistency and excellence on TV and I can only assume they associated those performances with emotionless, stripped-down, military-style preparation and execution. That couldn't be further from the truth. Simone resonated with so many because she smiled—not an artificial, pasted-on smirk that showed her teeth when the situation warranted it, but genuine joy that sparkled and touched the human spirit.

I imagine the parents were seeking a disciplined battalion of Karolyi girls they had seen on the NBC fluff pieces. What those segments didn't show was the danger a fall-in-line, never-speak-up, never-speak-out culture created in an environment where nobody felt safe or comfortable enough to question anything that felt wrong. When I was standing up to Martha throughout Simone's career, I didn't realize I was just one of many dating back to the 1970s. While the public viewed feel-good montages that showed gymnasts lining up with straight backs in the gym, quickly followed by images of them roasting marshmallows at the Karolyi Ranch, a more unsettling truth was being ignored.

In May 2021 the *GymCastic* podcast began to share details of an ongoing investigation they had embarked on with the assistance of a Romanian journalist. *GymCastic* had gained access to the secret police files the government had collected on the Karolyis, which included images, transcripts, handwritten notes, and more.

Back in 1976, after Nadia Comaneci had recorded the first-ever perfect 10 in the Montreal Olympics, she returned home and refused to be coached by the Karolyis moving forward. The communist regime wanted to know why. In response, the Socialist Republic of Romania launched a multiyear investigation (code name Operation Olympia) into the Karolyis by the Romanian Securitate, the secret police. During that time the Securitate tapped phones, spoke with informants, pulled government documents, interviewed colleagues, and much more. Through these files, *GymCastic* discovered that for years gymnasts and parents had been reporting the Karolyis for abuse, particularly Bela. The files even include one allegation of attempted sexual assault by Bela of one of his gymnasts. The secret police files also documented complaints against Bela that included "beatings, shoutings and vulgar expressions etc." The files show that parents had also contacted the Romanian Gymnastics Federation and specifically mentioned that Bela Karolyi had insulted and beaten their daughters.

Some action was taken against the couple, but ultimately their success as coaches drowned out any concerns. It turns out that a reputation is a powerful tool for suppressing the voices of those sounding an alarm. Tragically, a reputation was also a powerful weapon used by Larry Nassar when survivors began speaking out against him. In fact, just three years before USAG removed him from the competition floor, Nassar was inducted into the USAG Region 5 Hall of Fame. (He has since been removed.)

In 1997, Larissa Boyce was a gymnast participating in the Spartan youth gymnastics program at Michigan State, where Nassar worked as an athletic trainer and assistant professor. She was sixteen years old and was abused by Nassar. She knew it was wrong and told the head coach, Kathie Klages. In response, according to Larissa, Klages shot down her plea for help and "raised a piece of paper and said 'I can file this, but there's going to be very serious consequences for you and Larry Nassar.'" Larissa was confused and felt defeated. She didn't want anyone to get in trouble. Larissa went to Nassar, *apologized*, and continued getting abused. During her trial for lying to investigators, Klages said she didn't remember this incident.

It wasn't until a month after the Rio Olympics, nearly twenty years from when Larissa first reported the abuse to her coach, that Michigan State finally fired Nassar. Larissa wasn't the first or last survivor to speak up during those decades, but imagine how many would have been saved if her coach had handled that situation differently. In November of 2016, Nassar was charged with the first of his crimes: three counts of sexual abuse. The following month he was indicted on child pornography charges.

Nassar was also the team physician at a local Michigan gymnastics club, Twistars. The owner of the gym was the 2012 U.S. women's Olympic team head coach, John Geddert—the same job I held four years later. He was the personal coach of the incredible world and Olympic champion Jordyn Wieber. In addition to providing safe harbor for Nassar, Geddert was eventually charged in February of 2021 with a barrage of crimes including fourteen counts of human trafficking for forced labor resulting in injury, six counts of human trafficking of a minor for forced labor, two counts of sexual assault against children, and more. In non-legalese the human trafficking and forced labor charges meant he was taking gymnasts to competitions and forcing them to compete even though they were injured while profiting from those performances by receiving award money. The day he was required to appear in court for arraignment, Geddert took his own life.

As the news about Nassar unfolded and we learned more about what had happened and the scope of the abuse, I would occasionally reach out to Simone to see if she had anything to share. Over many, many months I probably asked her five or six times. I knew it wasn't something Simone wanted to talk about, and she would get a bit agitated if I broached the subject, so I would tread lightly and then drop it when she brushed off my inquiries. Each time she would say no. It was always short.

By June of 2017, Nassar had more than one hundred complaints against him, and the following month he pled guilty to child pornography charges. In October of 2017, McKayla Maroney came forward as a survivor and the following month Aly and Gabby joined the growing list.

Each revelation made my heart ache. These weren't just stories I was reading in the newspaper. These were young women I had coached and traveled with. We had laughed and shed tears of joy together. Now my tears were of heartbreak and sorrow. The realization that these young women had been secretly suffering from Nassar's abuses during the time we were traveling and training together sent my mind reeling.

I knew there was no reason or benefit for these young women to lie. If anything, they were exposing themselves to scrutiny—and perhaps more courageously, they were being truthful with themselves, opening up a Pandora's box of emotions and pain.

Sadly, like so many other women, I intimately understood the fear of speaking up. On September 25, 2018, I finally shared some very personal news with the world about something that had happened during my time in college. The #MeToo movement was near its peak in terms of online participation, while another poignant hashtag had also started trending and resonated with me: #WhyIDidntReport.

"Because I was in college, drunk at a party and I thought everyone would say it was my own fault. I told him NO, that should have been enough." #WhyIDidntReport ~ 9/25/2018

Was I the first woman this man assaulted? Was I the last? Could I have prevented this from happening to another woman if I had reported him?

These were questions I was once again wrestling with, but I was now feeling more empowered and less alone. So many women stay silent because they feel that they won't be believed or, even worse, that they will be blamed for an assault, implying that they somehow brought it upon themselves. Over many years, Nassar's victims told parents, coaches, and the police about their abuse and they were repeatedly rebuffed. But "No" means "No" and assault is assault. There is no room for interpretation.

I didn't speak up about my experience earlier because I didn't want to detract from the stories that were coming to light involving Nassar—and it's sad to acknowledge, but when a devastating number of women come forward to confirm that they have been assaulted, over time we as a society can become numb to the facts and their consequences. I wanted everyone to understand that you never know who is a survivor. Sadly, it's often the case that a single cry in a sea of tears is what resonates, which is why I thought it was important for me to put the description of my assault on Twitter. I had already seen the courage shown by the hundreds of women who had shared their stories of abuse, and I knew it was important to stand with a sisterhood that none of us had ever volunteered to join.

I was drunk and I was assaulted. If you can relate to this story, I'm truly and deeply sorry. In no scenario was being attacked my fault, and I hope if you have a similar story, you feel the same. I never let this moment define me, but I never forgot it either. If anything, the experience made me more compassionate and empathetic toward others. It wasn't that I had been hiding this information, but it wasn't until this movement that I felt empowered and hopeful that it might help make a difference to say something. Up until I posted that message on Twitter, I hadn't even told my husband or my mother.

***

Back at Evo, I was more than a year removed from the national team training camps and the whirlwind of regular elite competition, but I was getting sucked back in emotionally. I regularly talked with my old coaching friends. I began dissecting everything from the past and considered what I might have missed and how I had missed it. I wouldn't say that I knew Nassar well or that we even spent a great deal of time together, but I felt he was someone to be trusted. Early on, when I first met Nassar, I thought he was a genius. I considered him a friendly acquaintance. He would often compliment me on how I treated Simone with respect, not dictating to her but instead giving her a voice in her training process. He would praise me on how I protected Simone at camp when the days were especially physically demanding and how smart I was to have a bigger picture in mind by considering Simone's well-being. I look back on these words now knowing that it was all part of his method to get people to trust him. I had been groomed by Larry Nassar too. This knowledge creates an ache in my stomach that makes me want to cry and vomit at the same time. Nassar was emboldened in an environment where questioning authority, methods, and decisions was discouraged. In general, I'm a very trusting person and habitually think people are good, but if I could go back and talk to a younger Aimee, I would tell her not to trust everyone.

In November of 2017, Larry Nassar pled guilty to ten counts of first-degree criminal sexual conduct and the following month he was sentenced to sixty years in prison on child pornography charges. On January 9, 2018, Maggie Nichols, Simone's regular roommate at all the camps and competitions, revealed that she was Athlete A from the original investigation by the FBI looking into Nassar. (*Athlete A* is also the name of a heartbreaking and thoughtful Netflix documentary that helped spark the #gymnastalliance movement exposing abuses in other countries around the world.)

With Maggie's name public, I reached out to Simone. With her response, I burst into tears.

Simone was like my daughter, and knowing now what she went through and my feeling that I failed her—not even realizing she needed to be protected from that man—is crushing.

Less than a week later Simone came forward with a public statement, sharing the fact that she had been abused at the Karolyi Ranch. In her statement she wrote, "I'm not afraid to tell my story anymore. I too am one of the many survivors that was sexually abused by Larry Nassar." She went on, "It is impossibly difficult to relive these experiences and it breaks my heart even more to think that as I work towards my dream of competing in Tokyo 2020, I will have to continually return to the same training facility where I was abused." Three days later USAG terminated their lease agreement to hold national training camps at the Karolyi Ranch, essentially shutting it down.

As this was going on, I was coaching at Evo. Parents and athletes alike knew what was happening—at this point the whole world knew what was going on—and I was really beating myself up, constantly asking myself if there was something I could have done to prevent this atrocity from happening—if there was some sign I had missed, some red flag, something I had dismissed while I was consumed with the task at hand. The day after Simone posted her statement on social media, victim impact statements started to be delivered to a Michigan courtroom as part of Nassar's plea agreement. Judge Rosemarie Aquilina allowed each survivor to step forward and let her voice be heard. Every moment I was able to be off the floor at Evo, I would go into my office, watch the trial and sob uncontrollably. One after another, the survivors bravely spoke up to educate the world about the horrors they had endured, the trust that had been broken, the institutions and people who had failed them, and the power they were ready to reclaim. At first it was only supposed to be a handful of statements, but after each account was read, a collective courage grew. The sentencing hearing lasted eight days; 156 women came forward in the courtroom to read their impact statements, including Jordyn and Aly.

I felt like I had failed. The focus should absolutely be on the athletes, but I don't think many consider the impact this revelation had on coaches. I was supposed to protect Simone. All the girls (I hope) know I would have done anything to protect each and every one of them.

CHAPTER 18

Seeking Justice

During the time the impact statements were being read, I cried every day at work. When I got home, I would continue to cry. I would tell my kids, "Something happened and Mom's really sad." It was too much to try and explain the sexual abuse revelations to my ten-year-old son. James was very supportive, as he has been my entire coaching career. He let me talk and he just listened. It was like therapy.

It wasn't enough, though. I needed Simone to know how deeply sorry and ashamed I felt. I told her I was sorry I hadn't protected her and that I had failed to make sure that she was okay. Simone and Nellie both told me it wasn't my fault, that I didn't need to feel responsible for what had happened. That provided a bit of relief. It was healing for me to hear that from both of them.

While the sentencing hearing was emotionally devastating, it did make me hate myself less. Logically, I know there wasn't much, if anything, that I could have done. The sheer number of survivors in the courtroom proved what a prolific predator Nassar was. After hearing about all the people he had abused; all the people at Michigan State who had known; the father who had been told; the mother who was only a few feet away *in the same room* while Nassar committed the abuse and didn't realize what had been going on, thinking he was performing acceptable treatment just beyond her line of sight . . . it made me feel like I had personally failed Simone a little bit less. The Bileses' mercy and the volume of other stories provided the first step for me to forgive myself—or at least offered a path forward. It allowed me to backtrack in my mind and consider where and when I could have prevented things, and I realized that even if I had been in the room, it still could have happened and I might not have known it. I'm in constant amazement at the strength shown by the gymnasts and other survivors in demanding a healthier, safer future.

As for me, I'm still working through it. Whenever I send a message to Simone and I don't hear back promptly, my brain immediately jumps to *What's wrong? What's going on? What did I do?*

On January 24, Judge Aquilina sentenced Nassar to a possible 175 years in prison (in addition to the sixty-year federal sentence he had already received for child pornography). Over time, every single Olympian from the 2012 and 2016 teams (with the exception of Laurie) would announce that she had been a victim of Nassar's abuse. In total, more than five hundred survivors have come forward, including at least one who was just six years old when the abuse started.

When Tasha Schwikert spoke up—Tasha was the second member of the 2000 Olympic team to come forward, joining teammate Jamie Dantzscher—she added that Penny had pushed her to publicly support USAG, which had been showing itself to be a bad actor in its response to the abuse allegations with their actions of self-preservation over support of their own athletes.

Tasha's revelation coincided with the arrest of Penny for tampering with evidence in relation to the investigation into Nassar. Specifically, Penny was accused of ordering USAG employees to remove any documents with Nassar's name on them from the Ranch, including medical records that still have not been found. While Penny was awaiting trial and facing up to ten years in prison, the charges were dropped.

Had Kathie Klages believed and acted on the stories she was allegedly told, she wouldn't have been sentenced to serve ninety days in jail for lying to the police. However, a year and four months after her conviction, she won an appeal because the court determined that her interviews in 2018 to the police were not crucial to a state investigation: the judgment indicated her statements were inconsequential rather than material and did not say whether or not she'd been telling the truth.

As I go through the laundry list of issues that have been exposed through the worst crime in modern sports history, it becomes clear that none of these problems are specifically gymnastics problems. These are people problems. These are organizational and cultural problems. The sport of gymnastics remains an incredible vessel that fills athletes with strength, discipline, joy, courage, and so much more.

**

Coaches serve at the pleasure of the athlete. Without athletes, there are no coaches. With that said, good coaching matters. Being a good sports parent matters too. Actions—not just words—from leaders at every level of the sport, from your local gym to the CEO of the US Olympic Committee, will determine if a sport will live up to the ideals we know it should.

Around the time Michigan Circuit Court judge Janice Cunningham sentenced Nassar—in yet another criminal sexual conduct case—to up to another 125 years, I put out a personal statement on behalf of Evo. In it I wrote, "Without a doubt, we are all outraged by the situation at USA Gymnastics. Today, we must decide what comes next." My statement followed the resignation of the entire USAG board of directors. This was also many months before Penny's arrest and also before U.S. Olympic Committee CEO, Scott Blackmun, resigned, citing health concerns. Interestingly Blackmun's health problems seemed to surface after details in the 233-page Ropes & Gray law firm's report commissioned by the USOC became public. According to the report, Blackmun was told by Penny in July 2015 that "National Team members had lodged sexual abuse allegations" against Nassar, but he neither shared the information with anyone nor took any action for over a year, until the *Indianapolis Star* article in September 2016. The report made crystal clear that "USAG's and the USOC's inaction and concealment had consequences: dozens of girls and young women were abused during the year-long period between the summer of 2015 and September 2016."

On Twitter, Senator Richard Blumenthal (D-Conn.), a staunch supporter of survivors of sexual assault and who later authored the Empowering Olympic, Paralympic, and Amateur Athletes Act of 2020 with Senator Jerry Moran (R-Kan.), wrote, "Shocked to learn that former

USOC CEO Scott Blackmun—who enabled abuse of our Olympic athletes by Nassar & others & lied to Congress about it—received a $2.4M golden parachute, while survivors continue to be dragged through litigation." He followed this tweet with another saying he was requesting that the Department of Justice investigate Blackmun's conduct and a potential clawback of his severance. The bill he coauthored in 2020 introduced legislative mechanisms to decertify national governing bodies and prohibited retaliation against those who reported abuse or harassment, among other things. In 2021, Blumenthal went on to press for the investigation into the FBI's accountability concerning reports of abuse that had been filed against Nassar and were, by all accounts, mishandled.

My Evo statement went on:

> Rebuilding our organization will set an excellent example for our athletes: an example of pride, an example of leadership, and most importantly, an example of standing up for what is right. We can and will take back the organization we have invested our time and passion in.
>
> As leaders in this industry, we have a great opportunity before us to teach our athletes that even though evil exists in this world, evil will not win. We can teach them that injustice can be used as fuel for change and that positivity can and will grow again, even after the darkest of hours.

What I wasn't expecting when I wrote that statement was how few leaders would step forward. While not many coaches have been proactive in vocally advocating for change, I have used my public notoriety in interviews and online to share my views on how athletes deserve to be treated. I recognize it may have been easier for me to speak out because I had stepped away from the U.S. elite system for a while and therefore carried less fear of retribution for my comments. But I also didn't have a problem standing up to Martha when I was in the system, long before Simone was a champion, and faced the retaliation that resulted. After I had published my statement on behalf of Evo, I constantly wondered when the chorus from others was going to arrive. And isn't that part of the problem? Courage is never required from a position of comfort.

Martha and Bela have mostly kept quiet, but they did give an interview to *Dateline* on NBC. In the segment Martha said, "I feel extremely bad. I don't feel responsible."

I don't know how Martha could deny any responsibility when Olympian after Olympian revealed their darkest horrors to the world—a product of the repressive culture that Martha herself fostered as the leader of the elite system.

McKayla Maroney had a different perspective for the *Dateline* reporter: "That's what everyone says, it's not their responsibility." She added, "I feel like the reason I'm still alive is because we went through this together. I don't think I could have got through it alone. That's how we got to the Olympics and that's how we're going to get through this."

I further saw this strength while attending the premiere of the documentary *At the Heart of Gold: Inside the USA Gymnastics Scandal* at the Tribeca Film Festival in the beginning of 2019. I was asked to share my thoughts on the crimes and was the only elite coach alongside the roughly three dozen survivors at the premiere. *At the Heart of Gold* explores the culture at Twistars, Michigan State University, the Ranch, and the people who are to blame for that culture, including Klages, Geddert, and the Karolyis. It also brings the viewer into the courtroom to witness a few impact statements to highlight the power the survivors are reclaiming.

What couldn't be shown in the documentary were the tears in the crowd, the tissues that were getting passed around, the damage that had been done, and the wounds that had been opened and are still healing. When the lights went up, director Erin Lee Carr expressed her gratitude to those in attendance for sharing their story, and we all left for an afterparty hosted by HBO. As the night wore on, the gathering spilled into the hotel lounge and the demons for some began to rise. Their pain hadn't been mitigated. This gathering army of women—from teenagers to moms in their forties—still had to deal with a lot of unresolved trauma. While some were reminiscing with old teammates from decades past, I began to hear talk of a younger woman, Alexis, who was really struggling (and whose story I'm sharing with her permission). She was talking about committing suicide. I could see the physical scars on her arms from self-harm and now, in this environment, under these circumstances, it had become too much. I went over and sat next to her and started talking. More importantly, I listened. We were there for hours, and as the clock hands rotated, the unbearable pain for Alexis began to recede. We made it through the night.

I checked in on Alexis again the next day before I returned to Florida, and we exchanged contact information. We have stayed in touch since that evening and I'm happy to report that she is now thriving. Since that night, Alexis sought professional help, got married, and now has three beautiful sons.

I will never forget the lessons of that film premiere. We all have to pay attention, particularly when the cameras aren't around and the spotlight has faded. Just because a documentary covered the atrocities doesn't mean the pain scrolls away with the credits. We need to channel our energy in a productive and healthy direction.

***

At the end of 2018, Jason left Evo and started a new job as an assistant coach at Yale University. It was now down to me and Lydia to run the business, which really meant that I was the only coach left in charge to interact with the parents. Jason had a group of parents who had followed him to Evo, and when they couldn't follow him to Yale, they directed their anger and frustration at me. Some of them became downright nasty, as if swearing at me was going to bring back their coach. I didn't have an answer for them that would satisfy, just as I couldn't appease the moms who thought their level 4 gymnasts were just a few skills away from the Olympic trials. I had brought my expertise to Evo because I wanted to be a part of something new, I had a stake in the outcome, and I could build a gymnastics program from the ground up. I felt I was afforded some of that but by no means all of it.

When I joined the company, it had a clean slate. Clients had been migrating in from other local gyms, and then more joined after I arrived because of my track record. It was a true hodgepodge group, which was fantastic. There were many gymnasts who needed remedial coaching and there were a couple who had real elite potential.

I wanted the kids to have fun. I never expected our lower-level gymnasts to go out and win. Many if not most of the parents didn't like this. They thought the path to greatness was a series of wins all the way through an athlete's career. It's not. Sure, Simone would win on occasion at the lower levels, but even when she was a level 10 she finished tied for forty-fourth place at the Junior Olympic championships. A few months later she had a finish in the lower half of the CoverGirl Classic competition. I honestly didn't care about the placement. I had to look these finishes up for this book because I couldn't remember, and why would I? What I remember most about that Classic meet was the progress Simone made when she caught her Tkatchev for the first time in a competition.

As a coach, my goal is to teach gymnasts a good, solid foundation and, above all, to encourage a love for the sport. Unfortunately, I was having frustratingly repetitive conversations with parents whose main goal in putting their children in gymnastics was the desire to see them win.

I would tell a parent that if their goal was for their child to win at the lower levels, then my program wasn't the right one for them because that was not our focus. I often got exasperated looks in response. I'd continue, telling them I was not going to push their child to achieve something that I didn't believe in. If their kid was talented enough, they listened well, and they had fun, they were going to be successful, but there was no point in taking a level 4 and beating them into the ground if they didn't win because then they would end up quitting or hating the sport, and neither was the outcome I was looking for.

To be clear, if a gymnast quit because they didn't love doing gymnastics, I supported that. However, if a kid quit because of something destructive the coach said or did or there was too much pressure from their parents, or they kept getting injured because they were pushed too fast, then that was a problem that needed to be addressed.

Within three seasons at Evo, our lower levels *were* getting better. Our level 9s and 10s were winning. We even qualified our first elite gymnast. I loved coaching and I knew I was good at it, but I just wasn't sure I could spend any more time arguing with parents who wanted my coaching expertise without my coaching philosophy. In every program I have been in, I've made that philosophy clear to new members, but sometimes parents simply didn't want to hear it. At this stage in my career I felt I had earned enough respect to be heard, and it became increasingly frustrating when parents thought they knew better. Also weighing on me was how powerless I actually was when it came to the operation of Evo. The gymnastics program was thriving, but the profits of the program I was helping grow from nothing were supporting other programs under the Evo umbrella that were losing money. Those profits were supposed to be part of my compensation. Coming into the gym was not as much fun as it had once been. I felt more of my time was getting consumed with parental arguments and that my efforts were not being rewarded even as my responsibilities and the programs' successes increased. That wasn't what I envisioned when I came on as a partner of the company.

On the Wednesday after I returned from my trip to Tribeca, having seen the devastating impact of abuse and neglect, I was despondent when a mother of one of my gymnasts lashed out at me. She was angry that I hadn't asked her permission before departing on the trip, leaving her to practice with two of her other coaches during my two-day absence. The gym mom demanded a meeting with me and some of the other staff, including Lydia, and proceeded to spend close to two hours ripping into me. The fact that my business partner allowed this parent to do that and think it was okay didn't sit well with me. I no longer felt supported.

Parents should absolutely have a voice: their input is important. But I also believe there needs to be respect for the coaches and the other people at the gym. I recognized that I may not have been at my best as a coach while I was grappling with all of the victims of sexual abuse coming forward, but, still, I can't imagine another professional scenario where it would be okay for one adult to yell at another for hours.

The purpose of my trip was not a vacation but to participate in the screening of *At the Heart of Gold* and support others in the gymnastics community who were in serious need of compassion. To rebound from talking a woman from the edge of suicide to fielding complaints from a gym-mom who needed to inflict her wrath on me didn't just hurt; it broke me. That night I sat on my bathroom floor and cried for hours. I woke up the next morning and decided I didn't need to stay at Evo any longer. I felt the environment had become toxic, without a clear path forward, so I decided I was going to leave coaching. Being dedicated to my athletes, I told myself I would finish the season, which was about a month away, and then I was getting out of the sport. The thing that had brought me so much joy throughout my life was once again causing me anguish and tears. At the end of May 2019, I told Lydia I was leaving.

CHAPTER 19

A Family in Crisis

After the Olympic triumphs, a move to white sand beaches, and a new start at a new gym, I hit a wall. I wanted to spend more time with my kids and less time hearing complaints from other parents. After thirty-three years, I quit coaching.

I needed to focus on taking care of myself, and I felt it was time that I became a stay-at-home mom. I understood that not everyone had that option and I was lucky to have a partner with a very stable job and a reliable income, so it wasn't necessary for me to have a full-time job. Who knew that, less than a year into my shift, a pandemic would shut down gyms and force me to stay home with my kids anyway?

In February 2020, right before we went into a pandemic lockdown, there was a loud rapping on my door in the middle of the night. My first thought was that one of the boys had been out late and gotten in trouble with the police or, worse, that they were in the hospital. When I opened the door, there were three cops standing outside my door and five police cars lighting up the street of my gated community. They were there for my middle son, Chris. He and his girlfriend had been on the phone earlier that night when he told her he was sad and didn't have anything to live for. He was reaching out and looking for help but wasn't sure what he needed. With the way Chris was talking, his girlfriend was afraid suicide was a possibility, so after they hung up she called the police.

In Florida there is a law called the Baker Act, which provides emergency mental health services and temporary detention for those who are considered at risk. The cops arrived and asked my sixteen-year-old boy if he wanted to get emergency help, and he said yes. I was freaked out on the inside but kept my cool on the outside. The cops took Chris away for a mandatory forty-eight-hour hold in a county mental health facility. When the police officers drove away with my son, I didn't know where he was going or how long he was going to be gone, and I had no way to contact him.

Chris was depressed. I knew he could be melancholy, but I didn't realize it had gotten so bad. For all the years I have been coaching and dealing with the emotions of teenagers—even receiving praise for my handling of their sometimes volatile emotions—I had misread Chris's depression. Chris and I have had many conversations since that night and he has told me he was never suicidal but he definitely wanted help. More than anything he wanted to talk with someone.

My oldest, Jamie, was already seeing a therapist for anxiety, which he was very open about, and Chris wanted to talk with a professional too. In general, Chris's temperament was a bit more aggressive, but now when he got frustrated, he started to withdraw. I was still relating to Chris based on an impression he made on me when he was a toddler. When he was just two years old, he stood at the top of the stairs, trying to get the attention of the adults in the room. In the loudest voice he could muster, he screamed, "You're not listening to me!" Chris had always been outspoken about how he felt, which made the entire incident eye-opening because he had stopped sharing his feelings. I was expecting him to set things on fire if he ever got that emotional, not to tell his girlfriend he didn't have anything to live for. Even now I don't think we turned a blind eye to what was happening—we just expected his emotions to manifest differently. What a sobering lesson!

When Chris was taken away, my own emotions were flying all over the place, going from fear and sadness to combativeness and anger. I kept calling the county and couldn't get any answers as to where they had taken my son. I felt as though they were treating him like a criminal, not a child who needed help. It wasn't until the next afternoon that I received the information I needed to be able to visit him. I was relieved he was receiving aid, but I also wanted to take him out of the county facility, where they drew his blood and put him on medication without my permission, to see Jamie's therapist. Chris was still required to stay another twenty-four hours, and when I went back the following day to pick him up, he asked to stay one more day. He was an inpatient for seventy-two hours, and after he was released, we went straight to Jamie's therapist.

With all the guff I was giving the cops and county officials for not providing information, I was happy we went through what we did. The thought of having to bury our son because we didn't listen was beyond terrifying. The first night Chris was home, I was ready to sleep on his bedroom floor just to make sure he knew he was loved. I know people who have died by suicide, but I always felt they must have had some instability in their lives, with limited options. That's not my perception of my family, but I do wonder if my being gone all that time over the years had an impact.

I am grateful that just as I didn't need to lie to my mother because of our policy of openness and honesty, I know my kids can be honest with my husband and me—not that they don't fib on occasion. Still, I understand there are things Chris, Jamie, and Ben won't feel as comfortable talking about with us, which is why therapy is such an important tool for my kids.

James and I have made some changes too. Before making any decision that would impact our family, we make sure to talk with the kids. They don't necessarily have any decision-making power, but we want them to feel like they are being considered and their lives aren't being dictated to them. I check in more regularly now with all of them. I have made a conscious effort to include Chris in my day instead of assuming he is okay. I'm also spending more time with Ben—and did even before the pandemic struck—because I was home and not coaching.

Years from now, I hope that all my kids will be able to take this information to their families when they have them. I always felt like I was doing the right thing by having their grandmother here. I thought it would be enough, but Chris still needed his mother.

I want everyone reading this to know that I included this story only with Chris's permission. As a family, we believe mental health is important, and we share this story in the hope that it will help other families.

While writing this chapter, when I asked Chris about that night, he reaffirmed, "I needed to go." He then added, "I was just happy I got to eat pizza three days in a row." Yep, still working on getting them to eat more vegetables.

Before this scare with Chris, my oldest son, Jamie, had already moved out. He's still figuring out what he wants to do, but I have to brag that he's a bit of a piano savant. At sixteen he started playing the game Piano Tiles on his phone, began watching how-to YouTube videos, and then started playing on a Casio keyboard that we had had in our house for years. After about six months of continued interest, we broke down and got him a lesson. The instructor told us, "He's so talented!" Jamie expressed a desire to attend the performing arts school in Sarasota, and the school wanted him to audition, but we were still in Texas, so we sent a video instead. After only two months of official lessons, Jamie was accepted into the performing arts program at Booker High School in Sarasota. By Jamie's senior year in high school, he received a Steinway & Sons college scholarship.

One day I thought I heard Jamie playing in the other room and thought, *Wow, that's nice.* I turned the corner and saw it wasn't Jamie; it was Ben just messing around. I haven't pushed Ben in any direction, but one thing I do know is that, at sixteen years old, he is the most socially conscious of all three kids. He is constantly commenting out of concern for those around him. It's so sweet and encouraging. He is also a talented storyteller and writer. He recently disclosed to me that he wants to be an author. I can't wait to see where this new passion takes him.

Chris, now twenty-one, has an artistic gift like his father. He has considered animation and more recently blacksmithing. I know that whatever he ends up doing, he'll create amazing things. More than anything I'm grateful we listened and got him help so that he has a life to look forward to.

***

If you or someone you love is depressed or in need of assistance, here are some recommended suicide prevention resources:

988 SUICIDE & CRISIS LIFELINE
1-800-273-TALK
www.suicidepreventionlifeline.org

NATIONAL SUICIDE HOTLINE
988, a new three-digit number for emergencies

THE TREVOR PROJECT
1-866-488-7386
www.thetrevorproject.org

LOVE IS RESPECT
(NATIONAL TEEN DATING ABUSE HELPLINE)
1-866-331-9474
www.loveisrespect.org

CRISIS TEXT LINE
Text HOME to 741741
www.crisistextline.org

CHAPTER 20

Tokyo 2020(1)

When I left Evo, I thought I was done with gymnastics. I had competed, judged, and coached, and I had a small stake in trying to build something new. Gymnastics had been a part of my life for over four decades and it was time to move on. I was excited for the opportunity while Chris and Ben still had a few years left under our roof.

I started filling my days by cooking meals (a newly discovered talent of mine), lying out by my pool, reading books that I had put off for too long, and browsing the internet. Inevitably the majority of my social media connections were from the gymnastics world, and I couldn't escape the turmoil that was still ongoing. For the first time I was able to slow down and take in all the stories and recommendations, consider my experiences, and truly reflect on the sport as a whole. Every once in a while I would accept a request to teach a clinic or jump on an interview to share my thoughts. With each toe dipped back into the sport, my perspective sharpened.

With more time to myself, I consumed every bit of information that came out as part of the #GymnastAlliance movement. Started by British Olympian Jennifer Pinches, this movement was designed to bring to the forefront crucial conversations and reform in regard to gymnastics training. I would also hear from my coaching friends about what they were seeing in their gyms: mostly it wasn't good, especially if a parent was involved. Gymnastics is in the middle of a needed housecleaning, and while bad coaches need to be called out and held accountable, any semblance of grace is no longer offered for the good ones. Almost every coach I knew was now very scared to do their job—not because they were abusive but because their intentions no longer mattered. If an athlete became uncomfortable with common pain, which is inevitable when participating in a sport; if a gymnast's feelings were hurt or if a parent was upset, the coach became the target of a potential abuse allegation. I know many coaches who had become afraid to provide even remedial instruction and have had discussions about walking away from the sport. I say all of this from experience.

Throughout my career, I have always attempted to do the right thing and tried to treat my athletes with care and respect, but even the best-laid plans can fail. Sometime after I had stopped coaching, I was informed that there had been a SafeSport claim filed against me for words I had used during a competition. All I could think of at the moment was *Isn't SafeSport designed to protect athletes from abuse? Is someone claiming I abused them because I said something they didn't like during a meet?* This was shocking to me. I do take responsibility for the things that I say, and although I never intended to hurt a gymnast, apparently that had happened, according to a parent. I felt like this grievance could have been dealt with in a simple conversation between adults. If this parent had approached me and told me that they didn't like the words I was using, I would have chosen different words from that point on. I would have done what was best for the athlete, and in that circumstance the athlete's feelings were hurt. The SafeSport system has been bogged down with spurious complaints, causing it to take longer for the true abuses to be dealt with.

I am a supporter of SafeSport because I believe that athletes need to have protections; I also think that it is important that coaches have protections too. As a society, we need to be educated on the distinction between abuse and disagreements, what can be handled "in-house," and which situations need professional assistance. This is a global issue.

In 2011, Dutch gymnasts Suzanne Harmes, Verona van de Leur, Renske Endel, and Gabriella Wammes came forward with their own stories of abusive coaching. After hearing the collective complaint, the Dutch federation made sweeping changes to their program, including new training for the coaches. The response was swift and actionable, and the Dutch system has been heralded as a standard-bearer for the last decade.

The coaches—past and present—got the message. Gerrit Beltman, one of the original trainers who was highlighted for his abusive coaching, publicly admitted his faults to the Dutch newspaper *Noordhollands Dagblad*. "I mistreated and humiliated young gymnasts to win medals. I am deeply ashamed," Beltman said. "Never have I consciously intended to hit, to curse, to hurt, or to belittle. But it did happen. I was talked into that, to think it was the only way to cultivate a top-sport mentality. I blame myself for failing."

Beltman was accepting responsibility, a step too many coaches in the United States fail to take. I believe a big reason for this is that once a coach owns up to their role in a negative coaching situation, they have opened themselves up to being viewed as toxic. That leaves the alternative position of either remaining silent or digging their heels in and defending their actions—all but eliminating the possibility for change.

For decades, athletes have been expected to accept the "Do it because I said so" mentality. They never felt they had a voice regarding their training, and today's gymnasts finally do, which has created a precarious situation in the Netherlands. While the coaching style may have changed, the gymnasts from the past didn't feel they received the actual justice they deserved or desired. After all, some say they were physically abused (which Beltman even admitted). To quell the concern that not enough was being done to protect the gymnasts in the Netherlands, the technical director of the Dutch program, Mark Meijer, announced that none of the personal coaches from the national team who had allegations of abuse filed against them would be able to travel to the Tokyo Olympics. That included Vincent Wevers, father of Lieke and her twin sister Sanne, one of only two gymnasts in Rio to win an individual gold medal not named Simone Biles. The present-day gymnasts weren't happy their personal coaches were being punished for charges that had not yet been proven. Collectively, they signed a letter confirming the positive changes and how they no longer had to endure the abuses that past gymnasts described. By all indications, the changes over the past decade had stuck.

A few months before this decision, I had traveled to Amsterdam with my friend and coaching cohort, LaPrise Williams, to work with some of the national team athletes as they prepared for the European championships. Since I had formed a relationship with some of the coaches and gymnasts, as a temporary remedy to the coaching dilemma, I was asked to join the Dutch program. I was hired as an assistant coach for the Dutch national team to coach and accompany the gymnasts to the European championships, the Olympic Games, and world championships later in 2021. What's fun is this go-around in coaching: rather than being away from my family, my family traveled with me. James was able to visit, and my kids spent the entire summer with me in the Netherlands—their first time across the pond!

Traveling to the Netherlands had its challenges because it was during COVID. My family and I needed to have special permission from the Dutch government to even enter the country. Flying overseas on a wide-body plane with only about fifty passengers on it was also quite the experience. Economy seats were perfectly comfortable because we each had our own row on the plane.

During my four-month stay in the Netherlands, we lived in various parts of the country, including Amsterdam, Rotterdam, Gouda, and Heerenveen, which was designated as the home of the national training facility. Each part of the country had a different vibe. While Amsterdam was very historic, Rotterdam was much more industrial and urban, and Heerenveen was a pastoral paradise, with a slow pace of life. Every place had its adventures, ranging from walking the canals to doing a ropes course high in the treetops or gazing out on the hundreds of acres of magnificent tulips and windmills. I loved being able to provide this experience for my family, and I found it very fulfilling professionally to come into another country and help athletes have the best experience possible in a time of turmoil.

My time coaching the Dutch team was a mixed experience. Some coaches had come to terms with the fact that they were not going to be able to accompany their gymnasts to Tokyo, and other coaches fought the judgment to the very end. Ultimately, I was there to help the athletes, so I did what their coaches allowed me to do. I would collaborate with their trainers on techniques, and most of them helped me understand their gymnasts on a personal level. Walking into a meeting with an elite athlete for the first time, it is tough to understand what makes them tick. Most of the gymnasts had been with their coaches since they were young, and just like I knew what Simone needed in her high-stress periods, those coaches knew what their athletes needed. There was one particular coach who stood out as defensive, accusing me of being sent to sabotage the Dutch gymnasts so they couldn't beat Simone in Tokyo. That coach instructed me to speak to his athletes *only if* they asked me a question or if they requested technical help. I was told, "Speak only when spoken to." As absurdly as I took this accusation and his demands, I didn't let it affect the attention that I gave to the athletes.

One interesting thing about this team was their average age. This was a team of adult women, with the youngest being nineteen at the time and the oldest athletes turning thirty shortly after the Games. When you're coaching adults, the relationship is different than if you are coaching children. These women had their training plans and they had no intention of altering them. I was there to help the athletes who would be without their closest support system—their coaches—in Tokyo, not to dictate a new plan to them. So, in spite of my urge to alter some of their ingrained processes, I did my best to be a compassionate surrogate.

The COVID-19 pandemic threw a major monkey wrench into the lives of most elite athletes, like Simone, who had set their sights on the 2020 Olympic Games in Tokyo. They had to grapple with the fact that they now had to put in another year of training and another year of possible setbacks or injuries.

While I was living overseas, training the Dutch team, Simone was back in Texas, trying to hold on for one more year. She said she "didn't come this far to only come this far," so she was determined to be at the Games in Tokyo. When the schedule and groupings were released, the United States and the Netherlands had been placed in the same subdivision, meaning we would train and compete in qualifications in the same group. Simone and I were destined to run into each other again under the Olympic rings.

For two weeks prior to departing for Tokyo, the staff and athletes had to painstakingly take PCR tests every forty-eight hours to ensure that no one would be traveling with the COVID-19 virus. I had started to feel like my skull was a pin cushion after having so many swabs embedded as deeply into my nasal cavity as possible. Just once I'd like to attend an Olympic Games where a viral outbreak isn't stealing headlines. When we finally had the approval to travel, hundreds of Dutch athletes met up at the Schiphol Airport, where we were treated to VIP service in the KLM lounge. The flight to Japan would take thirteen and a half hours, so having a place to move around freely in before the flight was a bonus.

Narita Airport had planned well for the 30,000 athletes, staff, and officials traveling from around the globe. They had a dedicated terminal and access points that were designed to keep the Olympians separate from the other travelers. During the last hour of our flight, we were told not to drink anything because it could dilute the results of the antigen test we would be taking as soon as we got off the plane. Upon deplaning, we were escorted into makeshift booths for testing. Since we were all parched from the travel, there were little posters in the booth to show you how to create saliva for the test tubes. The signs told us to think about lemons or chocolate cake. This technique worked surprisingly well. Then we had to sit and wait until everyone's test was cleared. It was silly and surreal all at once.

Once the delegation was released from the testing area, we were allowed to retrieve our luggage and make our way to our hotel. We had a few days of instruction at a local university before the Olympic training halls were officially opened. As it turned out, not only were the U.S. gymnasts in our subdivision, but they were training at the same off-site facility that we were. Our workouts were scheduled back-to-back with the American delegation, but the university didn't want athletes to overlap in their training to prevent cross contamination, so we were ushered out of the building immediately after practice. The school staff would then come in and clean, ensuring that one country could not expose another to an illness if one existed. Once they finished cleaning, the next delegation could begin their session.

As most people know, Simone didn't retire after Rio and returned to competition to win her fourth and fifth world championships—extending her all-around unbeaten streak to eight years by the time the Tokyo Olympics rolled around. We hadn't seen each other in over a year, but at the university Simone and I had a glimpse of each other. We exchanged an awkward wave, but we were not allotted time to catch up because of the strict distancing policies. We weren't even allowed to get in close proximity to each other.

Finally, it was time for us to move to the Olympic Village. This Village experience would prove to be very different from my time in Rio. Due to the COVID-19 restrictions, delegations were not allowed to have all of their staff living in the Village. For the Netherlands gymnastics team, only the gymnasts and one trainer would reside in the Village during our time in Japan. The rest of the staff had to stay in hotels that were about a ten-minute ride from the hub of Olympic life.

The hotel was nice but our first room was tiny. My roommate, Jose, and I couldn't even fit our luggage past the door. We knew we couldn't live in such a small space for two weeks. Luckily, we were able to upgrade to rooms that were big enough for us not have to hold hands while we were sleeping.

For the next couple of weeks, my daily routine looked like this: open my eyes, spit into a tube, get ready for breakfast, drop off the COVID test in the lobby of the hotel, climb into our prearranged taxis, get dropped off at the Village, meet up with the athletes at the Team Netherlands house, then finally head to practice. After practice, it was everything in reverse . . . day in, day out. Due to the COVID restrictions, we were not allowed outside of our "bubble," which meant that any chance of sightseeing was off the table. Fortunately, I had been to Japan before, so I had less of a longing to do anything beyond our daily activities. What kept me occupied while in isolation was my obsession with the #TokyoToilets, which I proceeded to post about on social media daily in an attempt to share my fondness for the luxury they provided (heated seats, dryers, and soft melodies) for us savage Americans.

Even though the staff wasn't allowed to live in the Village, we were encouraged to hang out inside the gated community—that is, until some delegations started testing positive for COVID. Panic set in and most outdoor activities around the houses were canceled. The organizers no longer wanted people to sit outside and socialize. Suddenly we were all on lockdown. I didn't mind this too much because I had been trained to see the Olympics not as a social function but as a business trip.

As the team met each day to walk to the transportation hub, we knew it was almost game time. Even so, the Dutch women were much more relaxed than the high-stress U.S. women's team. The cultural differences were clear.

Now in the training halls, Simone and I had a lot more exposure to each other, and we had time to exchange hugs and chat a bit. But we were both still there to do a job, and time was limited, so we never found the right opportunity to grab a picture together, which I regret. One day, noticing that I was missing something from my left hand, Simone marched over to me and accusatorially asked, "Coach Aimee, where is your *wedding ring*???"

My ring had broken when I was in Switzerland for the European championships and I sent it back to the States with James to have it repaired. But at that moment Simone seemed truly concerned about my family and my personal life. After all, besides being her coach, she had known me as a wife to James and mom to Jamie, Chris, and Ben. I laughed and felt moved.

Back in the Olympic environment—this time across from Simone—I realized that when you work so closely with an athlete for so many years, you tend to see their greatness as normal. It had been several years since I'd coached Simone, and what I had become accustomed to—her aptitude, her difficulty, her sparkle—was now amplified. I could truly appreciate how magnificent she was as an athlete. She was unquestionably still the greatest gymnast on the planet and without a rival peer at the Games.

On July 23, the Olympic torch was lit. As usual, most gymnasts didn't participate in the opening ceremonies due to the competition starting the next day for the men and forty-eight hours later for the women. The Tokyo Games opening ceremony was unusual because, despite being held in a massive arena, there were no fans to welcome the athletes: spectators were not allowed. If you watched the fanfare from home, you probably would not have noticed that the athletes were waving to empty stands.

On July 25, I hopped on the bus to the competition hall with all of the competitors and coaches for the subdivision. They were silent during the ride. I looked out the window as we drove past the outdoor venues with no spectators in the stands and felt an eerie sense of isolation. Once inside the Ariake Gymnastics Centre, we proceeded with the normal ritual of competition, but without fans to cheer on the amazing athletes. It was unsettling to stand in the middle of a spectacle built for the world's gaze and then swim alone in what felt like an empty fishbowl. I tried to push this uneasiness out of my mind. Most athletes go into their personal bubbles when they are gearing up to perform, and I didn't want to project my feelings onto the gymnasts.

After getting ready in the warm-up hall, it was our turn to present to the judges in the arena. The seating area of the arena consisted of a series of beautiful cedar benches made of wood brought in from around the country. The competition floor was outlined with indigo blue draping with the Tokyo Games insignia stamped on it. As I basked in the warmth and smell of the wood, a feeling of dread came over me.

The 15,000-seat Ariake arena was mostly desolate. Just as every passenger on the flight to the Netherlands had their own row, it felt like every spectator at the gymnastics event had their own section. Under normal circumstances, when the teams are announced, the athletes get a chance to wave and flash their brilliant smiles while the crowd blows the roof off the building with excitement. But this was different: there was no crowd and there was no communal energy to pump them up. The American gymnasts were not used to this, and even though they tried to hide it, I could see their forced smiles as they waved to the empty stands. I believe the quiet in the stadium hurt the performance of the U.S. team. They qualified for the team finals in second place behind athletes from the Russian Gymnastics Federation.

The Dutch team did not have any standout performances during the preliminaries and, finishing in eleventh place as a team, had only one gymnast make it to the individual finals. Since the competition was over for most of the Dutch women, we were able to watch from the stands for the remaining days of the competition.

We arrived at the Ariake Gymnastics Centre on July 27 while the athletes in the team final were completing their preparation in the warm-up gym. As I walked through the hall, Simone and I locked eyes. She gave me a sideways smirk and a slight eye roll. I could tell something was wrong. Fighting my almost maternal urge to remedy any problem she might be having, I gave her a reassuring smile and made my way up into the arena stands to watch the grandeur that is the team finals.

The teams marched in, were introduced, and then quickly began their one-touch warm-up. I was sitting above the end of the vault runway. Simone's back was to me, but I could see she wasn't in her comfort zone. From the very first step she took, drifting to one side, she was out of her normal running cadence. I held my breath as she pushed into her hurdle and inverted herself up onto the vault table. Nothing about that moment seemed right. Simone appeared to be lost in the air. She bailed out of her two-and-a-half twist and came down on the landing mat with a thud. My heart was racing with concern. She rose from the mat looking shaken but not injured. Grateful that she was okay, I longed for her to look up at me in the stands so I could remind her that she was all right and to just do "normal." But I wasn't her coach anymore, and she didn't look to me to calm her.

Simone's next turn was for real. The competition had begun. With the stakes being incredibly high for a three-up, three-count format, even if Simone wasn't feeling confident, she still had to vault. I watched helplessly as she stood near her starting mark on the runway, rolling her ankle and looking more fidgety than usual. I couldn't see her face, but her body language said volumes.

The green light glowed on the scoreboard, signaling that it was time for Simone to take her turn. She anxiously stepped onto the runway. As if she was planning to get through this vault as quickly as possible, she leaned into her first step. Her rhythm was off. All I could do was watch—and pray. Simone initiated her round-off and reached back from the springboard onto the table. Rebounding sky-high, the novice observer would think that she would have no problem completing her Amanar. But I knew differently. I could tell that her twist timing was way off. In the blink of an eye, she opened up her arms from her chest, stalling her twisting speed, and landed in a deep squat on the mat. Her catlike instincts had taken over and prevented what could have been a catastrophic crash. She was safe but she was rattled. Saluting the judge, she came off the podium and appeared to be fighting back tears of frustration. Within minutes she headed under the bleachers toward the training hall with her coaches and the team doctor. I didn't know if she was hurt or if she had the twisties. All I wanted was to fix it, but there was nothing I could do.

Simone ended up withdrawing from the rest of the team final as well as several of the other finals she had qualified for. We connected the day after the team finals, when she reassured me that she was physically fine and that she just had a bad case of the twisties. After that brief encounter, we didn't see each other again in Japan. I could only presume to know what she was going through. She had been training for years for the opportunity to become Olympic all-around champion once more, only to have her mind betray her at the eleventh hour. In her 2024 interview with the *Call Her Daddy* podcast, Simone recalled thinking America hated her as she landed her vault in the team final. And, sadly, many ignorant Americans validated her fears, taking to social media to say how she "quit on her team" and that she "quit on America." Reading those comments broke my heart because no one except Simone knew what was going on in her heart or her mind at that moment. I felt compelled to come to her defense, so when the *Today* show and the *Unlocking the Cage* podcast reached out to me for comment, I took the opportunity to educate the public on what the twisties were and how detrimental they could be to an athlete.

When Simone was sixteen years old, I pulled her from a meet while she was struggling on vault. Eight years later Simone was able to protect herself with the entire planet watching. On the biggest stage in the world, Simone was presented with an opportunity to show she was more than a gymnast. She spoke up to advocate for her mental health, and I can tell you the whole process was both heartbreaking and inspiring to watch. Without her winning a single gold medal in Tokyo, Simone's advocacy and humanity became even larger than the Olympics. She was displaying to the world a strength of character that the sport of gymnastics had helped to cultivate. I'd like to think I had a part in that. And as her former coach, I couldn't have been more proud.

CHAPTER 21

Back to Japan

Unlike in Rio, once the gymnastics was done in Tokyo, we headed back home. The team and the rest of the staff boarded their flights back to Amsterdam, and I was on my way back to Florida. As I was flying east— and because I had gone east from Florida to Amsterdam to Japan—this flight would mark the end of an around-the-world trip for me. Another bucket list item checked!

I was eager to get back to the States to see my family and sleep in my own bed, but my time at home would be short. Two months after I returned, Mark Meijer from the Netherlands Gymnastics Federation reached out to me once again to see if I could meet up with the national team members in Japan, this time in Kitakyushu in October for the 2021 World Gymnastics Championships. The federation was standing firm on not letting accused coaches attend international competitions unless they had been cleared by a committee investigating the allegations. Since the world championships were only a couple of months after the Games, the tribunal had not had time to make their assessments.

Having worked with these women before, I was eager to help them again. I jumped on a plane and was on my way to Kyushu, one of the main Japanese islands, about 650 miles from the city of Tokyo. Kitakyushu is a city located on the northernmost part of the island and known for its cherry blossoms, but with COVID-19 protocols still in full effect, we were not allowed out of our hotels for any sightseeing.

This trip with the Dutch team was very different: the crop of athletes was a mix of 2020 Olympians and other gymnasts whom I had worked with during my time in their country. These athletes wanted my input and were intent on having a strong showing at world championships. The group was dedicated and hardworking, and made every effort to secure their spots in the finals. Of the four athletes the federation sent, Elze Geurts qualified for the vault finals in second place and Naomi Visser's eleventh-place score secured a qualifying spot for the all-around final.

With a few days before we were due back on the floor for finals, we needed to keep training, utilizing as much of the practice time as we could. Even the gymnasts who didn't qualify for the medal rounds showed up at each practice. On the day before the all-around finals, Naomi said she wanted to stay back at the hotel and skip going to the training hall. She didn't have any reason to stay back other than it was the process she was familiar with. I felt it was important for her not to just hang around, all alone for the day, so I encouraged her to attend the training with us. I told her that she didn't need to do any routines, but it would probably be best for her body if she went to the gym, stretched, and did some light conditioning instead of "rotting" in her room alone. She acquiesced and got on the bus with us to the training hall. She seemed to find solace in being around the equipment. Even the smell of the gym can trigger that competitive spirit in these elite athletes. Naomi ran through basics and kept her body and mind relaxed while cheering on her teammates. You'll often hear that at the elite level of sport it's just as much mental as it is physical. That's absolutely true, and I believe athletes at all levels would benefit from good mental hygiene. The next day at the all-around finals, Naomi finished in fifth place, recording the highest all-around finish in world championship history for a Dutch woman. Although neither of the two finalists went home with a medal, both showed how consistent training and mental rest can help you excel in the sport. Striking a balance between the U.S. system, which was ruled by one person, and the Dutch system, which was ruled by the athletes, reaffirmed the basis of my coaching philosophy. Athletes could absolutely succeed while being included in the decision-making process of their training and not simply dictated to.

***

With the Olympics and the world championships completed, a new opportunity presented itself. Every four years, post-Olympics, the FIG rules undergo subtle changes requiring all the current international brevet judges (again, the highest level of judge in the sport) to retest for the certification. This is also when new judges are brought into the fold. Each country has its own selection process to determine who it will send to test for the FIG exam. USA Gymnastics has a very strict protocol for who is eligible to sit for the test. Each applicant had to be an elite gymnast or coach at a world championship or an Olympic Games. I was honored to be nominated by a panel of top judges and officials in USAG to become a brevet judge. This intense assessment requires you to know all of the rules as well as all of the elements in the two-hundred-plus-page Code of Points, inside and out, not really something that you can just "wing." Luckily, my brain was still in study mode, having recently completed my bachelor's degree in management.

In March 2022, I received notice that I had passed my FIG test and have once again been filling my weekends judging—except this time in large arenas with the greatest athletes on the planet, instead of local gyms. Today there are only twenty-eight active brevet judges for the United States in women's artistic gymnastics.

In 2023, I judged Simone for the first time. I was at the U.S. Classic, back where it all started, in Chicago. With her on the stage and me sitting at the table, dressed in my judging blues, the air in the arena had changed. I was no longer standing by as her coach, twisting my wooden ring, I was sitting in an institutional capacity now. I had to remain objective. Simone had grown as a person and an athlete, adding new skills to her routines. It also seemed to me that since withdrawing from the Tokyo Games she carried a new maturity about her. It was apparent that this time around the circuit was going to be about doing it for herself and no one else. As her coach, I had to scrutinize her every day, every repetition. That was my job. I needed to see the errors so I could help her correct them. As a judge, I couldn't walk over and provide constructive advice. I was only watching, only critiquing.

Some people have asked me if it has been difficult for me to judge Simone, and the simple answer is no. When I'm judging, I'm watching for the skill requirements and evaluating the routine as a whole. I'm not watching the gymnast. It really doesn't matter to me who is up on the apparatus; what matters in that moment is how the gymnastics is being performed.

Judges often get ridiculed for arriving at scores that the fans disagree with because everyone wants their favorite athlete to come out on top. It's easy to be an armchair judge. Fans are usually watching a slow-motion version of a routine or vault on television, which is very different from the quick actions that a judge has to interpret up close on the competition floor. They are also seeing the skills from whatever the camera angle is for that routine, which I assure you is never the same angle the judges are getting.

Being able to judge at the highest level has been an exciting and complicated undertaking. Some experts say that the human eye can see thirty to sixty frames per second on film. When you consider that it takes an elite gymnast under two seconds to complete a vault, a judge's mind is required to take a snapshot of what they see before looking down at their paper to write down the deductions. For a vault alone, there are over twenty-five different category deductions that can be taken. We have to break down the vault into four phases: first flight, repulsion, second flight, and landing. Each error can yield either a one-tenth-of-a-point , three-tenths-of-a-point, or half-a-point deduction, with the largest deduction being for a fall at a full point. For example, if a gymnast has a knee bend, we have to decide how "bad" the bend is. That one action can incur a deduction of up to five-tenths. Is there human error in judging? Of course there is, because we *are* human, but we are also highly trained to do the job. To balance out human error, there are always at least four judges at each event at all of the major United States elite competitions.

Regardless of how I separate myself as a judge, I still feel a stab of concern for Simone's safety in my chest, but I remind myself that she won't do anything she isn't capable of performing. This came into play during the 2024 national championships. Simone was the last up to compete floor in her rotation. As soon as she saluted the judges, signaling the end of her routine, her group quickly moved over to the vault touch warm-up. Simone was visibly winded from her floor routine. While her group stood in presentation in front of the judges, Simone, not very gracefully, plopped down on the vault landing mats to catch her breath. This may have seemed unprofessional to some, but the reality was she had just performed the most difficult floor routine in women's gymnastics, and she was about to perform the most difficult, electrifying, and dangerous vault in women's gymnastics. The whole vault judging panel, including myself, was relieved to see her rest before she endeavored to perform her Yurchenko double pike (Biles II). The fifth eponymous skill in her repertoire begins with a roundoff onto the springboard with a back handspring onto the vault, launching her sky-high into the air, where she grabs the back of her knees to hold a piked position while she completes two backflips before descending out of the sky and landing. As of this writing, no other woman on the planet has ever attempted this vault in competition. With that said, if she crosses her feet in the air, I'm still taking the deduction.

***

As Simone's career thrives, one of the most satisfying things to witness is the growing appreciation toward her from fans and the general public. Her longevity and unwavering dominance have allowed for a mythicism to take root, and each competition she enters has become a celebration we collectively get to enjoy. Extending careers is a big reason why I'm excited to be a co-founder of the first women's professional gymnastics league (more on that shortly). Simone has become one of the rare single-name athletes synonymous with their sport and greatness, much like Serena and Jordan. For me, it feels like an eternity and the blink of an eye since my mom tried to drag me across the gym to notice a bouncy little kid. Today, Simone has everyone's attention.

Four weeks after judging Simone at the national championships, I was again sitting at the end of the vault runway inside the Target Center in Minneapolis, looking for those crossed toes. Simone was attempting to return to the Olympic games for the third time. As I've said a million times, nothing is guaranteed, because gymnastics is hard and anything can happen.

The competition had gotten off to an ominous start prior to even beginning. During a training session two days before the national anthem opened the event, one of the athletes favored to make the Olympic team, Skye Blakely, ruptured her Achilles tendon. Just like that, another dream postponed.

Once the competition was underway, things didn't get much better. In the first rotation, I sat in my judge's chair during the warmup and watched Shilese Jones, whom most fans considered the closest thing to a lock for the Olympic team next to Simone, land awkwardly and then grab her knee. She was clearly hurt, scratched the event, and was carried off the field of play. Shilese had been an all-around medalist at the past two world championships and would have been a favorite to reach the podium in Paris. It was later revealed that she tore her ACL on the vault landing. Remarkably, Shilese returned to the competition later in the afternoon and posted the highest-scoring bars routine of the day and the second-highest of the entire weekend. Gymnasts are tough! After that heroic routine, she withdrew from the remainder of the competition.

The first competitor up after Shilese's injury on vault was Kayla DiCello, a 2020 Olympic alternate and in the mix to be in Paris. When Kayla punched the vault table, I could see something was off, and she quickly abandoned any twisting and halted movement to a single flip to land as safely as she could, rolling onto her back. Kayla sat up and started shaking her head. She, too, had just ruptured her Achilles.

By the time Simone moved to vault in the final rotation, everyone's nerves were frayed. I knew if Simone stayed healthy she would make her third Olympic team—but Kayla, Shilese, and Skye had shown that was nothing to be taken for granted. I also knew that Simone was competing one of the most dangerous and the most difficult vault in the world for women's gymnastics.

Simone saluted the judging panel and began sprinting. Her entry was flawless. She punched the table with straight arms and catapulted into the air before flipping twice in a piked position. Before Simone came to a stop on her landing, which did include a large step back and slide of her right foot, she was already smiling. It was one of the best vaults I had ever seen. It was fun to look over and see Simone's former teammate Laurie Hernandez commentating in the booth for NBC with a big smile on her face. It was equally fun watching the replay later from the main broadcast and hearing Laurie's colleague Terry Gannon joyfully utter, "Oh my god," followed by giggles. The Biles II scored a 15.975, the highest score in the world for the entire quad. Inside the arena the fans rose to their feet to give Simone a raucous standing ovation, which subsided only because the crowd needed to hold their breath one more time for Simone's second vault.

Simone made it through the Olympic Trials and had once again guaranteed herself a spot on the Olympic team, through her first-place finish with more than a five-and-a-half-point margin. The rest of the named Olympic team of Sunisa Lee, Jordan Chiles, Jade Carey, and Hezly Rivera were all within 0.525 points of one another.

Off to Paris Team USA went, and for the first time in nearly a decade I was at home watching the Olympic Games along with four billion other people. I'm not going to lie; I had serious FOMO. I missed the energy you feel inside the arena and rubbing elbows with old friends within the sport. On the flip side, I was able to take in the spectacle and drama provided by the broadcast and view many more events than if I'd been there on a "business trip." Watching the culture of France spill out all over Paris in the opening ceremony was an incredible made-for-TV event, capped off with Celine Dion singing in the rain from the Eiffel Tower. I also loved watching the boulder rock-climbing event (who knew it was such a technical and thoughtful sport?) and fencing in the beautiful Grand Palais. Also, having been on the inside, I was more keen to notice headlines that I might not have paid much attention to otherwise.

Since I believe I was hacked at the 2014 World Championships in China and WADA was hacked in 2016 by the Russians, it caught my attention when I learned that more than 140 cyberattacks targeted the Paris Olympics. Fortunately, none disrupted the games.

Once the gymnastics began, I was on the edge of my seat. It didn't help that during the warmups for the floor exercise qualifications, Simone injured her calf and left the competition floor with Dr. Marcia Faustin, the team physician. With a look of concern on her face, but a "not today" posture in her body, Simone returned to the field of play and then put on a clinic, scoring a 14.600 and qualifying her into first place on floor. Then Simone went to vault and made sure all eyes were focused on her.

During her warmup, Simone completed her vault and while returning to the lineup about halfway down the runway, she dropped to all fours and began crawling. After a few feet she lifted herself up and then began hopping back to the lineup on one leg, avoiding all pressure on her left calf. Once again, I started spinning my wooden ring. Simone continued the competition and finished the all-around qualifications in first place by nearly two points. She made every final except for bars, where she placed ninth, making her an alternate.

Two days after qualification, Simone helped Team USA complete its mission of "redemption," a sentiment expressed at the Olympic Trials press conference while she sat next to her Olympic teammates, including three familiar faces from the Tokyo games. Each returning Olympian expressed they had more to show. I felt so excited for these athletes who had been deprived of the full Olympic experience in Tokyo because of the COVID-19 protocols. They deserved to hear the roaring crowds, to mingle with other athletes in the village, and to feel the singular energy of this unique, magical spectacle.

As had now become tradition, everyone wanted to know the new team name. During the Olympic team's final press conference, when Simone was asked by Aly, her Rio teammate and now an Olympic Channel commentator, she at first stumbled while attempting to deliver an acronym (FAAFO), then she said, "F Around and Find Out." The room burst into laughter. Later, on social media, Simone clarified that their official team name was "Golden Girls," a reference to the mid-eighties television comedy series featuring four older women, because this was the oldest women's artistic gymnastics Olympic team in American history. The name was also appropriate because beyond their team gold, it was the first time in Olympic history that a team fielded two all-around champions.

Two days later Simone continued her redemption tour, winning the all-around gold over Brazil's Rebeca Andrade by just over a point. Suni proved her Tokyo performance wasn't a fluke with her bronze medal performance. With this victory Simone became just the third gymnast ever to win two all-around gold medals and the first ever to win in nonconsecutive games. This golden girl also became the oldest champion in more than seventy years. In addition, Simone became only the fourth all-around champion to compete in three Olympics. No all-around champion has ever competed in four.

Remember the two-per-country rule? In Paris, it struck again, harshly! During the qualification round, Simone qualified for the all-around in first place, Andrade second, Suni third, and Jordan Chiles fourth. Even though the all-around final would feature twenty-four gymnasts, Jordan had the misfortune of being the fourth-best gymnast but the third-best American on that day. It was sad for me to watch the track competition later in the Olympics and see three athletes wear the same uniform and know our sport doesn't afford that opportunity. Sports just aren't fair sometimes, and it got even more complicated for Jordan at the end of the Games in the floor final.

The first event final was vault, where Simone was a big favorite. Because of her stratospheric scoring potential if she landed successfully on her feet, everyone else was competing for second. Simone nailed her eponymous skill and later posted online, "Getting up and not having to think about doing a yurchenko double pike is a blessing." Forty-eight hours after winning vault gold, Simone was joined by Suni and Jordan inside Bercy Arena one final time to compete in the beam and floor finals. Simone had entered this Olympics with the mental health training she lacked in Tokyo. Through the first five days of the women's competition, she had utilized her toolbox to stay grounded. Everything about her presence said *I'm doing this for me.* She was focused, confident, and taking her "calming" moments when she needed them, giving little regard to the cameras in her face. Even with all the training, the stress of the sport can still rear its ugly head.

During her multiple trips to World Championships, Simone regularly qualified to the medaling rounds on every event. In her Olympic run, Simone has qualified for every single final except for the Paris bars final! I cannot stress enough the absurdity of this fact. In her training sessions on beam, Simone could give a master class on precision and rhythm, but she could be hit or miss in competitions. I would be rich if I had a nickel for every time I heard her say, "It's so annoying," after a mistake in competition, referring to how she could regularly hit all her routines in practice without major errors. Simone holds four world championship titles on beam, but the Olympic title had eluded her. Even from nearly five thousand miles away, I could tell she wanted this one.

Maybe it was the pin-dropping quiet of the arena (I heard there was loud "shushing" during the routines, although it didn't come through on the broadcast), maybe it was physical strain of multiple days of competition, or maybe it was nerves, but the balance beam would claim multiple victims on that early August day. Following a beam grab from Zhou Yaqin of China and falls from Suni, Julia Soares from Brazil, and Sabrina Voinea from Romania, Simone got slightly out of her impeccable cadence during her routine, and she found herself standing on the floor next to the apparatus after a miscue on her flight series, landing her in fifth place in the overall standings and out of medal contention. When Simone's score was posted, there was a peculiar three-tenths deduction listed on her overall total. These deductions are generally for a rule violation such as overtime or out-of-bounds errors, but Simone had neither. I immediately considered that she had gotten an "unsportsmanlike conduct" infraction, as she had grown accustomed to cursing when she fell in competition. Turns out she was given the neutral deduction for not saluting or "acknowledging" the judges at the end of the routine, though she clearly had. I have never been on a judging panel where this deduction was taken at this level of competition.

For her final performance in France, Simone looked like she was ready to leave every ounce of energy she had on the beige floor. With Simone that sometimes means too much power. She landed out of bounds twice while trying to control her tumbling passes. Still, Simone's difficulty is so high that she has wiggle room. She also has a formidable new challenger in Andrade, who has squeezed that buffer to the point where Simone can't be careless in the tenths she can absorb. When Simone walked off the floor, she didn't want to receive another neutral deduction, so in a bit of defiance, rather than lifting her arms and then dropping them in a single saluting motion, she raised her hands in a salute toward the judges for what felt like thirty seconds and walked all the way off the podium while holding her arms over her head. Unfortunately, going out of bounds twice cost Simone a neutral deduction of 0.6 and pushed her out of the gold medal position—held by Andrade, who was very clean in her routine—by just .033 points. On the sidelines, I noticed Simone and her coach Cecile discussing what I assume was a potential inquiry. Video evidence later revealed that Simone's other coach, Laurent, had, in fact, attempted to lodge an inquiry, but in a bit of miscommunication with the officials it was never submitted to the superior jury for review. Later, on social media, Simone posted, "Honestly not a big deal for me, Rebeca had a better floor anyways . . . upsetting how it wasn't processed but I'm not mad at the results."

Submitting reviews is often a collaboration between the athlete and coach. They'll want you to challenge (or the coach might think about challenging a score), and a conference between the two will sway the decision. When I was in the Netherlands, some of the athletes would finish their routine, scribble down all the skills they performed, including the difficulty score they anticipated, and then look at me for my thoughts. I'd then give a simple head movement of yes or no on whether they should challenge the score.

That wouldn't be the case for Simone's teammate. Jordan's was the last routine of the Olympics. Just before she stepped on the floor, Sabrina Voinea walked off of it with a score of 13.700. Her teammate

Ana Bărbosu had posted the exact same score three routines earlier, but Ana received the tiebreak because of a better execution score. Sabrina's coach Camelia, a 1988 silver medalist and also her mom, submitted an inquiry challenging the score, thinking the judges missed a skill. The judges hadn't, and the inquiry was rejected. What her coach failed to inquire about, however, was that Sabrina was deducted for going out of bounds when video replay showed her foot sweeping above the out-of-bounds line but never touching the ground. Had any part of her foot touched the out-of-bounds line, it would have been a deduction, but since the out-of-bounds was not challenged, Sabrina's score was unchanged. Through no fault of her own, she was stuck with a 13.700 instead of a 13.800. And the real drama was about to begin.

Jordan performed a good routine, and her score flashed 13.666. A respectable fifth-place finish. Ana hopped up on the podium and began celebrating her bronze medal. While she was doing that, Cecile submitted an inquiry on Jordan's score. She noticed one of her skills didn't receive credit—not uncommon, but this was one of the best performances of that skill Jordan had ever competed. The judges agreed and accepted the inquiry, raising Jordan's score to a 13.766 and moving her into the bronze medal position. For the first time in Olympic history, there was an all-Black women's artistic gymnastics podium.

When Andrade walked up to accept her gold medal, Simone and Jordan, in a show of respect and sportsmanship, each got down on a knee and bowed in her direction. Remarkably, this was the first time in Simone's career at a World or Olympic Games that she competed on floor exercise and didn't win the gold medal.

Another Olympics in the books for Simone, and once again she was tasked with carrying the flag in the closing ceremony. This time she wasn't asked to carry her country's flag, but instead the Olympic flag—the symbolism wasn't lost on me, since she was already the face of the Games. So in the middle of the Stade de France, Simone, with her left foot and calf cradled in a black orthopedic boot, handed the large Olympic flag to megastar Tom Cruise, who had just jumped off the top of the stadium and rappelled down to collect the flag so he could bring it back to the United

States to kick off the transition to the LA 2028 Olympics. As of this writing, Simone has left the door open to compete. If history is any indicator, we might get more solid clues starting in 2026. How spectacular would it be to watch Simone compete on American soil in her fourth Olympic Games? If she makes that decision and qualifies, she would become the first women's all-around champion ever to compete in four Olympic Games.

Though the flame in Paris was extinguished, the drama around the floor final wasn't over just yet. Remember when I said earlier how stressful submitting an inquiry can be? Well, six days after the competition ended (on the same day as the closing ceremony), the Court of Arbitration for Sport ruled that Cecile had submitted her inquiry on Jordan's score four seconds beyond the sixty-second allowance; therefore it was reversed, her score went back down to 13.666, and she would go back down to fifth place, with Ana reinstated as the bronze medal winner. As of this writing, USAG has disputed that the inquiry was submitted late and has submitted irrefutable video evidence from a documentary crew that was following Simone and had a mic on Cecile. They have appealed the decision to the Swiss Federal Tribunal. In the meantime, Ana has her bronze medal and Jordan is holding on to her medal, too.

Perhaps the biggest winner of the Paris Olympics was NBC. If we've learned anything over the past few years, it's that Everyone Watches Women's Sports! A Gallup poll before the games started asked Americans what sport they were most looking forward to, and a massive 42 percent said women's gymnastics. The next closest response was men's track and field, with just 10 percent. So I wasn't surprised to learn that NBC reported a whopping 41.5 million viewers when the US women's team competed in the qualifying round during the first weekend. Nor was I shocked to learn that nearly thirteen million people tuned in live to watch Simone and Team USA compete in the team final on a Tuesday, making it one of the most-watched daytime Olympic broadcasts ever for the network, according to NBC.

Thriving sports need stars, and there's no bigger star of the Olympics or gymnastics than Simone. What makes her a star, more than just winning, is her longevity. With time fans have become invested in

Simone's success. Longevity, however, hasn't been synonymous with gymnastics—partly because of the abusive training that has broken athletes and partly because women haven't been afforded the opportunity to pursue long careers. Earlier I mentioned how the new NIL rules have enabled elite athletes to continue their careers into and beyond college. Competing in college includes the added benefit of providing athletes with world-class sports facilities, training, and medical treatment. When gymnasts finish college in their early twenties, many of them are still in incredible shape, only getting stronger, and not ready to say goodbye to their sport. I think of an athlete like University of Florida great Trinity Thomas, who finished her college career in 2023 tied with the most perfect 10s in NCAA history. Her only avenue to competitively continue in the sport at a high level was to pursue the Olympics. What if there were something in between? I think often about Trinity and the many, many other exceptional athletes with a lot of very high-level competitive gymnastics left in them, and how only five make it to the Olympics. I'm excited for them because of my next adventure.

I'm the co-founder of an upcoming professional women's gymnastics league called GIGA (Global Impact Gymnastics Alliance). As of this writing, we have multiple investors and have been building the foundation of what we want it to look like. We will use a 10.0 scoring system that will embrace a high focus on artistry and crowd appeal, with skills rated to encourage longevity in the sport. We are working with other companies to bring technology to gymnastics similar to the treatment other sports receive, like golf, where the viewer gets data on speed, height, the apex of the drive, and so on. Most exciting, we are working to make this a team-driven league where athletes train together and compete team against team, generating rivalries other sports take for granted. This will be familiar to many of the college athletes we anticipate joining the league, but will be new to the elite and international gymnasts who will also participate. As of this writing we don't have a season-opening date, but stay tuned.

***

Now I'm going to answer the big question so many parents and athletes have asked me over the years. Should they pursue an Olympic dream? My answer is simple: kids should stay in gymnastics because they love it. That should be the success they seek. A good coach will find what makes them passionate about hard work and progress. In order to be an Olympian, you need the perfect combination of talent, work ethic, family support, coaching, financial stability, health, desire—and luck.

When you consider there are more than 330 million people in the United States and at any time there are fewer than one hundred active elite female gymnasts, the idea of reaching that level is lofty. Then consider that there are only about twenty members on the national team and only five of them become members of the U.S. Olympic team—which of course is only assembled once every four years—and the thought becomes so improbable that it borders on fantasy. But it's not. It can happen. New elites rise every year and there are amazing coaches who continue to help gymnasts reach that level through the solid programs they have built.

Looking back at the run Simone and I had and calculating the odds, the outcome feels like a miracle. It wasn't. We were deliberate in approaching each day as a new adventure and challenge. Some days were tougher than others, but we kept progressing and smiling along the way.

A point of pride for me during my time with Simone was the fact that I never attempted to stifle who she was. When Simone was enjoying the process, she was the greatest on the planet. She grew up in the world of elite gymnastics and she's grown into an amazing woman. Today, Simone uses her social media platform and status to stand up for others and speak out against social injustices. She walked away from a deal with Nike to represent Gap's Athleta brand because, as Simone put it, "I like how they inspire me in the gym and out of the gym—not just as an athlete but as a person." Simone's infectious giggles are now part of the Olympic soundtrack. Never again can a coach claim that laughing and having fun will prevent you from reaching the pinnacle of success. Having fun is a true GOAT thing.

In truth, while winning is fun, it's not the goal. I know this sounds like a cliché, but it's true. If you ask any number of Olympians where they keep their medals, most will tell you that they don't have them on display. Most keep them in a safe or have given them to their parents. This should tell us something. Athletes and coaches simply want to soar. And for a special individual like Simone, she isn't just about discovering her own capabilities but about the limits of our species. That's a heavy burden when the world is watching, but time and again she has shown that her mind, body, and spirit are up to the challenge. This character was built during the quiet days in the gym when the final repetition wasn't satisfactory and she did one more. Achieving greatness was never inevitable; it was a process, a balancing act that was only possible because it was never grounded in winning but in perspective. *It's just gymnastics.*

AFTERWORD

Best Practices

Gymnastics has brought me so much joy over the years but also a lot of sorrow. I feel it is important not just to share my experiences in this book but also to offer some insight and solutions.

My favorite thing to do these days is help mentor young coaches on how to coach children differently than I was coached. Simone and I have shown that you can be great without training forty hours a week and that it's essential to have a healthy and cooperative training environment. In my time spent mentoring, I have taken my talents to other countries. In the summer of 2012, I made my first international trip for coaching, traveling with Luis to his home country of Argentina. We hosted a four-day clinic in Buenos Aires for South American coaches and gymnasts. This was quite the experience for me, since I didn't speak any Spanish, and most of the participants didn't speak any English. Luckily, gymnastics is a universal language and we all benefited from the training camp. Since then, I have worked with the federations of Brazil, Canada, Chile, Colombia, the Dominican Republic, Mexico, the Netherlands, Puerto Rico, and Venezuela, to name a few.

When I truly walk away from the sport someday, I want to leave it in a better place than I found it in. What good is all the wisdom I've gathered if I keep it to myself?

So how do we move forward? How do we provide justice to the gymnasts of the past while holding coaches accountable for their actions and allowing them to make the changes we seek? How do we offer further support to the current gymnasts who have benefited from the changed system? To be honest, I feel those who were not found guilty of egregious abuses should be offered counseling and allowed to atone for their past behaviors. After all, what good is asking for change if you don't allow it to take root?

What happened with the Netherlands gymnastics program is happening all over the world to varying degrees. Today there are still bad coaches who need to be removed from the sport. Some current coaches have made mistakes in the past and have made changes. And some good coaches are being unfairly accused of abuse for requiring strict but reasonable discipline and having high standards.

I think it's also important to distinguish between not being nice, being ineffective, and being abusive. Being a jerk is not a crime. Demanding discipline is not illegal. Setting an agreed-upon standard and enforcing team rules is not unjustified.

Repeatedly telling a gymnast they're worthless *is* abuse. Calling gymnasts belittling names *is* abuse. When wielded with malicious intent, words, like a physical assault, can leave lasting scars.

While considering how to move the sport forward, one issue keeps nagging at me: as a collective gymnastics community, we need to properly identify the parties involved—athletes, coaches, and parents—in order to create solutions that will offer a path to reforming the abuser and reconciliation with the victim and their family. I have been able to put my finger on a constant sticking point in this equation: high-conflict personalities.

"High-conflict people" (HCPs) is a non-diagnosable term used by psychologists when describing those with uncompromising, winner-take-all positions. It's the difference between a person exhibiting *contempt* and one exhibiting *anger*. Marriage therapists often say being angry is a positive sign because that means you still care. When a partner becomes contemptuous (or disgusted), they want nothing to do with their mate. They want to sever ties. At that point the relationship is all but dead. This dynamic is what we currently have in some circles of gymnastics. While we have groups who are angry, we also have more extreme groups who are HCPs and have moved their thinking beyond where a solution will satisfy. They want to annihilate the opposition.

As a community, we need to accept that some coaches don't belong in the sport. We have to also acknowledge that some gymnasts who have been wronged probably won't ever be satisfied. As journalist Amanda Ripley points out in her book, *High Conflict: Why We Get Trapped and How We Get Out*, "In high conflict, the conflict is the destination."

We need to treat these gymnasts with compassion. The justice system might be able to deliver a guilty verdict, but it can't always provide closure.

Before I share my solutions for the parties directly involved, I want to briefly acknowledge and comment on a forgotten group within the gymnastics community: the fans. They care deeply—after all, "fan" is derived from "fanatic"—and when we think of all the people in gymnastics who have been traumatized, we rarely (or never) consider the trauma suffered by the fans. In some cases, they have unwittingly rooted for the success of coaches causing harm, and then the rug was pulled out from under them. That can make you question everything you trusted. Some no longer want resolution; they want revenge. Of course, it's not the same as for those directly involved, but the pain is real, and fans can be the tinder that can torch an organization.

When we talk about public support for change, we're talking about fan support.

Once we realize these parties exist, we can envision a path forward. I believe we need to try to fix gymnastics from the inside rather than burn it all down. There is organizational wisdom you can't regain or manifest when you start from scratch. There are a lot of well-intentioned people who have made mistakes and want to do better; we should let them try. And if you're a coach who is unwilling to change, or an athlete who is ready to toss a Molotov cocktail, there's only going to be enough oxygen to burn or breathe, but I imagine the sport still has the possibility of a renewed life. And before anyone gets upset, I believe there is still justice to be served. Without that justice, none of this will work. USA Gymnastics will long be haunted by the shadow of its inaction whether it is remodeled or rebuilt. We can seek justice and renovate at the same time. We might need to strip the organization down to the bare studs, but I still think that's better than trying to mold something out of ashes. Today, USAG is well on its way to being overhauled.

Now, let's identify solutions and opportunities. Three main groups need to be addressed—each with its own responsibilities and checks on accountability: coaches, gymnasts, and parents.

These intersecting relationships are what I call the "athlete > parent > coach triangle." The athlete is at the top of the triangle and the coaches and parents are in the corners below, supporting the child.

COACHES

Good coaching is good communication and collaboration. Using the pyramid theory, everyone should be looking at what is in the best interest of the child. When the athlete becomes the focal point of each decision the answers more easily fall in place.

I have found that coaching is kind of like an addiction. Most coaches over time start to do very habitual things like an addict would do. For example, even when a smoker kicks the nicotine habit, they still need to work through the ritual of the smoke break because it's become a part of who they are. When an addict finally recognizes (or is told) that their actions are destructive, they enter rehabilitation to get better. After they've acknowledged they have a problem, work the issue, and go back out into the world, they remain in a state of recovery. The reason this metaphor resonates with me is because the best coaches are in a constant state of learning, whether they're addressing a bad habit or simply growing.

Let's consider what this might look like if a coach is a long-term belittler in the gym: the gym owner sees it, the parents know it, and the kids feel it. The idea that the coach would permanently stop diminishing kids because they were warned, without doing any self-reflection, reading, or listening, or undergoing reeducation, is very unlikely. The coach will need to evolve to the point of being able to identify when they're putting kids down and then make the adjustment before it happens. They will need to do this over and over again.

There is a common belief that it takes twenty-one days to form a habit, but psychologists acknowledge this is a myth. Each situation is different, and it might happen on day twenty-one or day thirty-four.

The importance of, say, a twenty-one-day timeline is that it establishes a goal and a routine. It's no wonder today's apps include "streak" trackers to incentivize habitual usage. Once you've been successful for twenty-one days, you've invested enough into the commitment that you'll want to keep it going on day twenty-two and are more likely to do so. When this habit continues over the course of weeks and months, it can then become automatic. When that magical day clicks depends on the individual.

Some rehabilitation programs go on for ninety days to establish a healthy routine. I believe we should establish a coaching rehabilitation system. This could include instruction in everything from coaching techniques and training ideology to pedagogy, philosophy, and courses in child psychology. Depending on the offense the coach committed, they might even need to be suspended from coaching while they take their classes. It's important that coaches learn and change when it's possible. We can't expect them to be perfect but we can expect them not to be abusive. If a coach is committing a crime against a child, they have no place in the gym. Period.

If a coach isn't a criminal but is guilty of repeatedly committing a lesser offense (e.g., retaliation for not performing well), I propose a probation period. Like a restaurant health inspector, an organizational representative could then pop into any gym or competition to observe and take action if necessary during the probationary period. If the offender is cited again, they should be suspended. The path back from that point isn't based on time but on learning. The coach will need to demonstrate an understanding of and contrition for their offenses. If they're unwilling to do the work, they're likely unwilling to make a change. As in the judicial system in the United States, a coach should be allowed to appeal any decisions and also be afforded a speedy hearing before their peers. I believe the hearing panels should include coaches, physical/mental health professionals, and former athletes. In the end, once a coach becomes aware of a problem within themselves, they will begin to notice this same behavior in others. Then the now-enlightened coach will become part of the solution.

This brings me to another essential ingredient in maintaining the stability of coaching in the triangle: coaches need protection too! Sports are hard. Athletes get injured. It happens. Athletes experience physical discomfort, sometimes even pain. Gymnastics class might be the first time a kid's muscles burn as they hang on the bars and push themselves to do one more kip. Kids need to work through that pain, and they need to learn how to work through their emotions. Some athletes might think this is abuse. It's not. It's adversity. It's essential to building physical and mental strength. An athlete won't be able to reach their full potential if they don't first identify their limit. One of the coach's jobs is to help the athlete safely navigate toward that goal— and that doesn't mean it will be painless.

There needs to be realistic expectations and understanding from the gymnasts and their parents. Just because a parent or gymnast complains doesn't mean the coach is being abusive. Should the coach listen to their concerns? Absolutely. Should a disagreement devolve into threats and screaming? No. Gymnastics is a voluntary activity and if a parent, gymnast, and coach can't be on the same page in regard to expectations, the relationship might not be a good fit.

Of course, all of these are gray areas and nuances. For example, it's possible for a coach to spot too aggressively. They grab a gymnast a little too hard and it physically hurts them. It might not cause injury, but it is painful and unnecessary. That should be addressed. In another scenario, a coach might gently poke a gymnast on the stomach to get them to feel a muscle that needs to be tightened. They might unintentionally poke too hard. What's too hard? That's where this gets really difficult. Some kids might wince at very little discomfort, while others will never complain no matter how hard the jab. If a kid complains, they should be listened to and considered. If multiple athletes complain, then there's most certainly a problem with what the coach is doing. And in that case there's a simple solution: Don't poke so hard! Remember, most coaches are in the profession because they want to help kids achieve their goals, not hurt them. Coaches should constantly be working to improve their techniques, just as they expect their athletes to do. The core goal of a coach should be making their athletes feel safe and promoting a healthy balance between hard work and fun.

In another scenario, a coach might actually hurt an athlete, but for a noble reason. Gyms are busy places, with kids of various ages moving around stationary equipment. In just one example, imagine a gymnast sprinting down the vault runway when a teammate—not paying attention—steps right in front of them, which is bound to result in a horrific crash. An attentive coach sees this accident unfolding and quickly grabs the wandering kid's arm, injuring their shoulder as they jerk them off the runway. The child's shoulder is now hurt, but a much worse fate was avoided because of this laudable split-second action.

Some issues are simply the result of coaches not knowing any better. That's not an excuse but it's an acknowledgment that there's a path forward with a bit of education. Going back to marriage research, world-renowned relationship expert Dr. John Gottman identified the "Four Horsemen of the Apocalypse" as telltale warnings of toxic interactions. The metaphorical horsemen are Criticism, Contempt, Defensiveness, and Stonewalling. In fact, these four types of interactions are so powerful that Gottman is able to identify with 90 percent accuracy the likelihood a couple will divorce after observing just fifteen minutes of conversation. If even one horseman appears within fifteen minutes, he knows there's real trouble in the way the couple interacts, and this is likely a comfortable pattern for them.

This brings me to stonewalling. This is what Coach Jeremy did to me after I had broken my leg. He withdrew. He ignored me. He figuratively and literally turned his back on me without any conversation or encouragement. I've seen this many, many times in gyms and at competitions. A gymnast will make a mistake and the coach will stonewall. They will turn around and walk away without saying a word and maintain that silence. When you stonewall, you are shutting down. You've severed the connection you have with the athlete, and they feel it. This isn't the type of abuse we often think about and this also isn't good coaching. This is bad coaching that creates an unhealthy environment.

There's a healthy way to step away so that you don't let your own emotions get the better of you.

And here's where I put my foot down. I don't just think more education should be considered—I believe it should be required. From here on out all coaches should be required to have a baseline comprehension of child psychology, anatomy, physics, abuse education, and first aid. I believe this should be required at all levels (and, in fact, in all sports). If you don't pass your tests, you don't interact with kids. At present, there are no such requirements in the United States. To provide instruction in a gym, coaches aren't even required to be members of USAG, which is the official governing body for gymnasts in the United States. As a condition for receiving a professional membership with USAG, applicants must pass a background check, complete a course in safety and risk management, and become certified with SafeSport, a nonprofit organization that protects minors and athletes in Olympic sports. This seems like the bare minimum that can be done.

In 2020, I posted a link for an anonymous survey of coaches that I had created. I received 120 responses while the link was active. Ninety-five of the respondents had been coaching for ten or more years. One question posted on the survey was "If a higher degree or continuing education was required to coach, would you go back to school?" Over 85 percent of the coaches affirmed they would be willing to pursue further education if required. When you become a professional coach, you are not simply a babysitter; you are responsible for shaping young lives, both physically and mentally.

GYMNASTS

One of the most tragic revelations from the *Athlete A* documentary came when 2000 Olympic bronze medalist Jamie Dantzscher revealed, "I wasn't proud to be an Olympian." The Olympics are the wildest aspiration a young athlete can have—and to be talented enough, work hard enough, and endure the grueling commitment to make that dream come true and then not be proud is beyond heartbreaking. My first recommendation to gymnasts is to find the fun! Ask yourself, "Why do

I love gymnastics?" Get a journal and write it down if it helps. When things aren't going your way or you feel unmotivated or dispirited, take a peek at your journal and remember why you enjoy going to the gym. I realize this doesn't solve every problem, but it should be repeated over and over that gymnastics is supposed to be fun.

One way to make gymnastics more fun is to reframe the idea of losing. There is no such thing as losing. You went out there, competed, gained experience, and—many times—someone placed higher than you did. The results you should consider are: Did I do my best? Did I improve? Did I learn anything? And did I have fun? If you can answer any of those four questions affirmatively, you should be happy with your performance. Yes, gymnastics is a sport, and in the very basic sense the goal is to stand atop the podium. However, there are so many factors that lead to that outcome that wrapping your identity and/or self-worth in a result that is based on a judge's interpretation is not productive. You can't control the outcome, but you can control your effort and joy. Celebrate your wins but accept other finishes as gained experience and learned opportunities. Early in Simone's career, a double-digit placement at an event wasn't uncommon. You'd never know by how quickly her smile and giggles filled the gym—and they don't come any more competitive than Simone.

I have another secret for gymnasts. You won't find lasting happiness staring at your screen. Kids today live in a digital era. I'm not naive enough to think smartphones are going to get thrown in the trash and teens are going to shun social media. I think it's amazing that today's kids have the world's knowledge at their fingertips—but unfortunately they also have the world's opinions. One of the things I've noticed as a coach over the years is that today's gymnasts seem to be far more empathetic toward others than previous generations, but they also seem to be more sensitive to criticism—or at the very least more demonstrative of the impact. If we, parents and coaches, accept that online influence isn't going to magically disappear, then we need to educate kids on how to participate in a healthy manner and what the limits of that look like. This is tough, because gymnasts can achieve instant gratification online with a single post, while achieving the same emotional high in the gym might take weeks as they struggle to learn a new skill. Each "like" they receive online is giving their developing brains a hit of dopamine, giving a temporary feeling of pleasure and satisfaction, the same as if a judge flashed a 10 on the scorecard. So what's the solution?

I don't believe there's a one-size-fits-all answer. I do think the smartphone can be embraced for certain things and prohibited in other instances. For example, I do think it's okay for you to use your smartphone to record routines so you can review if you're using proper techniques on your skill. But you should not be scrolling through social media or posting during practice. What I will say is we're never going to return to a life where the virtual world doesn't exist. How each coach and gym handles their online code of conduct policy will need consideration, which brings me to my next point.

There is a program and coach out there for everyone. One more time for the people in the back: gymnastics is supposed to be fun! That doesn't mean it won't be hard, but you shouldn't feel bad about yourself when you finish practice and head home. If you're in an environment where you don't feel joy, I'm here to tell you it's okay to find another gym where you do. This doesn't make the coach or gym you're leaving a bad program. Some personalities or coaching styles simply complement others more effortlessly. If you're in a situation where the coaching is fine, but the chemistry isn't working, there is never a bad time to speak up. One of the greatest lessons of the last few years is the need for gymnasts to have a voice and to be heard.

Let your coaches know if something doesn't feel right, if you feel neglected, not heard, or if the demands of the training are just too much for your body. Remember, coaching is a constant learning process. And great coaches will always be open to your input.

PARENTS

Baked into the process of coaching kids is the parental middlemen. Parents have the ability to facilitate a happy, healthy experience or to become a deterrent by overwhelming the athlete and poisoning the environment and relationships that their children must navigate regularly. Creating positive change in the parent/coach/gym relationship may be the easiest issue to tackle while at the same time the most difficult to take root.

Most of the problems I've encountered with parents could be resolved with a code of conduct that discourages bad behavior. Yep, it's that simple. I say this can be difficult to implement because it's the parents who are writing the checks that keep gyms open. Standing up to the hand that feeds you can be difficult.

Too often parents feel they are the ultimate authority because they are paying for the service. Most people would find it intolerable to see a parent berate or harass a doctor for diagnosing their child with an ailment. That same mentality should be afforded to coaches—particularly since parents voluntarily choose to place their child in a gym. The deferential question would be "How do we get better?" Parents, you absolutely should have an open line of communication with coaches and gyms and expect a level of accountability; however, you should remember that you're paying the gym and by extension, the coaches for their expertise and experience. Each month you write a check for tuition, you can regard it as agreeing to a contract for expertise that needs to be respected.

Parents should be supportive and understanding. Kids sometimes have bad days and parents need to understand that it might just be an emotional moment for a child. When they speak to the coach it should be with a very open mind. Start by presuming the coach wants the best for the child. If you can't make that assumption, you should reconsider the gym and the care your child is receiving.

***

I recognize there are 1,001 examples of bad coaches doing bad things. Obviously, if you hear a coach tell your eight-year-old, "You're worthless," there's a serious problem. Because of my poor word choice when I was a younger coach, I learned to never use the word "stupid" again when I was in the gym. I also became hyper-attentive to all the language I use—whether or not I thought it might harm athletes. This gets back to the number one consideration for kids participating in sports: What is best for the child?

There are times when it is okay for you and the coach to agree to disagree. In these cases, a stalemate should default to what is best for the athlete, even though the parent and coach don't see eye to eye. If what's best for the athlete directly pertains to the sport, defer to the expertise of the coach. If the disagreement is more personal, such as the athlete needs downtime or is struggling with emotions, then the parent's decision should carry the weight of the outcome.

This can be a delicate process, and many parents will want to make a public spectacle out of their grievance. If you, as a parent, have a problem with a coach, there should be a meeting set up for a future time. Things should never be addressed in the heat of the moment unless the child's safety and well-being are at immediate risk. These interactions should also be done in a private setting, preferably with a third-party witness, for the protection of all involved.

Coaches, if parents are out of line, they should be warned and then placed on probation if they commit a second infraction. If they repeat their poor behavior, they should be removed from the gym because the environment is obviously not the best for that family or for the business. This should all be codified in a code of conduct.

Of course, coaches are human and make mistakes. We should be accountable for our actions while also being shown grace as we work to improve ourselves. If the complaint is truly about an error or lapse in judgment, the coach should be afforded the opportunity to learn, apologize, and make an adjustment. Again, I go back to thirty years to when I flippantly said, "Well, that was stupid," when referring to a mistake a gymnast made. I wasn't talking about the gymnast, but it didn't matter, because that was how she interpreted my words. Of course, I could have fought to prove my point and demanded I had a right to say *something* was stupid, but when I thought for a half second about what was best for the child, I knew I needed to adjust my language so there wouldn't be a misunderstanding in the future. The language had become an impediment to the lessons I was trying to teach. There was no shame in me making the change.

As time goes on, a sound relationship develops between coaches and athletes (and parents) and there are fewer of these miscommunications. That's important, because in gymnastics it's impossible to be on the elite circuit and not have relationships with an athlete's family—in fact, you *need* to have a relationship with the family because the athlete will regularly be in your company and care often more time during the week than they will be with their own family. Case in point: on a few occasions when we had an early flight, I would stay in the casita at the Bileses' house because they lived closer to the airport. This is not something that the SafeSport rules would allow today, but it worked for us at the time.

While a relationship with parents will happen, my approach includes boundaries. I see myself as a coach first and foremost. I want to have a friendly relationship with every parent in the gym, but I don't need to be their friend outside the facility. I know the gymnasts will learn a ton of lessons under my supervision, and I'm always willing to share advice when asked, but I don't believe it's my primary role to be a surrogate parent. I know coaches who bring lunches to school for their athletes. I know coaches who attend their gymnasts' family parties. As a general rule, I don't do any of that.

I had been coaching Simone for over seven years before I attended a private family function. It was Ron's sixtieth birthday party, and for me, attending the party was a big deal. However, this was not my habit, and I hadn't done it before. In this rare situation where our relationship was already almost a decade old, the Biles family had become part of my life, and this type of private celebration was important. Knowing that Ron is really, really big on family, I was honored to be included. Some of my fondest memories during those years were getting to know Ron while chatting about non-gymnastics events and finding a shared passion in football. (Bear Down!)

If I tried to maintain this type of close relationship with every promising gymnast who walked through the doors, I would cease to have a personal life. I wish I could explain how to handle each situation, but I can say parents demand the same personal engagement as gymnasts. There isn't one right approach, but there are some basic rules that should be observed, the first being the setting of personal boundaries. (Where those lines are drawn is up to you.) The other is respect. Coaches should show respect toward the parents and the parents should reciprocate.

Gymnastics is a unique sport in that a coach and athlete often transition together rather than the athlete moving on to the next coach or team as they progress. This happens when a gymnast shows promise and is moving toward becoming an elite. When Simone was coming up, her parents knew I didn't have experience coaching a gymnast into the elite world. I told them I believed I could do it but if they felt I wasn't getting the job done or if I recognized I wasn't able to keep up with her abilities, I would help them find another coach for her. There were plenty of gyms with elite programs in our area, but I knew it would be essential to find Simone a coach who would be right for her personality. After all, I wanted what was best for Simone. Ron and Nellie allowed me to grow with her and I'm forever grateful. Their trust allowed me to push myself. I knew I could do it and I believe the opportunity showed others there was more than one way to practice and compete at the highest level.

A final best practice for parents and coaches to remember is patience. Excellence won't happen all at once. For most, it won't happen at all. When a few starry-eyed parents don't see a prodigy after a few weeks, they will begin to look around for someone to blame. When the kids don't start winning early on, it's a common criticism that the coaches are the problem. Parents often want instant gratification, not recognizing the varying timelines of development and skill levels that help determine progress. Parents need to repeatedly ask themselves why their kid is participating in gymnastics.

If it's to be the best and earn medals, then every metric of measurement they apply to the coach, the gym, and their child is inherently polluted. What they should be asking is if their child is having fun. Did their kid learn something that day? Did they push themselves? Will their experiences from being involved in gymnastics help them develop as a human being? Did their child smile? Only when the proper goal is understood can a healthy path toward that destination be plotted. I want to stress: this was our approach with Simone, and she developed into the greatest gymnast of all time.

The goal gets fuzzier as the child moves up in competition. It shouldn't. Parents (and coaches!) often slide into the belief that a child's goal shifts to winning so that they can move up the ladder. *Winning isn't the goal, it's the byproduct.* I promise, competitive athletes won't desire victory any less if they're treated well and are having fun. Gymnastics is technique, strength, conditioning, and mental fortitude. There's no reason any of these aspects need to feel torturous.

What helps in this process is balance. Life is about balance. When I hear parents wanting their child to focus exclusively on gymnastics—not because the athlete wants to but because the parent believes it's what is required to excel—I get very uneasy. If a kid is truly good enough to make a run at elite, it will be obvious when more time is needed to hone their skills. Most kids will benefit from a variety of sports and experiences outside of the gym. I had my best competitive years when I was balancing multiple sports at one time. Children should not be forced to choose: they will decide on their own.

Parents just need to make sure their child is in the right environment. It's important when you walk into a gym to notice if the kids are laughing and talking. This isn't to be confused with horseplay, which can be distracting and unsafe; rather, kids should feel comfortable talking with each other and their coaches. Parents should also be able to see other parents observing practice. Parental supervision is usually a good sign. Equally important, parents should feel comfortable leaving their children at the gym without their supervision. (The door should always be open!) If the environment is right and the kid is having fun, I'm not sure you could ask for much more.

ACKNOWLEDGMENTS

To James, for sticking by me through this wild journey. Your commitment to our family and your constant patience have allowed me to spread my wings and pursue my dreams.

To my boys, Jamie, Chris, and Ben. Thank you for bringing so much joy into my life and forgiving me for being gone more than I would have liked. I hope that my journey has taught you about following your dreams, working hard, and doing the right thing, even when it's not the easiest thing to do.

To Rebekah, for being my steadfast friend. Your companionship has always made me feel safe and accepted. Thank you for teaching me to let things roll off of me.

To LaPrise, for never giving up on me, even when I wanted to give up on myself. Your support has been dynamic if not downright pushy, and I love you for it.

To Coop, for always taking the call, talking it out, and working tirelessly on this book. We were brought together through the mutual love of the Great O'Beirne, and we leave this venture as friends.

To my Delta Phi Epsilon sisters, for helping frame who I am. Even in college, when I looked like I might turn out to be a disaster, you always stood by my side, offering more support than anyone could possibly ask for.

To Ron and Nellie, for trusting me to guide Simone during the years that I coached her. Our lives will forever be linked and I am grateful for that.

And finally, to my dear Simone. This adventure wouldn't have been possible if you and I hadn't come into each other's lives at the right moment. It was serendipitous. Together, we grew through the process of tackling elite gymnastics, and even though I don't coach you anymore,

I still watch you perform with pride. I think the song "Whenever You Remember" by Carrie Underwood perfectly encapsulates our journey. You have grown into a beautiful, strong woman who has proven she can take on any challenge. No matter how much time or distance separates us, I will always be ready to stand by your side.